For our
Jim, Julie, Patty
David, Laura, Billy
who will need to know
all that we know and more.

ARE YOU LIVING IN A BUILDING THAT IS ABOUT TO BE CONVERTED TO A CO-OP OR CONDOMINIUM?

ARE YOU SEEKING A HOME OF YOUR OWN BUT CAN'T AFFORD TODAY'S HIGH-COST SINGLE-FAMILY HOUSING?

DO YOU WANT A SHARE IN A PART-TIME VACATION HOME, A SOLID FINANCIAL INVESTMENT, OR A SIMPLE TAX DEDUCTION?

Whether you're a buyer, a seller, or an investor, this is the book that can answer all your questions about co-ops and condominiums. As a tenant in a building that is being converted, you will find out exactly how the conversion process works, how to deal with a "red herring," and what your rights, options, and strengths are. As a buyer or seller, you will learn about all the important points to look for in legal documents, how to negotiate, how to choose an agent, methods of financing available, how to set prices, and all the pros and cons of co-op and condominium living. As an investor, you will discover how to make solid profits at extremely low financial risk. And if you are interested in a vacation property, you will get a thorough grounding in what time-sharing is all about, its pluses and its pitfalls. It's all included in—

THE COMPLETE GUIDE TO
CO-OPS
AND
CONDOMINIUMS

DAVID T. GOLDSTICK is senior partner in the law firm Goldstick, Weinberger, Feldman, Alperstein & Taishoff, which specializes in co-op and condominium conversions. He is a frequent consultant to banks, tenants, and investor groups throughout the metropolitan New York area.

CAROLYN JANIK has been a licensed real estate salesperson since 1968 and is the author of THE HOUSE HUNT GAME, SELLING YOUR HOME, and numerous magazine articles. She has appeared on *Good Morning, America, Cable News Network, Good Morning Carolinas,* and several local TV shows, and on over 100 radio shows including CBS' *Second Sunday.* She has also spoken extensively at home-buying seminars.

THE COMPLETE GUIDE TO
CO-OPS
—————AND—————
CONDOMINIUMS

DAVID T. GOLDSTICK AND CAROLYN JANIK

A PLUME BOOK
NEW AMERICAN LIBRARY
TIMES MIRROR
NEW YORK AND SCARBOROUGH, ONTARIO

Publisher's Note

This publication is designed to provide accurate and authoritative information in regard to the subject matter covered. It is published and put on sale with the understanding that the publisher is not engaged in rendering legal, accounting, financial, or other professional service. If expert assistance is required, the services of a professional should be sought.

NAL BOOKS ARE AVAILABLE AT QUANTITY DISCOUNTS WHEN USED TO PROMOTE PRODUCTS OR SERVICES. FOR INFORMATION PLEASE WRITE PREMIUM MARKETING DIVISION, THE NEW AMERICAN LIBRARY, INC., 1633 BROADWAY, NEW YORK, NEW YORK 10019.

PLUME TRADEMARK REG. U.S. PAT. OFF. AND FOREIGN COUNTRIES REGISTERED TRADEMARK—MARCA REGISTRADA HECHO EN WESTFORD, MASS., U.S.A.

SIGNET, SIGNET CLASSICS, MENTOR, PLUME, MERIDIAN AND NAL BOOKS are published *in the United States* by The New American Library, Inc., 1633 Broadway, New York, New York 10019, *in Canada* by The New American Library of Canada Limited, 81 Mack Avenue, Scarborough, Ontario M1L 1M8

Library of Congress Cataloging in Publication Data

Goldstick, David.
   The complete guide to co-ops and condominiums.

   1. Apartment houses, Cooperative.   2. Condominiums.
I. Janik, Carolyn.   II. Title.
HD1390.5.G64   1983   643'.2   82-22513
ISBN 0-452-25400-0

First Printing, April, 1983

1 2 3 4 5 6 7 8 9

PRINTED IN THE UNITED STATES OF AMERICA

Acknowledgments

I wish to thank my partners Goldie Rotenberg and Lewis Taishoff for their helpful criticisms and contributions; my friends Arlene and Daniel Neiditz for their patience and good humor; and my wife Deedy for her encouragement and invaluable assistance.   —David T. Goldstick

Every book is the work of many hands, but this one especially so. I'd like to thank Rick Balkin for the spark that started it all; the National Association of Realtors for research and survey material; Carole Hall for a light and sensitive editorial touch; Rich Rossiter, Scott Osborne, and Jim Plumeri for a just-right cover design; the copyeditors for many diligent hours; Maryann Palumbo for enthusiastic publicity work; and most of all my husband, Joe, for listening.

—Carolyn Janik

Contents

CHAPTER 1

The Shared-Space Concept: What Do You Get For Your Money?

Shared-space housing is *not* new. Prehistoric cave communities may have been the world's first cooperative apartments, and the ever-efficient Romans, from whom we get the word *condominium,* even recorded the deeds of their multiunit dwellings. Most were rentals or slave quarters, but surviving records show that in some buildings the apartments were owned by individuals; and the courtyards, the passageways, and yes, the baths, were owned collectively and shared.

Later the shared-space concept became a part of life throughout medieval Europe. Walled cities could not expand outward upon the surrounding land without inviting attack from roving bands of robbers, and therefore grew upward. People, being what they were and are, claimed ownership to whole stories or sections of these early high-rises. Some of their legal codes and entanglements survive even to this day. On this continent, a prime example of ancient shared-space housing survives in the great and beautiful communities of the Pueblo people.

Today—in the late-twentieth-century world of titles, deeds, mortgages (and *creative* mortgages), vacillating interest rates, leases, municipal taxes, computerized house-hunting, liens, encroachments, suits, depreciation allowances, necessary open space and recreational facilities, air space, maintenance assessments, rent control, Internal Revenue codes, "baby boom" demographics, *recurrent* recessions, state legislators who would make the proverbial jack-of-all-trades look like a specialist, and more legal paperwork than any person could be expected to read, much less understand—we still have shared-space, mutually and severally owned housing. Most of it we call either *condominiums* or *cooperatives*.

Twenty-five years ago only a handful of our population knew those words; today hardly a cocktail party or barbecue ends without one or the other becoming a focal point of discussion. In fact, if you *can't* talk about condos and co-ops, you operate at dire social risk of being labeled incredibly unsophisticated.

But that won't happen. By the time you turn the last pages of this book, you'll be able not only to talk about shared-space housing, but to talk so others will listen.

Beyond the talking, however, is the buying and the selling. Here's where both your money and your happiness come into the picture. Given the current housing trends, the odds are a condo or co-op apartment will become a factor in your life during the next decade even if you happened to start reading this book purely as an inducement to sleep.

Your apartment experience may be your first home or an investment property, or you may be caught into the conversion of the rental apartment building in which you now live, or you may purchase a vacation apartment or a retirement apartment, or you may want to fight against (or for) a condominium community proposed for the vacant land next door. Whatever your particular interest or involvement, you will want and/or need to know what makes a condominium or cooperative community work, how the property value of an apartment is determined, and how to avoid all the potential thistle snags of buying and selling.

To borrow an old sales saw: "You've come to the right place." We hope you will enjoy reading this book, and we know it will save you money, keep you out of trouble, and dramatically reduce the amount of aspirin you'll need to get through your particular condominium or cooperative decisions.

What's a Co-op

Some cooperative buildings—co-ops—date back to the 1880s, others to the 1920s, and yet another group to the late 1940s. The current boom (increasing numbers, demand, and value) started in the late 1960s, slowed with the economy in the early 1970s, and is strong now despite a depressed real estate market.

People talk about "buying a co-op," but in fact *no one* actually owns the co-op apartment he or she occupies. You buy *into* a co-op, and when you do, you own shares of stock in the corporation that owns the building in which you live.

Like stockholders everywhere, you have voting rights in electing the management (called a board of directors) of your corporation. Unlike most other corporate stockholding, however, your co-op purchase carries with it a financial responsibility to share in keeping that co-op corporation solvent. You must contribute to the building's mortgage payments, municipal tax payments, and operating expenses such as heat, repairs and renovations, and janitorial services. These expenses are usually lumped together in a *maintenance fee* assigned to your apartment.

The amount of that fee may or may not be the same as your next-door neighbor's since it is determined not only by the cost of running the building, but also by the number of shares allocated to a specific apartment. Some units carry more shares and pay a larger percentage of the building's expenses, some carry less.

The number of shares in the corporation attached to each apartment is established when a building becomes a cooperative. It is usually determined by relative size, desirability of location, and/or some other special feature or detriment. Those apartments holding a larger number of shares are usually, but not necessarily, the more expensive units in the building.

The number of shares attached to each apartment cannot be changed without the *unanimous* approval of the stockholders. Even when an apartment changes in desirability and resale value, change in the number of shares and therefore the portion of the building's expenses that that apartment pays is extremely rare.

But all this is very theoretical. Let's look at some specific stories that should make share allocation crystal-clear.

A ground-floor apartment that we'll call 1-A in Midcity Manor was somewhat larger than most of the other apartments in the building and had the extra advantage of having an outside door that opened upon a small city park. When the rental apartment building was converted to a co-op, 1-A was allocated extra shares because of its size and selling appeal.

Three years later city fathers voted to exchange the park for a multitiered parking garage and local bus depot. The view from 1-A's windows became traffic, and opening those windows meant noise and carbon monoxide. Yes, 1-A was still larger than the other apartments in the building, but it was no longer more desirable or more salable. In fact, selling would be difficult because *now undesirable* 1-A carried a larger maintenance fee than quieter, more private 1-E on the other side of the building. The owner/occupants of

1-A requested a change in the number of shares allocated to their apartment. But the request was denied.

"That's not fair!" you say. In the eyes of God and in the name of justice, you're probably right. But that's the way it was in Midcity Manor and generally *is* everywhere. The other shareholders in that or any cooperative are not about to take on a larger portion of the building's expenses just because of 1-A's hard luck. After all, it was the hard luck of everyone on that side of the building. One-A just had it a little worse than most, being on the ground floor and all. Or so the arguments went at the shareholders' meeting.

As bad as all this may sound, remember that the reverse may also be true. An undesirable apartment with a smaller number of shares allocated to it may suddenly become more desirable. The occupants then usually become very quiet and obscure at shareholders' meetings. Look for example at the story of West-104 in Bayside Bungalows.

Here we have another ground-floor apartment, but an apartment in a building that was once a warehouse. At the time of conversion to a co-op apartment building, West-104 was a back corner unit whose windows faced the trash bins of Fresh Catch Fish Market and Tiddy-Bits for Your Kitty, Inc. Its share allocation and therefore its monthly maintenance fee were the lowest in the building.

A year later, though, the corporation that owned both the fish market and the canning company declared bankruptcy. The city claimed the building for back taxes and with a little government financial assistance razed it and installed a beautiful sculpture garden to display the works of local artists.

The value of everyone's apartment in Bayside Bungalows went up significantly, but West-104 became most salable of all *and* the number of shares allocated to it remained the same. (A change in share allocation would require a unanimous vote of the shareholders, and the owner of West-104 was not about to vote himself out of a protfitable situation.)

All this sounds as though the occupants of 1-A and West-104 did actually own specific apartments, and we said that in a co-op you never own the apartment you occupy.

You don't. When you buy into a co-op apartment building, you buy the number of shares assigned to a *specific* apartment and you receive a proprietary lease (sometimes called a Certificate of Beneficial Interest) that defines exactly which apartment and what space in the building you have the exclusive right to occupy. So although you don't *own* the apartment, you have the keys to it, the exclusive right to use it, the right to sell its shares, and the right to assign its proprietary lease to the purchaser of those shares, usually, however, subject to the board of directors' approval of that new purchaser.

In addition to the exclusive right to occupy *your* apartment, buying into a co-op also carries with it the right to use all the areas of the building, buildings, and grounds owned by the corporation that are not specifically allocated to other shareholders by their own proprietary leases. You have the right to use the hallways, staircases, elevators, common sitting areas, pool or recreation facilities, parking areas (although specific spaces may be allocated to each apartment by mutual agreement), and basement storage areas (which again are usually divided and allocated one to each apartment).

But you have the right to use these common areas *only* in the manner that is outlined in the co-op's lease, rules, and regulations, and within the limits of commonly acceptable social practice. You cannot skinny-dip in the pool at 3 A.M. just because you own a "share" in the pool. Nor can you string your laundry across the hallway because your dryer is broken. And you can't hold your daughter's wedding reception in a corner of the lobby of Garden of Eden Apartments without the approval and permission of the board of directors. You do not own, let's say, 12 percent of the Garden of Eden's lobby; you own a 12-percent share in the whole lobby, including the air space in the room.

Let's go on for a bit using this 12-percent figure. Twelve percent ownership means that you own twelve shares in a co-op of a hundred shares. Those twelve shares give you twelve votes in electing a board of directors.

A co-op apartment house is in many ways a miniature community and its board of directors is its governing body. Day-to-day decisions are made by this group, which supervises both the financial management and maintenance of the building. (A maintenance company may actually do both the bookkeeping and the yard and building work, but always under the supervision of the board of directors.) Shareholder meetings are held infrequently, often annually or semiannually. In larger cooperatives, however, owner/occupants wishing to partake in the corporation's management while not serving on the board of directors may volunteer to serve on one or more of the various subcommittees (grounds, recreation, interior decoration and maintenance, budget, and so forth) that the board establishes.

The principle of owning shares in a corporation that owns and runs a building, yet owning *no part* of that building separately, is the major difference between cooperatives and condominiums. In a condominium community, you hold recorded title to certain specifically defined space and an undivided interest in common areas, but we'll get into this in just a while.

Meantime, it is important to understand that cooperative ownership means not only sharing space with your neighbors but also sharing investment opportunity and liability. The co-op community is more tightly interdependent financially and at the same time more capable of controlling its investment than the condominium community.

Your Money and the Co-op

After you agree to the purchase price on a co-op, sign the contract, get the approval of the board of directors, and take possession of your apartment, you take on certain obligations and reap certain benefits. We have already briefly mentioned most of them, but since we're dealing with *your* money, let's take a closer, step-by-step look.

Because round numbers are easier to work with, we'll assume you paid $50,000 for your apartment. Of that $50,000 you had $10,000 in ready cash that you had saved over the past three years. Ten thousand dollars is 20 percent of the purchase price, and a local commercial bank seeing the good judgment in your investment purchase and approving of your stable and/or upwardly mobile financial status granted you a $40,000 loan that was written similar to, but not exactly like, a home mortgage. You are obliged to make the regular monthly payments on that bank loan just as faithfully as homeowners make their mortgage payments each month.

The check that you write to the bank will eventually repay the loan that you took out in order to buy the seller's shares in the cooperative building. The purchase of those shares, however, also bought you the right and obligation to assume that seller's proprietary lease and therefore his portion of the financial obligations of the cooperative. In other words, you bought his monthly maintenance fee, and this payment is every bit as important as your bank-loan payment, maybe more important!

Your maintenance fee, as it is called virtually everywhere, contributes to paying the mortgage on your building, its municipal taxes, insurance, the cost of heating and maintenance, labor and management charges, and sometimes a portion of the reserve fund for major repairs. If you do not pay this maintenance fee, there is a provision in most proprietary leases that you can be evicted from the building within a specified number of days (usually no longer than any ordinary rental tenant who didn't pay his rent would have). The co-op corporation can then sublet your apartment pending the sale of its shares and proprietary lease. (This is a protective device for the co-op corporation. If a tenant/shareholder defaults, the co-op has a ready means of recouping most of the income lost by the nonpayment of monthly fees.) If you are evicted and lose your lease, you will recover the $10,000 you invested in the co-op only if the sale price of your apartment is adequate to cover your back maintenance fees and the loan you took out from the bank, with money left over.

"Are we returning to the days of debtor's prison?" you ask. No, but the cooperative must set up such provisions to protect itself. It runs on the contributions of its shareholders and those shareholders must therefore regard the maintenance fee as crucial. Stay with us and we'll tell you why.

One of the much-discussed disadvantages of cooperative ownership is joint liability. If a co-op's expenses are not met, its mortgage can be foreclosed or it can be sold by the municipality for nonpayment of taxes. In this case *all* the shareholders in the building lose their proprietary leases and their investment in the fair market value of the building. The remaining shareholders therefore must increase their monthly payments to cover the portions not being paid by the departed owner/occupants, or sublet those vacant apartments.

If the times are such that no sublet tenants can be found and if the increase in monthly payments to the remaining shareholders is high, it may force some of them to default on their payments since they cannot afford a larger percentage of the building's operating costs. Their default would further increase the monthly fees to those still remaining owner/occupants. This domino effect could go on, in fact it could escalate, until the co-op was forced to fold. Exactly this scenario did take place during the Great Depression of the 1930s and forced some people to lose their homes and their lifetime investments.

Could it happen again? In theory, yes. In all probability, we don't think so. Both government and private citizens have learned much from the economics of the Depression. Admittedly the Federal Reserve Board is not infallible, but it *can* affect the economy, and we have to believe that it operates in good faith. Banks, having learned that multiple foreclosures in extremely difficult times are not profitable, usually try to make some accommodation (at least on a temporary basis) to individuals or corporations having difficulty with mortgage payments. And tax sales, complicated and slowed by a goodly number of legal loopholes, take forever.

But no co-op board of directors wants to get into the hassle of trying to keep a faltering building afloat. Protection therefore is written into the proprietary lease. The right to screen and approve prospective purchasers is another of the protective devices. It isn't usually mistrust or social prejudice that prompts cooperatives to reserve this right; it's just good financial policy. Most boards don't care if new purchasers have green skin and pointed ears; they do care that these future neighbors earn enough money to carry their share of the expenses.

Let's switch the focus for a moment and look at the board of directors' approval from the other side (yours). If it makes you nervous and you're not sure you really like the idea or even the principle behind having to be "approved" before you can buy something, you are giving yourself a needless headache. If you feel angered by the necessity of board approval, you are taking business practice too personally.

Of course it's O.K. to be nervous. Everyone is. But rationally, you must accept and respect the role of the co-op board of directors in screening buyers as a financial necessity. Condominiums do not offer this protection, for each owner has the right to sell his space as he sees fit without regard to his neighbors.

The mutual ownership and liability of a co-op building also limits to some degree the amount of renovation that a tenant/shareholder can undertake within a given apartment. Here again the element of control is tighter than that of a condominium because the co-op corporation actually *owns* the building and all its space, merely leasing the right to use both the space and the building. All alterations to interior space, therefore, must be approved by the board of directors. In most cases decisions are based upon the possible effects of the alterations on the monetary worth of the apartment and the effects (if any) on the structural soundness of the building.

For example, a board of directors would probably disapprove of your putting up interior walls to divide a bedroom into three padded and sound-proof reading cubicles. Although you may put a premium upon privacy and silence while reading, most of the other shareholders would think that an apartment with such cubicles might be very hard to sell indeed. And the corporation *might* have to sell it, were you to default and disappear.

You may well complain that your finances have never been better and that you intend to live in the building for the next fifty years, but your special interior walls would probably still be disallowed. On the other hand, however, you as an investor in the co-op would be protected by the same need for board approval when the people in the apartment above you petitioned to add extra plumbing to their apartment so that they could install a hot tub for six in their living room.

Most of the topics we've talked about so far in this section are obligations. You're probably wondering when we're going to get to the benefits. We're there. To give you an overview: the primary benefits of co-op ownership are potential investment appreciation, tax deductions, and the pride and security of ownership. Some people would add the opportunity to live and own property in the city to that list.

We're going to discuss the investment potential of co-ops and condos in the next chapter, but for now we'd like you to think about the documented fact that homeownership (and that includes co-ops and condos) was one of the best hedges available against the runaway inflation of the 1970s. People who bought houses in 1970 have seen their investments triple and more. The same is true of condos in Florida; New Mexico; Arizona; California; Washington, D.C.; Chicago . . . We could go on and on. And in New York City, co-ops bought at that same time have increased in value 400 and 500 percent!

And taxes. As a co-op apartment ''owner'' you'll also share the same tax benefits as single-family homeowners across the nation, despite the fact that you own shares in a corporation that owns the building in which you live. Congress has enacted an Internal Revenue Service code (Sec. 216) that permits cooperative apartment building tenant/shareholders to deduct their share of the building's municipal property taxes and mortgage interest payments as well as the interest paid to a lending institution for their co-op purchase loan from their gross income on federal tax returns. Besides lowering the amount of income upon which you must pay taxes, these deductions can sometimes shift you to a lower tax bracket and thus save even more dollars by lowering the percentage of your income that must be paid to Uncle Sam. There are no comparable benefits for those who rent.

But this brings up restrictions again, although these restrictions work to protect the value of your *residential* property. The provisions of the IRS code stipulate that in order for tenant/shareholders to claim homeowner-type deductions on their co-op apartments, at least 80 percent of the gross income of the cooperative corporation must be derived from the tenant/stockholders. This 80-percent restriction, the 80/20 rule, must be met in each fiscal year.

What if a cooperative gets the chance to lease its entire roof space to Executive Sunbaths, Inc., for example, at a price that would pay 20 percent of the building's expenses, while still keeping as ground-floor commercial tenants Poodle Palace, Forelock Wigs, Over the Horizon Maternity Clothes, and Footloose Shoe Store, the rent from each of which pays 5 percent of the building's expenses. The total income from nonshareholders then would be 40 percent of the building's expenses. Is this an offer too good to refuse? The tenant/shareholders would have to decide which was the better financial deal, leasing the extra space to lower the cost of monthly maintenance fees or taking the tax deductions.

This is an important decision because if a building should fail to meet the

80/20 rule, all the tenant/shareholders in it lose their homeowner-type tax deductions. You must understand, however, that the 80/20 rule does *not* prohibit a tenant/shareholder from subletting his apartment. Many bylaws of cooperative corporations *do* prohibit subletting or require the approval of the board of directors to sublet, but this is internal to the cooperative's management and not a factor in taxation policies.

The 80/20 rule is not the only Internal Revenue code limitation on cooperatives, however. In order to qualify as a cooperative corporation, the government also requires that there be only one class of stock issued and that each stockholder be entitled to occupy an apartment in which to live. There can be only three types of stockholders in a cooperative: individuals, lending institutions that acquire stock through foreclosure, and the sellers of the building to the cooperative corporation (even if this seller happens to be a corporation). Primarily these Internal Revenue code restrictions have kept cooperative buildings *residential* investments, much to the benefit of the "little guy," the tenant/shareholder who calls the place home, since the building is controlled primarily by those who live there and care most about it.

Not least among the benefits of owning a co-op apartment is pride in ownership, with its accompanying sense of security. But coming now to discuss this particular benefit, we feel relieved that we never promised you a book of statistics.

Everyone is well aware that man is a possessive animal, claiming as his own both space and objects (and sometimes other people). Whether standing at a bar waiting for beer, or opening his doorway to guests, a person says in a thousand ways, "This is mine!" Sometimes the "This is mine" is a temporary and shifting claim, but at other times it rings with the hope of permanence and exclusiveness, especially when the claim concerns mates, children, and homes.

Housing surveys show homeownership as a primary life goal of most Americans. The feelings that develop *after* that goal is achieved can turn even a shoddy, grimy building into an attractive place to live after it's converted to cooperative or condominium ownership.

Life in a Co-op

Co-ops are primarily city creations. They are also usually older buildings that become co-ops through conversion.

Only a tiny percentage of *new* shared-space construction is cooperative apartment housing. Most of it is condominiums. A Department of Housing and Urban Development (HUD) study done in the mid-1970s shows that even then 85 percent of all co-ops had been built before 1970. If the study were to be repeated in 1983, the percentage would be much higher. The conversion rate has doubled, and redoubled, and is on the way to redoubling again; and conversions are *not* new construction.

The conversion rate is highest and strongest in New York City, which also has the largest number of cooperatives in the country. Chicago, the Greater Miami area, San Francisco, and Buffalo all also have significant co-op populations. There is a recorded scattering in Connecticut, Illinois, Massachusetts, Michigan, New Jersey, and South Dakota, and a token few in most states. But essentially buying a co-op means buying in a major city and buying in an older building. Most conversions were once rental apartments, but some are remodeled factories, warehouses, hotels, motels, schools, mansions, and lofts.

Already you've begun to imagine the problems, right? Well, they do exist. Maintenance work and high-density living are at the top of the list.

In a cooperative apartment building, the corporation is responsible for all necessary maintenance and repair work to the building and its working systems. It is not responsible for your personal property or for problems caused by your negligence or destructiveness. For example, if your dishwasher breaks, that's your problem. If you put your fist through the wall in a rage over an umpire's call, that's your problem too, and you are responsible for repair work.

However, if a window falls out of your apartment while you are away at work, the corporation is responsible for replacing the window and repairing the faulty frame. It is also responsible for any liability incurred by the falling glass.

But what if a water pipe that serves the apartment next door breaks and the only access to the pipe is through *your* apartment? Who repairs your walls, replaces your wallpaper, and cleans up the mess? Or what if the people upstairs leave the bathtub water running and go out? The water overflows and soon the ceiling in *your* kitchen comes crashing down. Who is responsible then?

The following letter, written by a prominent real estate firm to the shareholders of a cooperative that it manages will give you some insights into how co-op "insiders" would answer that question.

Dear Shareholders:

The question of responsibility for leaks in apartments and tenants' responsibility for repairs and decorations arises periodically, indicating some confusion and misunderstanding on the part of some of the stockholders.

Those of you who have recently purchased apartments may not be aware of the provisions of your Proprietary Lease. It has been suggested, therefore, that a notice be issued in explanation.

While leaks alone are bothersome, the problem arises primarily from the uncertainty as to who is responsible (1) for finding the cause of the leak; (2) for curing the condition; and (3) for repairing the resultant damage to walls, floors, or ceilings in the apartments. Therefore we set forth the following:

1. It is the Corporation's responsibility to find the cause of the leak.

2. It is the Corporation's responsibility to cure the condition if the leak emanates from any of the main or branch lines serving the apartments. (The leak would be inside the walls.)

3. The Corporation has the responsibility for repairing the pipes and plaster, but the expense of redecoration is that of the Tenant/Shareholder, unless the Corporation is, in fact, negligent. (Negligence does not mean leaks resultant from normal wear and tear and deterioration over a number of years.)

4. It is the Shareholder's obligation to give access to his apartment so that all inspection and necessary and/or emergency repairs may be made expeditiously, and refusal to grant such access imposes upon the Tenant/Shareholder full responsibility for all the damages which may ensue. It is for this reason that all Shareholders are required to turn over keys to the superintendent to be used for emergency purposes.

5. If, in order to repair the leak, the wall in a tenant's apartment other than in an apartment which is being damaged by the leak, must be broken through, the Corporation's responsibility to that Tenant/Shareholder is *no different* than the apartment that is being damaged by the leak. Therefore, the Corporation is responsible only for repairing the plaster and pipes and leaving the area broom clean. The Corporation does not have the responsibility to redecorate.

Because of the above, it is strongly suggested that each Shareholder obtain both liability insurance and a policy covering betterments and improvements, commonly called a ''Homeowner's Policy,'' so that if a leak should occur, whether in the walls in your apartment or in the apartment above you, you may be protected against damage claims by other tenants in the building and redecorating costs necessitated by the Corporation's breaking through your walls. Bear in mind that while neither the Corporation nor the Tenant/Shareholder will have any reason to suspect that a leak will occur, and therefore cannot be guilty of negligence, persons damaged may still sue, claiming negligence. Adequate insurance protects those sued not only against ultimate liability, but also against the expense of a lawsuit. Bear in mind, too, that while the likelihood of a leak may not be foreseen, once it occurs, if correction is delayed, liability will surely ensue for any increased damage.

Does the letter intimidate you? Don't let it. Pipes burst in single-family houses too, and then there's no question about who's responsible and who has to pay for repairs.

Perhaps even more important than the specifics of this letter is its unstated insight into the closeness, the interdependence, and the potential irritation of one neighbor upon another living in and owning shares of the same building. To some extent the management company and the board of directors (or in larger cooperatives the grievance committee) must act as mediators, legislators, and judges. But even with the best of rules and most careful enforcements, disputes will come up, just as they will come up in suburbia, for example, when one neighbor's dog decides that a newly sodded lawn is a great place to dig.

Speaking of pets, typically dogs, cats, parrots, and canaries—another HUD survey found them to be the primary source of discord among owners in shared-space housing. Many cooperatives forbid them and many co-op owners secretly break the rules. Next to pets, come children. Do we need to say more?

In a court of law, what restrictive cooperative bylaws will hold up against a challenge? That depends on the court and the state that it is in. Some states seem to favor the individual rights of shareholders whereas other states seem to lean toward the "common good" as a ruling principle.

Among the restrictions that have generally been upheld by courts in both cooperative and condominium cases are the right to forbid pets or limit their kind and number; the right to exclude children as full-time residents or to limit the sale of units to a particular age group; the right to forbid or limit the subletting of apartments or to require board of directors' approval; the right to require board of directors' approval of new buyers (co-ops only); the right to require board of directors' approval for changes in the design or floor plan of an apartment; the right to require board of directors' approval for decorative or structural changes on the outside of an apartment; the right to assign or limit the use of parking areas; the right to control the consumption of alcohol in the common areas; and the right to set hours for the use of the pool, tennis courts, or other recreational facilities.

If you're a city person, not particularly fond of Irish wolfhounds or Great

Danes, willing to put up with the personality quirks of others in return for their tolerance of yours, and interested in building equity, in depriving the government of as many tax dollars as you legally can, and in beating inflation, co-ops may be right for you. But let's take a look at condominiums too.

What's a Condo?

In 1961 legislation was enacted at the federal level that defined and permitted condominium ownership throughout the United States. Each of the fifty states, not to be outdone, enacted their own rules and regulations. Today you can buy condos in every state, the District of Columbia, the Virgin Islands, Guam, and Puerto Rico.

Condominium legislation is sometimes referred to as "horizontal property acts." The wording of this legislation differs somewhat as you travel across the country. Some states are more strict and demanding than others; some are more detailed; and a few are rather vague or permissive. But essentially the laws all boil down to one definition: *Condominium ownership is the right to own interior or specifically designated space while also holding an undivided interest in the common elements of a piece of property.*

But exactly what is "interior or specifically designated space," what does "undivided interest" mean, and what are "common elements"?

Let's take those phrases one at a time, starting with "interior." When you purchase a condo, you buy air. You receive recordable title to the space within certain walls; usually you do not own the walls. You own everything within the finished interior surface of the walls that encompass your total space, including the wallpaper on those walls. You own the walls that are totally within your designated space and do not support any common elements. You also own all the space between finished floor and finished ceiling, including carpeting and lighting fixtures. You do not own the floor or the ceiling unless again they are totally within your space and do not support any common elements.

You do not, for example, own carrying timbers and cannot remove them, but you may in most cases add new walls within your designated interior space. You could have those padded reading cubicles you wanted if you were to own a condo. (They might not help you sell your condo later, but you *could* have them.)

On the other hand, the people upstairs might be able to have their hot tub for six in their living room. You do not own the pipes that supply your condo with water, but you do own the plumbing and fixtures within your designated interior space. Now, if the hot tub came crashing through your ceiling because the carrying timbers could not take the added weight, or if you could prove that it might, that would be yet another problem, a question of improper use of the common elements, which would probably stop the hot tub.

This definition of owned space works just fine if you have a high-rise or mid-rise condominium, but you'll run into trouble applying it to the letter in garden-style (sometimes called "patio plan") condominiums, or in condominium communities of detached units such as the mobile/manufactured home developments that are now being built in the western part of this country. This is where the "or specifically designated" part of our definition comes in. It bears directly on the answers to questions like the following: If your corner townhouse condo has a basement, do you own the air space in that basement, part of the air space in that basement, or is the entire foundation and all its space considered a common element? In other words, is the basement divided, and can it be divided?

If you have a patio, do you own it, or only the right to use the air space on top of it? Is your balcony owned by *all* the condominium unit owners in common, or do *you* own it—or do you own only the exclusive right to stand on it? And in the case of detached units, do you own the outside walls and foundation and roof, but not the land, or do you own only the interior space—or do you own the house *and* the land it stands upon with a shared ownership of roads, sewers, street lighting, some landscaping, and all the recreational facilities?

"Specifically designated" means exactly that. Conceivably you can own almost anything, so long as that ownership is written down. For example, you might own a garage or some space within a garage that is two hundred yards from your condominium unit, but that space must be stated as yours in your deed.

Many contracts between people can be sealed with a handshake (or a kiss) and be enforceable in a court of law, but all real estate contracts *must* be in writing. That was decided in England in 1677 and still holds in this country today. If you want to be certain of your ownership in a condominium, you must be certain that exactly what you own and what you share is *written down*.

Now to "common elements." In a co-op the corporation owns everything—therefore, everything is a common element—but you as a tenant/shareholder are assigned the exclusive right to use certain space. In a condominium, you *own* certain space and share the ownership of everything else.

But exactly what "everything else" is has to be written down too. Everything else might include, among other things, foundations; roofs; water pipes but not the fixtures in your apartment; heating systems and ducts; air-conditioning systems, but not room air-conditioners unless they are built into the walls, and then there is a question of who owns the working parts; hallways, stairs, and the space in the stair wells; electrical wiring that serves multiple units or is within the walls; the lobby, foyer, game room, laundry room, and maintenance staff apartment; land and landscaping; parking lots, although you might own the air space over a particular spot; recreation facilities including swimming pools, clubhouses, tennis courts, stables, golf courses, and so forth; and sometimes even the roads, sewers, sewerage processing plant, drainage systems, and special security facilities. "Common elements" are those structures, land, working systems, and facilities that serve the common usage of the members of the community.

To complicate matters just a little more (although in practice this complication clarifies who can use what), many condominiums also include areas that are called "limited common elements." A limited common element is one that is reserved for the exclusive use of one or more but less than all of the unit owners. Your seventeenth-floor balcony may be a limited common element. The structure of the balcony is part of the building and as such belongs to the common elements of the condominium, however only you, the owner of the unit, can use it or decide who will use it.

The basement of a building that contains four units could also qualify as a limited common element. The walls of the building's foundation are common elements; the space inside the walls, however, is reserved for the use of the four unit owners of that particular building. Often storage bins are built and basement laundry facilities are shared by those four unit owners.

So you own an "undivided interest" in the common elements. With an undivided interest you don't exactly own any *thing*, you own a share in each and every *thing* in the common elements. That does not mean that there is a tile in the swimming pool that is yours, or a tree tagged "Planted for Jane and Allen Forest." And the grate over the storm sewer in front of your apartment does not belong to you alone, even if you happen to think it would make an interesting sculpture hanging on the brick wall above your fireplace. Everybody owns a share of everything. You can get down to counting atoms if you like, but no one atom can have any individual name on it. An undivided interest is one that cannot be severed or separated.

Some condominium complexes handle this undivided share ownership of common elements by incorporating a homeowners' association. Individual condo owners then own shares in the homeowners' association much as co-op owners do. Like cooperatives, some units carry more shares, have more voting power, and pay a higher portion of the common expenses than others.

In other condominium communities the control of shared space is not incorporated but established in the condominium documents. The owners of the individual condominium units form a unit owners' association, homeowners' association, owners' association, or whatever they wish to call their group, and elect a board of managers (sometimes also called a board of directors). A specific number of votes in the association is assigned to each condo unit just as a specific number of shares is assigned to a particular apartment in a cooperative. Also as in a co-op, more votes equal more of a share in common expenses.

The condominium board of managers has virtually the same duties and powers as the cooperative's board of directors, except that it cannot rule on the sale of a unit or approve or disapprove of the buyers. Also, except in cases where the condominium documents set limits on subletting, the board of managers has no control over to whom or when the unit is sublet.

Some condominium communities, in an effort to establish a degree of control over the members of their association, include a right-of-first-refusal clause in their bylaws. In a right-of-first-refusal situation, the unit owners' association or its board of managers would have the opportunity to match any sale price that was agreed upon between seller and buyer and purchase the unit, thus closing out the perspective buyer. This procedure has little effect upon the seller since he/she still gets the agreed-upon sales price.

In order to assure the funds to support and maintain the common elements of a condominium community, its condominium documents establish the obligation of each unit owner to contribute to the maintenance costs of these areas. This financial responsibility is passed to the new owners with the sale of the unit. Most condominium documents also establish penalty fees for nonpayment or late payment, and these unpaid fees can become a lien on the individual unit itself.

Your Money and the Condo

Condominiums are usually considered easier to sell or trade than cooperative apartments because you, the owner, can determine when, if, and to whom you want to sell. They are also somewhat easier to mortgage because lending institutions use exactly the same mortgage instruments for condos that they use for detached single-family homes. Most banks therefore feel comfortable with condominium loans. In large urban areas where co-op loans are common practice, you won't have any problem arranging this type of financing either, but in a small- or medium-sized town where you are buying into the only cooperative building around, you may run into considerable red tape. Red tape usually born of ignorance, but still difficult to cut through.

Some "experts" maintain that condos are a safer investment than co-ops. Your investment, they say, is not tied to your neighbors as tightly as in a cooperative. If six of your condo neighbors "go under" and disappear, the banks that hold the mortgages on their units could all foreclose. In foreclosing, they obtain the right to occupy the space of that unit and must also take on the financial obligations that go with the ownership of common elements—that is, pay that apartment's share of maintenance costs. In practice, however, this does not always occur. Foreclosure proceedings must be started (which can drag out for what seems like eons) and maintenance charges are often *not* paid but simply added as a lien on the unit.

The people who do the maintenance work for the condominium still want to get paid, however, and the heating bills still come in. Granted the total amount of these expenses is smaller than in a co-op, where the mortgage on the building and real estate taxes must also be paid, but the default of several condominium owners could add the burden of higher maintenance fees to the shoulders of the remaining members (at least temporarily). Once the delinquent units are sold, however, the liens for unpaid maintenance fees are usually covered. The money is restored to the coffers of the condominium community and no one is too much the worse for wear.

The domino effect described in the section on co-ops could not occur in a condominium, but in difficult times or through mismanagement, maintenance of the common areas could deteriorate to such an extent that owning the space inside a near shambles would be worth very little. The risks therefore in a condominium and a cooperative are slightly different, but it would be very difficult to say which is the "safer" investment. So many other factors come into play when determining the security and potential appreciation of a building (which we'll talk about when we get to how to choose *your* apartment) that it is impossible to base a judgment solely upon the type of ownership offered. With good management, both condominiums and cooperatives can and will be safe and profitable investments.

Personal income-tax returns are perhaps a little simpler when you own a condo than a co-op. Since you *own* your space, you are directly assessed for property taxes by the municipality in which you live. These taxes and the interest on your condo mortgage are deductible from your gross personal income when filing for the IRS. Your maintenance fee to the condominium unit owners' association, however, is *not* deductible because no part of that fee is used to pay interest on a mortgage or municipal taxes. (In the same way only the *portion* of maintenance fees in a cooperative that is used to pay mortgage interest and municipal taxes is deductible.)

Because property taxes and mortgage interest are not included, condominium maintenance fees may appear considerably lower than co-op fees. To make an accurate comparison of living costs between a condo and a co-op, you must compare them on an equal basis. To do this, use the two forms in Chapter 9, pages 158–160.

As for investment potential—it's fabulous. Condominiums are the fastest-growing type of housing in this country today.

Life in a Condo

Once you get past the legal intricacies, life in a condo is little different from life in a co-op. Though you may own your own space, you live in close proximity with other people and share certain facilities with them. You therefore must respect their rights and needs, and you have the right to ask them to respect yours. You must also abide by the rules of your condominium documents.

Condos differ from co-ops in that they are being built in the suburbs, even in the country, as well as in the cities. This allows for more spacial spread, and therefore more variety in style. Most of the new condominium communities are bright and attractive in their youthful splendor, and even the older conversions often have open green space attached and owned by the community.

The newest fad in condo building is the "theme community." Yes, a bit like Disney World. You can buy into a New England fishing village in San Mateo, California; a cluster of *Great Gatsby* mansions in New Caanan, Connecticut; and what looks like the set from *Star Wars* or *Superman* in Tulsa, Oklahoma, to name only a few. And you pay for your fantasy.

Like co-op ownership, condominium ownership carries restrictions, virtually the same as those we listed under co-ops. What may be a restriction to one person, however, is a protection to another. What is an attraction for one (no maintenance work) may be a deprivation (I can't even plant a garden) for another. If reading the bylaws and operating guidelines of a community aroused little reaction in your gut, you probably are in the right place. If you have strong objections, look elsewhere rather than try to change your life-style to fit the community. Both newly built condos and renovated conversions are opening up everywhere, every day.

CHAPTER 2

Crystal Balls and Computers: How Good an Investment Are Co-ops and Condos?

The direction that real estate takes in the next decade will affect the economic health and physical comfort of every person in our nation. And there is no crystal ball into which we can gaze or massive computer into which we can punch codes that will provide us with a certain and accurate vision of that direction.

We can only evaluate, estimate, and predict, which is a sophisticated way of saying we can only guess. A serious guess, however, requires glancing backward into history to learn where we're coming from, evaluating the reality of what's happening today, then using that knowledge to answer the basic question of this book: *Are condominiums and cooperatives a good investment in this decade?*

Let's begin with the look backward. A home of your own as the American Dream has become a cliché. But anyone can understand where the concept got its strength. People came to this country from crowded European cities or from rural areas where the overwhelming portion of the available land was passed from generation to generation in the hands of a few families. In this country, the early settlers built houses and claimed a share of land as their own. Later, with westward expansion, the government offered free land to homesteaders.

Our early heritage, therefore, was based in the idea of "I want, I'll work, and I can own."

"It's not so easy nowadays!" you say. And we agree. But the I-can-own dream still lives for most Americans, although the specific vision in the dream has, of necessity, changed.

In the nineteenth century the dream was farmland. In the twentieth century it shifted to the city and was sweetened with Horatio Alger–style success stories. After World War II, the goal became escape from the city to suburbia, the new utopia, with a single-family home just like every other single-family home on the street, a white picket fence around a third of an acre, and perhaps a garage for the family car.

More than ever, homeownership became a goal, an investment, and a status symbol. In 1948, Hollywood enshrined this American Dream in celluloid. The film was called *Mr. Blandings Builds His Dream House*. With Cary Grant in the title role, it became a tremendous hit. Savvy builders put up models at the outer limits of their tracts and set out bright signs that read: MR. BLANDINGS' DREAM HOUSE OPEN FOR INSPECTION. Crowds flocked through.

Perhaps *Mr. Blandings Builds His Dream House* was a box-office success in 1948 because it captured and dramatized a life situation common to the social climate of its day. The movie depicts the flight of an upwardly mobile husband and wife and their two children out of the city and into the suburbs in search of a better life. They contract to build a house in Connecticut for $14,000, and after several plot complications, end up paying a whopping $24,000 for their dream house. All ends happily, however. Finances don't seem to be an overwhelming problem. The children have "fresh air and good schools," Mrs. Blandings has her home and her clubs, and Mr. Blandings is certainly king of his castle.

Now we watch the film with the condescending amusement usually reserved for the Bumsteads, because the problems it examines with light-handed satire are so removed from today's concerns.

If Hollywood or, more likely, a TV network were to attempt a contemporary film dealing with American housing, there would be little room for clowning. The producers would probably choose to do a documentary. It would be shot in a variety of cities and suburbs across the country and people from every socioeconomic level would be given a chance to voice their opinions. And we'd hear the recurrent theme of disillusion and difficulty and the cry for change that would make a new dream possible.

The following housing stories are typical of what we'd hear. They sharpen our focus on the housing scene today and clarify where today's demands will take us in the next decade.

Locked-out First-home Buyers

Peggy and Tom Starter live in the kind of apartment complex often advertised as *Garden Apartments*. There are no gardens. Their back door looks out upon paved parking areas. Their front door is separated from the road by fifty feet of grass.

Peggy is very pregnant. Tom is lean, dressed in jeans and a cotton shirt. He is pushing a stroller that seats a curly-haired toddler, and he is pushing a little too fast. The family is out for a walk, but both Tom and Peggy are angry, at each other and at *things*.

It had started the evening before when Peggy's mother (visiting from Florida) said sweetly to Tom over after-dinner coffee, "Wouldn't you like to move, Tom, now that *another* baby's coming?"

Tom's voice started out in measured tones. "Yes, we'd like very much to move. We've been looking for a place for almost two years, *you know that*, we've told you. Look, Mom, we're caught. We had saved twenty thousand dollars for the down payment on a house while we were both working. Everything was great, we were going to buy right after the baby came. We got caught by the crazy mortgage market. We're trapped, don't you understand?"

An argument had flared. Peggy's voice became strained as she tried to explain to her mother that they had been the victims of circumstance.

Her mother couldn't seem to understand. With Tom in programming and Peggy in nursing, she thought, they should have enough to make it. She started one of her stories. "In our day, your father and I worked harder, saved more, sacrificed. A *home* for our children was important to us . . ."

The words flew, Tom trying to explain that they couldn't save enough, fast enough, Peggy trying to tell her mother that she too wanted a *home* for her children but to her that meant being with her children while they were young!

Under pressure, Peggy and Tom finally told Peggy's mother that they were considering buying a condominium apartment or refurbishing an old house near the center of town. But the older woman, still in a world of years ago, didn't approve. Emotions got mixed with divided loyalties and everyone got angry.

Forty-two million Americans will reach the prime home buying age of thirty in the 1980s; the majority of them are like Peggy and Tom Starter. Data compiled in 1980 by the United States League of Savings Associations showed that in 1979 (when interest rates hovered between 8 and 9 percent) fewer than one in five mortgages went to first-time buyers. Price was the squeezing factor then. Today? Statistics indicate that with interest rates in the mid teens, 95 percent of American families cannot qualify for the mortgages they would like, even when the lending institutions are willing to consider up to 35 percent of gross family income toward housing costs.

So what are people doing? Some are waiting, uncertain about the economy. Others are realizing that they must be flexible and willing to embrace new dreams.

Changing Attitudes and the Corporate Scene

In a New Jersey suburb on the edge of the affluent hill country of Jackie Onassis, June and Paul Travelor, a couple in their forties with no children, are walking away from a rather sleezy Cape Cod on a large, irregular, and poorly kept lot. The real estate agent is still talking with the owners at the front door.

"What do you think of it?" asks Paul.

"Think of it!" replies his wife. "I couldn't believe it. It made me sick in the pit of my stomach. Ninety-two thousand dollars for that!"

"I know what you mean. Our house in Memphis is probably worth only $85,000 and it is twice the size of this one, only two years old, and in a prestige neighborhood. The prices out here are absolutely unreal. They're trying to sell New York City with an acre of land per household! If I had known my job change would cost us so much, I don't think I would have taken it."

The real estate agent joins the couple. "Now isn't this a magnificent piece of land, Mr. Travelor?"

Paul isn't completely sure he's serious. "Oh, yeah! It'll take two years to get the crabgrass out or two hours a week to keep it mowed short enough to look like unspecific greenery."

June breaks in. "You know, I think we're doing this all wrong. We could get a decent co-op in Brooklyn or Queens for $85,000."

There is a strained moment of silence. The kind of quiet that's just a little too long. Logically Paul is the only one who can break it, and finally he does. He sounds as though he wants to talk very fast and is therefore talking *very* slowly. "You mean you'd move back *into New York City?* When we went to Memphis you said you wanted a place in the country."

June doesn't answer immediately. The real estate agent looks both uncomfortable and worried. Three people are standing in front of a FOR SALE sign, saying nothing, and being watched by the owners of the house from behind the curtains of the bedroom window.

June kicks some pebbles. "Maybe I'm disillusioned." Her voice is rising. "Maybe I'm sick and tired of driving the damn car miles and miles every time I want anything! Look, I guess deep down I miss the city. And besides, there are some very good reasons for going back."

Before she can go on, the agent breaks in, determined not to let things get any more out of hand. "We have some lovely older homes in the next town that have rather small yards to mow."

Paul laughs. ". . . And furnaces to fix and pipes that leak. No, thanks."

With her back to the agent, June begins speaking again, seeming to throw ideas into the air. "If we move into a co-op, we won't need two cars, and you won't have an hour-and-a-half commute each way every day. I'm sure the heating costs will be less than on a godforsaken open hill like this, and we'll have some time for fun in our lives instead of being slaves to the house every weekend."

Paul is not quite convinced, but interested. "I still hate the subways," he mutters.

June says nothing. The real estate agent is flipping the pages of his book trying to find a dream home for this couple.

There are two important insights to glean from this story. The first is the dilemma of the executive transferee. In certain areas of the country, principally surrounding major cities, housing has appreciated much faster than the national average, and it continues to appreciate despite the housing recession. Families transferred from areas of lower housing appreciation are being cut by a double-edge sword. First their dollars buy much less house in their new location, and second, they must often turn in low-interest-rate mortgages to take on variable rate loans at double their old interest.

This phenomenon is making management personnel reluctant to move. Only a few years ago, a raise and a promotion were incentive enough to send family and furniture across the country. Today the benefits and extras offered by the company are more crucial than salary in the decision to accept or reject a promotion requiring a move. "Will the company pay me the difference in interest costs?" is becoming a common question. And "No, I don't think I want the transfer" is becoming an even more common answer.

The result? Fewer houses for sale and fewer house-hunters. And more important, those who do accept transfers are weighing the advantages and disadvantages of a larger variety of housing options. Especially in the highest-priced metropolitan areas, condominiums and cooperatives are much in demand.

The second insight apparent in the story concerns a changing buyer attitude. June and Paul are representative of a rapidly growing number of couples who see the city as a realistic alternative to suburban living. Their thinking is being voiced in living rooms, parks, committee meetings, and church socials across the country. Newspaper and magazine articles are headlining the "Renaissance of the City."

Gentrification is a term they bandy about. Briefly it means the buying of run-down inner-city houses or apartment buildings by well-educated, upwardly mobile young individuals or groups who intend to rejuvenate their buildings and eventually their neighborhoods. Some of these buildings are brownstones, some old frame houses that were once considered elegant, some small apartment houses that the new owners intend to convert to co-ops or condominiums. Even the four- and six-family houses of the 1930s are being bought up by small groups for conversion.

In California, for example, duplexes, triplexes, and fourplexes led a condominium conversion craze in the late 1960s. Today, lofts, warehouses, and abandoned office buildings are appealing to creative gentrifiers. Gentrification creates more beautiful and more expensive city neighborhoods, but it raises another question. As neighborhoods become more expensive, the poor are moved out. Where and how will *they* be housed? No one has yet found an adequate solution.

The Crisis in Rental Housing

In Dallas, Texas, Joe Pedpower, a young man in his early thirties, is jogging in a city park. He is joined by a woman acquaintance from the office. Between puffs, she complains about the delayed closing on a small house in the suburbs that she is about to buy. A good place for her and the children, she says, and she wants to get in.

Joe stops and turns to her. He is feeling just a little envious of her alimony and her down-payment money.

"You're damned lucky," he says. "I can't even find a decent place to rent. Right now I'm sharing this three-room flat, two bedrooms and a kitchen, with some guy I don't even know. Just until I can find a place I can afford, you understand. And you know what, there *are* no decent places. Not that I can afford anyway."

He starts jogging again, just fast enough that his woman friend has difficulty keeping pace.

The rental situation in the United States is reaching crisis proportions. In July 1981 the nationwide vacancy rate reached 5 percent, the lowest on record. In many cities, however, it was even lower. New York has been hovering between 2 and 2.5 percent for several years. Palo Alto, California, has been *under* 2 percent since the early 1970s!

A study by Advance Mortgage Corporation, the nation's fourth-largest lender, blames the shortage on the virtual collapse in production. Approximately 75,000 unsubsidized rental starts in 1981 marked the lowest record since World War II, and to make matters worse, nearly a third of those starts were in two market areas, Houston and Dallas-Fort Worth. Even after adding government-subsidized starts, the total only approaches 250,000, still the lowest figure since 1958. New starts do not even come close to filling the demand.

George Sternlieb, director of the Center for Urban Policy Research at Rutgers University, has found that 40 percent of today's rental housing is over forty years old. Each year the nation loses about 2 percent of that rental housing stock (500,000 units) to deterioration and demolition. In addition to the need to replace this 500,000-unit-a-year loss, Mr. Sternlieb estimates that the nation needs to build 4.1 million new units during the decade of the 1980s. We are not doing it.

Why so little building activity when there is such a demonstrated demand? Interest rates again. Advance Mortgage cites the unavailability of standard apartment mortgages as the chief bottleneck to more building. Like "creative financing" in the single-family marketplace, today's apartment houses are being financed with standby commitments, five-year construction loans, joint ventures with saving associations or life insurance companies, or, rarely, with all cash.

And where does this leave the renter? Doubling up and looking for a place to live. For anyone who can scrape together the money necessary, the security of owning a condo or co-op begins to look very appealing. But let's take a look at rental apartment building from the other side of the desk.

Builders and the Dollar

In a well-decorated office that overlooks the Hartford skyline from its two corner walls of glass, an obviously wealthy businessman sits behind an antique carved desk. His secretary brings in two cups of coffee, offering one to a young reporter from the local newspaper.

The businessman, Jonathan G. Stonecutter, started out in jeans and flannel shirts ten years ago to be the "biggest builder in New England." He has almost made it.

He leans back in his chair and responds to the reporter's question. "No, I'm not putting up any more rental apartment buildings in this city or anywhere else either."

The reporter is a little anxious. He *knows* that Stonecutter has stopped building rental buildings; now he wants to know *why*. But he had done his homework, and he throws out a lead.

"I just read a bunch of statistics that say the country has a shortage of rental housing and that the shortage is getting worse. With so much demand, why not build?"

"Money."

The reporter laughs with a sarcastic edge. "It's hard to believe that you're hurting for money."

"Not my money," replies Stonecutter earnestly, "other people's. Let me explain something to you. If I decide to put up a new high-rise rental building in a prime area of this city, it will cost me approximately two hundred dollars a square foot to build it. At that rate a fifteen-hundred-square-foot apartment will cost me three hundred thousand dollars to build. Now multiply that times 100 apartments. Think about the kind of rent I'll have to charge to service the mortgage debt, pay taxes, management costs, maintenance costs, insurance, and make some small (and it gets smaller every year) profit. Only the wealthiest could afford that rent, and the trend among the upper socioeconomic classes is to buy condos or co-ops rather than rent. So either I have to cut rental prices or the apartments go begging, even with the low vacancy rates in this area. That's why new, non-government-subsidized rental apartment construction just doesn't pay. In this business the dollar is the bottom line. Which is why we're building three gorgeous condominium complexes just outside of town. I can build and sell those at a profit and I don't have to worry about carrying costs."

The high cost of land and construction, the scarcity of apartment financing, and the inability of rental income to profitably service the mortgage debt and maintenance expenses of new buildings are all deterrents to new rental construction. And in some cities entrepreneurs are further deterred from new projects by rent control.

As of this writing, rent control is operating in New York City and surrounding counties; Boston; Washington, D.C.; Los Angeles; San Francisco; at least 130 communities in New Jersey; and a dozen other California cities. It is also a recurrent topic of discussion and controversy in hundreds of other cities throughout the country. Long before the current escalation in interest rates, rent control and rent stabilization were a contributing factor to unprofitable apartment building ownership. They were also a contributing factor, therefore, to deterioration and abandonment, and the conversion to condominium or cooperative ownership. Rent control, however, does protect the poor, the middle class, and the elderly in times and places where the demand for living space is so great that the potential profits in unregulated rental would tempt even the most humanistic landlord to gather in higher profits.

Doubling Up and Overcrowding

On a tennis court that might be Anywhere, USA, a man in his late twenties grabs the ball and shouts to the woman across the net, "Let's call it a night, O.K.?"

As he walks off the court, he's stopped by a professional pollster. "Do you think the President is effectively handling the housing crisis?"

The man looks surprised, then incredulous.

"Housing? Are you kidding? That's a joke. You know where we're living? Downstairs in my parents' house, that's where. Not exactly the cellar—they call the place a raised ranch and we even have a little kitchen and our own outside door. But every week or so we have to listen to 'So when are you two going to get married?' or some variation on that theme like how nice it would be to have a little grandchild!"

The dark-haired young woman from the other side of the net has joined the group and caught the gist of the conversation. She slips her racquet into a needlepoint case saying, "I'll tell you one thing, being born in this baby-boom generation is a bummer. Every time we get to a stage of our lives, it's always overcrowded. Sure we'd like a place of our own. We can't find one and we can't afford it if we could."

Between 1947 and 1957 this country experienced the highest birth rate in its history. In the 1950s towns across the nation were building elementary schools and taxing their residents for them. Many are now closed. In the 1960s and 1970s, it was tough getting into college; now recruiters are just a step away from going door-to-door in search of students to fill their dorms. And then the boom moved into housing. Part of the price spiral of the 1970s was caused by the nearly thirty-two million Americans who reached home-buying age during that decade. And now those high prices and the mortgage crunch are forcing the second half of the "boom" to double up and overcrowd existing housing.

Add this to the fact that apartment building has virtually stopped and that new single-family housing starts touched new lows in each of the succeeding years between 1979 and 1982, and you have documented evidence of the most explosive pent-up demand for housing in our history.

What will that mean for the future? No one can be absolutely sure, but we see pressure for construction of smaller, more space- and energy-efficient living units and a search for methods of construction that will take less time and cost less money. Modular and manufactured housing should become more acceptable and widely used. More people will live in shared-space housing. There will be more rehabilitation of existing housing. Condominium and cooperative homeownership will become more common and more popular than detached single-family homeownership.

The Retirement Plight

At the same tennis court, the couple who were doubling up with his parents leaves, but the pollster is approached by a man in his late sixties. He introduces himself as John Elder and begins a nonstop tirade, his resentment and frustration overflowing into his voice.

"I couldn't help hearing you talk with those kids. Baby boom, hell! I don't feel sorry for them. They're young. They ought to get out and work a little harder instead of playing tennis in their little white suits.

"Now us older folks, we've really got troubles. How would you like to try to live on a fixed income in these times, huh? Oh, yeah, there's Social Security, but even with their raises, it isn't enough. There's no money left over for *us* to buy fancy tennis clothes!

"Me and the missus, we want to sell our house and move down near Phoenix, where it's a little warmer and maybe a little cheaper to live. We want to get one of those condo apartments so we don't have to do yard work. But do you think we can sell our house? No, sir! No one can afford the mortgage payments, that's what those real estate agents keep telling us. They want us to say we'll give the mortgage and then, they say, we'll sell real quick. We've been thinking about it too. I suppose it's all right if whoever buys the place makes the payments on time 'cause then we could make our payments down south. But my Martha, she's worried what'll happen if they don't pay."

The lengthened life span of Americans is contributing to the nation's housing problems. Many municipalities across the country protect senior citizens from real estate tax increases, rent increases, and from eviction when
a rental building is converted to a condo or co-op. These are the lucky seniors,
but they are also a statistically significant problem. Often rent- and tax-
protected older people live alone in units that once housed whole families.
No one would ask them to move, but we must acknowledge their effect
upon the housing marketplace.

For those senior citizens selling their homes, however, the market is
difficult. Many are forced to hold mortgages, thus effectively lowering their
profits on the houses they are selling and limiting their buying power or
rental limits in a retirement community. Those who do buy again after the
sale of their houses are buying condominiums and co-ops overwhelmingly.
They have contributed to both the population growth and the price escalation of housing in the Sun Belt.

Single-person Households

At a restaurant table in San Francisco, a young woman—say,
twenty-five—is talking with a man of nearly fifty. Her expression could
only be described as earnest.

"I think trying to get started is the toughest thing in this society today.
Being young, a woman, and inexperienced puts three strikes against me
before I even walk into a business interview. I don't know which is worse,
finding a job or a place to live. But I do know one thing, I want to be
on my own."

Her companion smiles. "It's pretty tough. Especially for young people.
But I know what you mean about being on your own. Thing is, though, *you*
have a lot of choices in where you live. You can get a one-room studio and
really make it work. Now me, I'm divorced and I have kids. *That* means
restrictions. I needed a place that was nice but not too expensive and with
extra rooms for the kids when they're with me. I had to take one of those
townhouses on Maple Street. It's really big for me when I'm alone, but I
love it when it's full."

Demographics show that the number of single-person households in this
country is increasing rapidly. In statistics released by the United States
Census Bureau comparing 1970 to 1980, the number of persons living alone

increased by 58.5 percent. In a housing survey conducted by Advance Mortgage Corporation, studies showed that if single-person nonfamily households continue to grow at the 1970s rate, the 1980s could record a demand by singles of 2.7 million units a year, 10 percent above the average of the 1970s. And even if the growth of these single-person households levels off, it is likely to average a demand of 2.3 million units a year—a good deal of added pressure on the housing scene in a time when other factors are also contributing to increased housing demand.

Single-person households comprise a high percentage of condominium and cooperative owners. A HUD survey released in 1980 showed that 57 percent of the conversion condo or co-op owners in major cities were single. (Thirty-six percent were women, 21 percent were men.) The figures would certainly be lower if suburban shared-space housing were included in the study, but even there, singles comprise a significant portion of owners and should continue to increase the demand for owned shared-space units.

Foreign Investment

In the parking lot of a shopping center lined with royal palms, a middle-aged man in a gray double-knit suit is arguing with another man. He shakes his finger in the air to make his point.

"Listen to me, I know about housing! I know right where the bottom of the problem is too. It's the foreigners. We've got foreigners buying up the best places. Not just here in Florida, I'm telling you. Everywhere, all over the country! Those guys know this is a great country and they're putting their money in real estate here for safekeeping. And that's what makes it hard on us Americans. We have to pay more because there's a scarcity. Not enough good places for us to live, never mind them foreigners."

The increase in foreign investment in the United States over the past several years has prompted the passage of three new laws in Congress:
The International Investment Survey Act of 1976;
The International Agricultural Investment Disclosure Act of 1979; and
The Foreign Investment Real Property Tax Act of 1980.
In addition to these federal laws, forty-five states have also enacted restriction or disclosure legislation on foreign investment. Prior to this legislation, neither the federal nor state government had any way of knowing how extensive foreign investment was in this country.

The fact is that United States real estate is an appealing investment. According to a study done by the National Association of Realtors, foreign direct investment in the United States amounts to $53 billion, or 1 percent of all the nation's capital. And still it grows, with Australia, New Zealand, and South America as the most active investors currently, and Germany close behind.

In terms of residential purchases, condominiums are the preferred form of investment among the foreign resident population. There are no statistics available that testify to the demand or extra pressure put upon shared-space housing by foreign residents or investors, but that demand is both real and growing.

Housing in the United States is in trouble. And change is inevitable. Why? The answer is as ancient as trade itself: *supply and demand.* What drives up the price of anything is shortage. A shortage when there is a demand means the "thing" becomes more dear, and that means more expensive and more valuable.

We see a growing demand for condominiums and cooperatives in this decade *and* a growing shortage. Let's briefly summarize the reasons.

Supply:

1. The number of single-family housing starts has fallen off to the lowest levels since World War II.

2. New rental apartment building construction is slowing to a turtle walk.

3. We are losing approximately 2 percent of our rental housing stock to deterioration and demolition each year.

4. New condominium starts have been the only segment of the housing industry to show a slight increase in activity from 1980 through 1982.

Demand:

1. Homeownership is a part of "the American dream" and will remain so. The particulars of the dream are changing but not its intensity, and tax laws still encourage and support the dream.

2. The "baby boom" needs housing.

3. Senior citizens need housing.

4. The number of single-person households is increasing, thus increasing the number of dwelling units required.

5. High mortgage rates have made single-family home purchases impossible for the majority of first-home buyers; shared-space housing is less expensive and puts homeownership within their reach.

6. Cities are becoming attractive places to live again and apartment building conversions put city homeownership within the reach of people who have rented most of their lives and probably never thought of ownership as a possibility.

7. Energy-efficient housing is a major buyer concern; multi-unit buildings are more energy efficient than single-family houses.

8. Vacation condominiums are a preferred ownership scheme in the Sun Belt and ski regions.

9. Foreign investment in real estate is increaing.

So here we have the situation: Housing supply is shrinking, housing demand is increasing. Condominiums and cooperatives are a desirable and affordable housing option. And there are not and will not be enough of them in the next decade.

This would be a nice place to end this chapter, but there's one more important point to be made. Yes, we are saying that the long-term investment outlook for condos and co-ops is excellent. We are not saying, however, that every person who buys a condo or co-op will make a fortune on it. Shortage *is* the major determinant of value, but it is not the *only* factor, especially when we stop talking about the national picture and look at the particular condo or co-op that you are considering. It's one thing to know that the national mural is magnificent, but quite another to evaluate the snapshot you just took of a particular building or a particular apartment.

Hold supply and demand in one hand, then, and in the other hold location (area of the country, municipality, and neighborhood), price, appearance, quality and cost of maintenance, and desirability. These are the elements you must juggle and evaluate in making your decision about a condo or co-op purchase. And while you're juggling, a few other questions might pop into your head. How would you evaluate a conversion offering? Is it a good idea to buy on paper before construction even begins? How can you find out the fair market value of a resale? What about condos or co-ops purely as investment property?

We've spent a chapter telling you that condos and co-ops look vibrantly healthy for the future. Now we need the rest of this book to tell you how to choose the good ones, and then how to come up smiling as an investor and a homeowner.

CHAPTER 3

Smart-Money Variables: Key Factors in Judging Property Value

Have you ever watched people betting at the racetrack? Sometimes it's more fun than watching the races. Each person has his own system: numbers, names, colors, birthdays. Some racing fans even swear they can smell a winner. But scattered about the park, usually in lawn chairs under trees, are some very quiet people with their copies of *Racing Forum* and a pencil. They often bet just before the bell; they win more often than most people.

Why? Usually because they add knowledge to intuition. They have learned to read all the records before betting a race and they have learned how to weigh, consider, and compare the variables. Theirs is the proverbial "smart money."

Many people buy real estate the way they bet horses. Gut feelings rule. And just as at the races, they win sometimes and they lose sometimes. Also at the real estate marketplace, however, are buyers who have learned to read the facts and weigh the variables. To a certain extent their purchases are also bets, but usually best bets. They win much more often, and they win bigger.

This chapter is your initiation into that smart-money set. We'll introduce you to the variables that affect and determine the value of a piece of property. There is no magic Green Card that will guarantee a winner every time, but the how-to-judge and what's-important knowledge that we'll give you will add confidence to your investing and dramatically increase your odds for substantial profits. To tie theory to substance, we're going to compare two typical apartments—horses, if you will—and show you where we'd place our bet.

We've chosen a location in south Florida where there are literally thousands of apartments, both condominiums and cooperatives. These are the advertisements for our two places as they might appear in the classified section of the *Miami Herald*.

Two bedroom, 2 bath condominium apartment with balcony and view. Convenience, abundant recreational facilities nearby, tremendous investment potential. $84,900. Financing available. Call Ten Palms, The Condo Company! 555-5434.

Two bedroom, 2 bath co-op apartment. Poolside location. By owner, $119,000. 555-1234.

From these ads you guess we will be comparing two apartments of about the same size and amenities, yet you see a $34,000 + difference in asking price. Should these apartments, in fact, be compared by the same buyer? Why is one so much more expensive? Which is the better deal? Let's look at them.

The condominium is on the seventeenth floor of The Flamingo, a nine-year-old high-rise located just off U.S. 1, south of the center of Miami. Route 1 in this area is an unlimited-access highway with many traffic lights and extensive commercial development. The Flamingo stands alone above the highway and the businesses, a pale pink tower with white wrought-iron balconies stepped floor-by-floor upward at each corner.

It is a beautiful building, yet we have a sense that it is out of place. There is a vacant lot on its right side, and a once stately but now rather shabby house on the left with a chiropractor's shingle hanging from the porch. A huge, but well-maintained and attractive mobile-home park spreads over most of the land on the other side of the street. Small stucco houses populate the remaining area with the exception of a Quick Check grocery on the corner. The street is zoned for commercial use despite its primarily residential appearance.

Construction was started on The Flamingo in 1973. It was almost complete when the condominium bubble burst in 1974. Since the Miami/Fort Lauderdale area was extensively overbuilt, the recession and the virtual shutdown of the mortgage marketplace brought sales to a halt. The Flamingo's builder was forced to declare bankruptcy; the property went into receivership; and it was finally purchased by a huge real estate management and sales

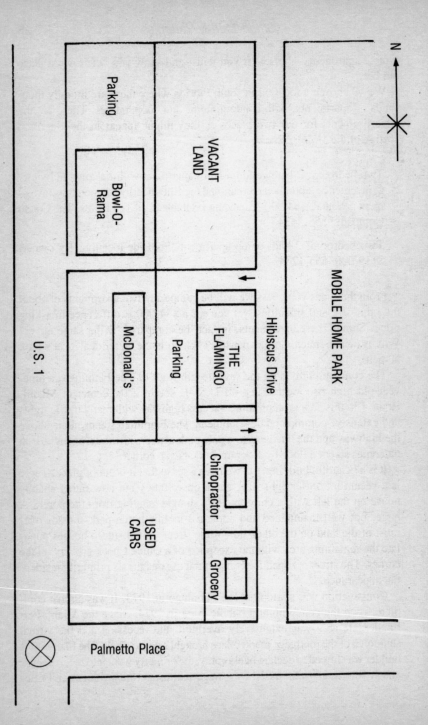

corporation, Ten Palms Inc., which finished construction and rented the apartments.

Development surrounding The Flamingo, however, took an unexpected turn. Instead of new condominiums or apartment buildings, the land on both sides of U.S. 1 was built up with commercial establishments. McDonald's took the piece immediately behind the pink high-rise, a bowling alley came in next to McDonald's on one side, a used-car dealer on the other.

In 1981 Ten Palms began the conversion process. By the time of our visit, 55 percent of the apartments had been sold. The one advertised was recently vacated.

Some readers may be wondering by now how an ordinary buyer would ever find out all this background. What if we were just transferred to the Miami area? We'd have no way to know all this beforehand. How would we get this kind of information?

It's easier than you might think. Most of the information could have been pieced together by anyone asking questions of the real estate agents handling the condo sale. Or if they had been silent or evasive (which they might well have been considering that they work for the seller), one could gather all the information by asking questions of competing real estate agents in the area. Questions are one of a buyer's most powerful tools; don't hesitate to ask them again and again. And compare the answers that you get to the same questions from different sources.

But let's move on to the inspection of that two-bedroom, two-bath apartment. Inside, everything is spotlessly clean, newly painted, and newly carpeted. The appliances in the eat-in kitchen are new. The bathrooms were recently done over with Formica panels. Both bedrooms are about the same size, and the dining area could easily be converted into a third bedroom. We can just catch a glimpse of the ocean from the balcony.

On the main floor of the building is a foyer, a larger common room with its own kitchen ("just right for association parties," the real estate agent tells us), a recreation room with a pool table, table tennis, and several bridge tables, and an apartment occupied by the building superintendent and his family. In the brochures spread across the foyer table we read that maintenance fees for the unit advertised are set at $165 a month. "No reserve fund fees are included in this maintenance charge," says the brochure, "since the sponsor has deposited a generous reserve fund of $10,000 against future repairs." Further down the page it says, "The management company has been contracted for the next ten years in order to continue the finest available condominium management for unit owners of The Flamingo."

Outdoors there is no pool (the original builder never got that far), but ample parking between the building and the back fence of McDonald's property. Two shuffleboard courts and a sitting area complete the complex.

Are we ready to buy? Definitely not after seeing only one apartment. So let's inspect the co-op advertised by owners in Hollywood-by-the-Sea.

Crystal Sands is a twenty-year-old cluster of buildings that was once an oceanside resort apartment motel. Three two-story buildings form a U that faces the ocean with a grassy sitting area in the center. Across Sea View Road two four-story buildings form an L that sets off a pool and gardens.

Crystal Sands has been a co-op for twelve years; eight years remain on its 7-percent self-amortizing mortgage. Only the one unit advertised in the newspaper is currently for sale.

High-rise condominiums surround Crystal Sands on three sides. A time share resort and a motel stand on either side of the waterfront buildings. Parking is at the door of the L-shaped building and in a lot owned by the co-op across yet another street.

There is a walk of two short blocks from some parking spaces to the waterfront buildings. The zoning is commercial.

Anyone approaching the cooperative could not help but be impressed by the beautifully maintained gardens, the cleanliness of the buildings and walkways, and the tasteful and inviting arrangements of chairs, lounges, and tables by the pool and near the beach.

A management company is employed by the board of directors and a superintendent lives in one of the units. Maintenance fees for the two-bedroom co-op apartment that we came to see are $225 a month. (Low because of the small mortgage being carried at a low interest rate and the carefully supervised budgeting that has characterized Crystal Sands over the years.)

Inside the apartment, we find the kitchen small, pullman-style, with just enough working space for one, but with sufficient cabinets and a good-sized storage closet. One bedroom is very large with two closets and its own bath, the other is smaller but will hold twin beds comfortably. The main bathroom is interior; a fan turns on with the light switch. It seems a little musty. The tiles are faded pink, and the fixtures really need replacing.

The dining L is mirrored to give the illusion of more space. It could not be converted into a bedroom or den since it is the only walkway to the large living room. The front door (the one that opens from the living room) leads to the poolside.

Without inquiry, the sellers volunteer the information that they are willing to take back a purchase money straight mortgage of $60,000 at 12 percent for a term of five years. (An explanation of mortgaging terms is in Chapter 8.) We get the feeling that they are quite eager to sell.

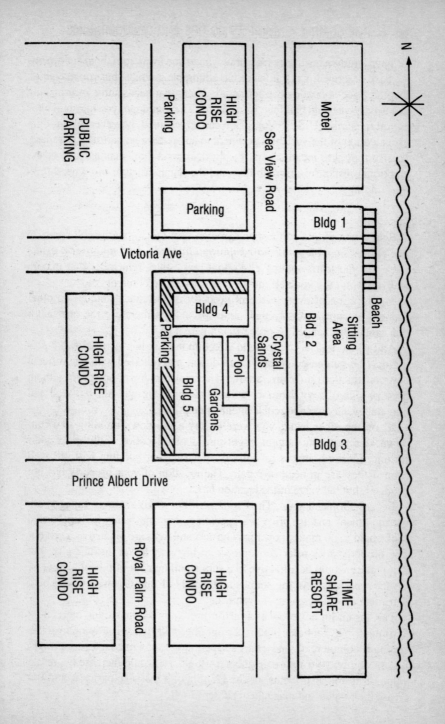

Your intuitive responses may draw you to and away from both apartments we have described. Crystal Sands has admirable grounds, but you may think that the price is rather steep for an apartment that needs some refurbishing in a twenty-year-old building. Considering The Flamingo, you may pull back as you remember U.S. 1. Confusion can be resolved, however, by a rational evaluation of the variables pertinent to any potential apartment purchase. Briefly they are: location, space, physical condition, maintenance costs, emotional response, affordability, and the legal structure of ownership in the building.

Location

Real estate people don't often agree on very much, but they all agree on one point: *Location is the most important factor in determining real estate value*. If you learn nothing else about real estate, remember that maxim and you won't dig yourself into trouble too deep to climb out of.

The location of every piece of property is absolutely unique; no other property occupies exactly that same space. It is therefore the one factor that cannot be changed. A property is where it is.

And where it is has a profound effect upon its value. A run-down building may be purchased cheaply, torn down, and replaced with magnificent new construction. If the area around it remains run-down, however, without hope or sign of revitalization, units in the building will not sell well and may not even command replacement value prices.

If, on the other hand, you were to buy a run-down building in a run-down area that you thought might turn about, location could make your fortune. Once an area is revitalized, units in your building will sell well even if they are in need of repair. The location of your property has not changed, but the value of the location *has*.

Because of its location, The Flamingo is not a bargain, even though both the apartment and its price are appealing. No one wants to live behind McDonald's, no matter how many bushes and trees are planted as a screen. The property does offer convenience to highway travel into the city, but that feature would be attractive to a very small number of potential buyers. To the vast majority, the sounds and smells of that highway would be a detriment far outweighing convenience.

The vacant lot next door is a factor of unknown impact, and therefore a detriment. Yes, another high-rise might be built there. But remember the zoning is commercial, and a bar, a supermarket, or a massage parlor might just as well be your future neighbor. A high-rise would increase the resale value of all the apartments in The Flamingo; a massage parlor would decrease their value and make them harder to sell.

The mobile home park across the street, though well-maintained and attractive, is a detriment to other residential real estate appreciation because the properties there (mobile homes on rented lots) are less valuable than the condominium apartments in The Flamingo or even the small stucco single-family homes on the street. *Residential property appreciates best when surrounded by like or more valuable residential property.*

The location of Crystal Sands is a major factor in supporting its higher price for an apartment of relatively the same size. The proximity to the ocean accounts for at least part of that premium price. Coastline, usually being limited to what nature put in place, is a finite commodity and therefore relatively scarce. In an area of the country where recreation facilities are in high demand, oceanside is worth many thousands of dollars. The bit of ocean view that one catches from the balcony of the apartment in The Flamingo can't compete.

Like The Flamingo, Crystal Sands is located in a commercially zoned area, but all the land surrounding it is either built upon or accounted for and in use. The new high-rise condominiums in the immediate area increase the value of the older co-op apartments in the building we have come to inspect. The resort motel next door does property values in Crystal Sands no harm since its use is residential (and rather expensive) as opposed to the eating, sales, and recreational uses of the commercial properties near The Flamingo.

But we've been talking about the condominium and cooperative as wholes; what about the two individual units? *The location of an apartment within the building or buildings of a co-op or condominium complex usually has some effect on its desirability and/or value.* In The Flamingo the apartment we have inspected is one of the most desirable, located near the top of the building and looking away from the commercial highway toward the ocean. This desirability is not reflected in the maintenance fee since all two-bedroom, two-bath apartments pay the same fee. (The percentage of undivided interest was determined by square feet alone. We'll explain in detail in the next chapter.) The location of the advertised apartment in The Flamingo, therefore, is a genuine plus since its desirability is not reflected in its monthly cost. Don't be overly impressed, however; you can still hear the street noise from the balcony.

In Crystal Sands the apartment we have inspected is one of the least desirable. Poolside is a mixed factor, convenient but noisy. Ground floor may be attractive to older or handicapped buyers, but upper floors are usually preferable, since they are quieter. Distance from the beach is a minus, compounded in this case by the necessity of crossing a road (even though its speed limit is 25 mph). The proximity of parking spaces is another mixed blessing, some prospective buyers may like it, others may be turned off by it. The most desirable, the most salable, and without doubt the most expensive apartments in Crystal Sands are those in the building on the ocean with ocean views.

The advertised apartment, however, pays a smaller maintenance fee than others of like size, since its location was taken into consideration when share allocations were made. For someone who does not object to its first-floor poolside site, therefore, it is all the more a bargain.

The effects and importance of location, however, are not limited exclusively to what can be seen at an on-site inspection. The character of the city or town is also a major factor. *The economic health and stability, demographics, tax structure, municipal services (including schools), recreational facilities, and transportation facilities of a municipality all affect the value of the residential real estate within it.*

Evaluating these factors takes some digging. A trip to the town hall may be necessary to look at zoning maps or master plans for future development. Perhaps an inspection of one or two of the schools and an interview with a principal would be advisable for families with children. Certainly a driving tour of the whole town, hopefully guided by a knowledgeable resident or real estate agent is indispensable.

Real estate agents can be of tremendous help in evaluating and comparing municipalities as well as individual properties, and their services should be used. Besides their personal knowledge of the area in which they do business, they can provide printed statistics on population, taxes, schools, and municipal facilities. Again we urge you to ask questions. And ask the agent to get you the information you want if it is not readily available in his/her office. In the event that your agent doesn't answer your questions or provide the information you request, *change agents*. Most real estate offices also have street maps in their closets that are available for the asking. Take one.

Space

Space is the second most important factor in determining real estate value, but it can only be compared to like space in a like environment. In other words, the fact that you can get about the same amount of space at The Flamingo for less money than at Crystal Sands is irrelevant. It's the old story of comparing apples and oranges. The very different nature of the two locations makes the apartments unlike commodities; comparison of space as a determinant of value is therefore impossible.

Let's say for the sake of this discussion that we have decided that $85,000 is the most we can afford to spend for an apartment. Crystal Sands, therefore, is out. Should we buy in The Flamingo? Is it a good deal?

You know that the location isn't so great for resale potential, but you really aren't bothered by the highway or the commercial development. After all, you think, it's a place to live, the space is certainly adequate, and if it's convenient to work, why *not* buy it?

We don't know what it's worth, that's why! The price looks great compared to the price of the co-op in Crystal Sands, but how does it look when The Flamingo is compared to other condominiums located near it, or in similar areas of neighboring communities? Comparison is essential to the accurate estimation of property value.

Maybe you're thinking, I'm not a real estate agent, much less an appraiser. How am I supposed to accurately estimate property value?

It's easier than you imagine and you can use some of the very same tools an appraiser would use. *The best method of calculating the value of residential space is the market comparison*.

First, go out with another real estate agent (not associated with the one selling The Flamingo) and look at other apartments at approximately the same asking price in the area. Check how the apartment that you are interested in stands up to its competition. Make lists, charts, anything that will help you compare on a space-for-the-dollar-in-a-similar-location basis. Then use the tool of the appraiser: comparables.

Comparables—or *comps*—are words frequently heard in real estate offices. They refer to sheets or books containing all the listing information on properties that have sold in the real estate company's working area during the past year or two. Using them, an agent can tell you the exact selling price of all the units similar to yours that have sold within the past year or so. He or she can also tell you how long the properties were on the market, whether or not there were price reductions during the course of the listing, and usually the length of time between contract and closing.

With this information you can compare "your" property to others like it and make an accurate evaluation of value. You can also evaluate how soft or firm the real estate market is. Is there a great deal of negotiating space? Are apartments selling far below their asking prices and taking many months to sell? Or should you act quickly in a fast market where apartments are selling near their original asking prices and soon after their listing dates? This information may help you to get a bargain or keep you from losing an apartment that you really want by haggling too long over the price.

Going out with another agent, looking at comparable properties, and examining the comparable sales file will take perhaps two days of your time. We can't think of time better spent. And you might even find a place that you like much better.

Exactly the same process would be employed to evaluate the worth of the for-sale-by-owner apartment in Crystal Sands. We might use one or two real estate agents working in that area, see a dozen other apartments, and then work through the comparables for the past year.

Once the value is established for each apartment in its own neighborhood, then value for the dollar can be compared. For example, if the apartment in Crystal Sands is thousands of dollars lower in asking price than comparable apartments around it and the apartment in The Flamingo is higher in asking price than comparable space in its area, the unit in Crystal Sands would be far out in front of the unit in The Flamingo as a best-bet investment.

Physical Condition

For decades wise home buyers have hunted out handyman specials, run-down properties in good neighborhoods. Why? The answer goes back to location and space as the most important factors in determining value. *The physical condition of a property affects its selling price out of proportion to the cost of repair and future sales price.*

In other words, you may buy a property cheaply because it is run-down, but once the time and money is spent to refurbish it, its value will be comparable to other properties of similar space in the neighborhood. The trick is to find properties where the price is low but the cost of repairs is considerably less than the difference between that price and the value of comparable neighborhood properties.

It is important not to let the numbers scare you when you are buying one apartment but calculating the cost of refurbishing an entire building. Remember you need only contribute *your* share of the fix-up costs as determined by your proportionate undivided interest in the common elements of a condominium or the number of shares you hold in a cooperative.

For example, if $500,000 in fix-up costs are needed to refurbish an apartment building being converted to a co-op, you might well be overwhelmed. Half a million dollars is a lot of money, no matter what your income. But wait. You hold .5 percent (five-tenths of 1 percent) of the shares in the corporation that owns the building (or five shares in a thousand). Your share of the half-million dollars therefore will be a special assessment of $2,500.

In a co-op the fix-up costs might well be financed over many years if the board of directors chooses to use a second mortgage or other long-term financing for the project rather than a special assessment. Your real costs then would be .5 percent of the cost of carrying and repaying the loan, which would usually add but a small amount to your monthly maintenance fee. In a condo, you would have to obtain the $2,500 on your own since the common elements cannot be mortgaged by the unit owners' association, but you could take out a second mortgage on your individual unit.

Meanwhile the renovation may well increase the value of the individual units within the building by $20,000 each. Thus you invest $2,500 (possibly over a long term) that immediately increases the value of your unit by almost ten times the amount of your assessed share in the repairs and fix-up costs.

But what about a situation like Crystal Sands, where the co-op complex seems to be in good condition, but the interior of the apartment advertised needs help badly? Let's look around the apartment more closely first.

The carpet is so worn that the nap is completely gone in the areas of high traffic. The stove looks as though it has cooked an army through a siege, and the refrigerator is barely breathing—all this, besides the faded bathroom tile and fixtures and a desperate need for fresh paint everywhere. It would cost a good many dollars to make the apartment an attractive place to live.

But the real estate agent says that the last two-bedroom apartment in this building that was sold pulled $135,000 from an asking price of $139,000. Some quick arithmetic reveals that even with its not-so-great location within the complex, this apartment is a bargain at $119,000. The real estate market is currently slow; the owners are apparently eager to sell; and they seem self-conscious about their apartment's need for fix-up and redecorating. We decide that they may have underpriced the unit, and resolve to do some comparable hunting quickly.

Meanwhile, we try to evaluate the cost of fix-up. A quick guess-timate brings a price of about $5,000. If we could get the place for $115,000 and put the $5,000 into it, we'd probably have a place worth $130,000 at least and be $10,000 ahead. Not as good as the return on the share investment of $2,500 in the conversion, but still a good return.

On the other hand, what if we're not really certain of the condition of the common elements in Crystal Sands? After all, the building *is* twenty years old. Everything looks good from outward appearances, but what about the out-of-sight heating and plumbing systems, the roof, and the wiring?

We would hire a home inspection service. For a fee that ranges quite widely across the country, a trained inspector will observe and test as far as possible the working systems, the structural elements of the building, and the appliances and fixtures within the apartment. We will get a written report on the inspector's findings within days, but we can make our offer and even sign contracts conditional upon an acceptable report. For an additional fee, some home inspection services also offer insurance against appliance breakdown.

If we were buying into a condo or co-op conversion building like The Flamingo, however, we might have much more detailed information on structure and working systems available to us. Many states require that an engineering report on the condition of the building be submitted with the conversion application. At the same time many tenants' committees in a building being converted pay to have their own engineers' report done to be used in negotiating with the sponsor. We, as buyers, might well have access to two professional engineering reports. Sounds great, doesn't it? How could we possibly go wrong?

Well, actually having two reports sometimes causes a good deal of confusion. The report of the sponsor's engineering firm usually paints a rosy picture. The report of the engineering firm hired by the tenants usually paints a very bleak one. Read them both, note where they agree (those statements are probably accurate), and then compare the disagreements. The reality of the points of disagreement is probably somewhere in between the two reports.

Maintenance Costs

Maintenance costs and potential maintenance costs must be considered as part of the "price" of a piece of property.

Let's test this variable at our two apartments. First The Flamingo. Some maintenance repair and remodeling work has obviously been done to make this rental apartment building ready for conversion sale. Some of the work probably remains under warranty policies; the kitchen appliances, for example. We should ask about these policies. Are they transferable to a buyer or limited to the sponsor? If they are transferable, they represent potential costs that we need not worry about, for a while anyway.

The value of the other items of renovation work is not so clear, however. What's behind the Formica panels in the bathroom? Strange that these should be put up in a building only nine years old. Have leaks been covered over? What shape is the wiring in? What's under those brand-new carpets? In fact, what are the carpets made of? Who made them? Will they disintegrate in a preprogrammed period of time (under two years)? Has anyone looked at the roof? Does the parking area need repaving or repair?

No, we're not nit-picking. We're trying to point out potential trouble spots. If you move into an $85,000 apartment, and then must pay out $3,000 in unexpected repair bills plus a $50-a-month increase in monthly maintenance fees six months into the first year, that apartment did not cost you $85,000. It cost you $88,300. And to add insult to injury, the cost of repairs may not be added to the cost of your apartment for income-tax purposes; only the cost of "improvements."

In a conversion such as The Flamingo, the sponsor may provide a list of approximate operating costs upon which your estimated maintenance fee is based, but *you* must judge these estimated operating costs for accuracy. A difficult job for a novice! A good professional property manager can help. Comparison with the operating costs of similar, functioning condominiums will be your best insight. Your real estate agent may be able to help you get in touch with the property managers of other buildings.

And just to give you something else to think about: Who owns the management company hired to run The Flamingo for the next *ten years?* Could it be that the real estate company that sponsored the conversion and handled the sale of the units will be around in another capacity for a while? Also: Is $10,000 a ''generous reserve fund'' as the brochure asserts? Or is it really a token allowance?

In Crystal Sands the question of maintenance costs is a little easier to evaluate. We may request copies of the operating budget from previous years and compare that budget with the financial statement of the corporation, which will list its actual expenditures. We may ask if there is a reserve fund, and what part of the monthly maintenance fee is apportioned to it. We may ask if major improvements are planned and how they will be financed.

Evaluating the maintenance costs of an operating building is always easier than evaluating ''projected'' expenses. It will be especially important that you remember this section if you decide to buy a new or yet-to-be-built condominium or cooperative.

Emotional Response

When buying a piece of property that is to be your home, you should give due weight to your emotional response to it. In other words, don't buy an apartment you dislike just because it checks out well on the rational judgment scales. Besides being unhappy, you may well end up selling too soon and you will pay moving expenses and closing costs when you sell. This maxim does *not* apply to investment purchases, however. When you buy an apartment with the intention of renting it and then selling for a profit, rational evaluations, rate of return on your investment, and potential capital gains should rule unquestioned.

In terms of our two-apartment marketplace: If we hate pink buildings, are terrified of heights, and allergic to noise, we should not buy the apartment in The Flamingo even if the figures show that it is the best bargain in all south Florida. If you are faced with a similar decision and there is nothing else you can afford, wait, starve, stop going to the movies, give up cigarettes, walk rather than ride, do anything to save money until you can find and buy something that you like at least a little. On the other hand, even if you can easily afford the price and you *know* the apartment is a bargain, you should *not* buy in a building like Crystal Sands if being near the ocean makes you think of hurricanes and swimming in it makes you think of sharks.

Affordability

The affordability of a piece of property is not determined solely by its price tag. Rather it is a complex relationship between price, capital investment (down payment), the terms and cost of financing, maintenance costs, municipal taxes, federal tax benefits, the stability and/or mobility of the buyer's income, and the spending demands on that income.

Old mortgaging rules-of-thumb—such as "One week's pay should cover monthly housing expenses," or "The principal of the loan should not be more than twice your annual income," or "The bank will finance 2½ times your annual salary," or even the newer guideline "The lender will grant you a loan whose monthly payments will require up to 32 percent of your combined monthly income"—are no longer accurate.

As financing becomes more creative (that is, varied and complex), each financing situation is more likely to be unique. Each therefore is also more likely to raise the questions, "What will this really cost me?" and "Can I really afford it?"

We'll take you through some hypothetical situations and work out the numbers for you in Chapter 9, but for now we'd like to show you how inaccurate a first reaction to price can be. Again we'll use our two apartments.

After negotiating, the sponsor at The Flamingo agreed to take $80,000 for the two-bedroom apartment on the seventeenth floor. At Crystal Sands the seller agreed to take $110,000, grateful that he did not have to pay a real estate commission. He also agreed to take back a purchase money note for $90,000, interest only at 11 percent for five years. Let's see how the numbers work.

The bank that is financing The Flamingo with a buy-down from the sponsor (buy-downs are explained in Chapter 8) has agreed to an interest rate of 13 percent for the first three years of a twenty-five-year Adjustable Rate Mortgage (ARM). A down payment of 25 percent is required and there is a mortgage origination fee of 4 points. To buy this apartment, therefore, we would need $20,000 in cash as the down payment plus $2,400 in cash to pay the 4 points (4 percent of the face amount of the mortgage), plus closing costs. (For the sake of this comparison, we'll assume that closing costs are approximately the same for both apartments and eliminate those figures.) So the cash investment in The Flamingo is $22,400. The cash investment in Crystal Sands is $20,000.

Mortgage payments at The Flamingo are $677 a month, maintenance fees are $139 a month, and taxes are $100 a month. Total monthly payment: $916. At Crystal Sands total yearly interest is $9,900 or $825 a month. Maintenance fees, which include municipal taxes since the apartment is part of a cooperative, are $225 a month. Total monthly payment is $1050.

There is a $134-a-month difference in the monthly housing cost between The Flamingo and Crystal Sands, but The Flamingo requires $2,240 more in initial out-of-pocket monies to be paid to the bank. Even without earned interest, the $2,240 would pay the difference in monthly costs between the two apartments for seventeen months. Or it could be used toward fix-up costs in the Crystal Sands apartment.

So which apartment is more affordable? Which is the better deal? We bet your answer is different from the one you would have offered at the beginning of this chapter. And, yes, we know we stacked the deck in favor of Crystal Sands, but this was just a demonstration.

The Legal Structure of Ownership

Which to buy, a condo or a co-op? Either. *The legal structure of ownership in an apartment complex is not as important as its financial soundness, efficiency of management, location, and resalability.* Both condominium ownership and cooperative ownership have advantages and disadvantages, but the form of ownership should not be a factor in your decision between two apartments unless it affects salability or financial security.

For example, Crystal Sands could compete with condominium sales in Hollywood, Florida, because both co-ops and condos are accepted and commonly used forms of property ownership in that area. If, however, the same apartment were located in Bangor, Maine, or Denver, Colorado, where co-ops are *not* common, it might not be able to compete effectively in the marketplace. Potential buyers and lending institutions alike would be unfamiliar with the cooperative concept and therefore wary of it. This negative attitude, although intangible, could affect the value and potential appreciation of an apartment.

In The Flamingo the problem is financial security. There is a sense of cover-up in the remodeling. The estimate of operating expenses could be inaccurate, or a major repair such as an elevator failure might necessitate a large out-of-pocket cash assessment to each unit owner.

What we're saying is: Look at the whole property as a piece of property and base your decision to buy or not to buy on the weighing of variables one against another, not upon the legal structure of ownership in the apartment complex.

...recapitulate the variables and their effects upon your purchase:

- Location is the most important factor in determining real estate value.
- Residential property appreciates best when surrounded by like or more valuable residential property.
- The location of an apartment within the building or buildings of a co-op or condominium complex usually has some effect upon its desirability and/or value.
- The economic health and stability, demographics, tax structure, municipal services (including schools), recreational facilities, and transportation facilities of a municipality all affect the value of the residential real estate within it.
- Space is the second most important factor in determining real-estate value, but it can be compared only to like space in a like environment.
- The best method of calculating the value of residential space is the market comparison.
- The physical condition of a property affects its selling price out of proportion to the cost of repair and future potential sales price.
- Maintenance costs and potential maintenance costs must be considered as part of the price of a piece of property.
- When buying a piece of property that is to be your home, you should give due weight to your emotional response to it.
- The affordability of a piece of property is not determined solely by its price tag.
- The legal structure of ownership in an apartment complex is not as important as its financial soundness, efficiency of management, location, and resalability.

Based upon our evaluation of the variables in these two apartments, we would buy in Crystal Sands. The location is much better for a residential investment and more likely to appreciate significantly. The space-for-the-dollar is a bargain relative to similar apartments in the area and the fix-up necessary is primarily cosmetic. The co-op has been operating successfully for many years and the property is exceptionally well-maintained. There are no foreseeable major expenditures in the next three to five years, and most important, the underlying five-year straight mortgage offered by the sellers is a financing bargain that rivals the apartment itself. There is some risk in refinancing at the end of that term, but with the likely appreciation in the apartment's value, new financing from a conventional lender should not be a problem.

The Flamingo, on the other hand, is the most expensive residential building in its area. Its value as an investment is hampered by its location in a busy commercial area, the vacant lot next door, the absence of a swimming pool, its uncertain maintenance as a rental building, and its lack of operating records as a condominium.

But these are only stories. The Flamingo and Crystal Sands do not exist. Choosing one or the other can neither give us shelter nor make us a profit. If you are really serious about your investment in an apartment, you must remember these two fictional apartments and go out to look at real ones. Successful real estate purchasing requires on-the-job experience.

So even if your building is being converted and you are considering the purchase of the apartment in which you have lived as a tenant for ten years, go out and look at other apartments. Get some standards of comparison. Ask questions. Even negotiate a little. You can make an offer on any apartment that appeals to you and try to negotiate toward *your* ideal price. You are not obligated to buy the apartment unless and until you sign a contract to purchase.

It's a game, and the prizes are happiness in your home and potentially great appreciation on your investment. But you cannot learn this game sitting in your easy chair. It requires time and physical movement. Your skills in the marketplace will be honed only *in* the marketplace.

To help you, we've included a comparison chart that you might want to take along on your apartment hunting trips.

Rating the Variables

10 Excellent ≧ 1 Poor

Factor	Apt #1	Apt #2	Apt #3	Apt #4
Asking Price				
Address				
LOCATION				
Neighborhood				
Convenience				
Municipal services				
Taxes (enter mill rate, annual taxes, and tax dollars per month)				
View				
Location of the unit in the complex				
SPACE				
Square footage (enter actual number)				
Floor plan and traffic pattern				
Kitchen				
Baths (enter number and evaluation)				
PHYSICAL CONDITION				
Condition of condo or co-op complex				

Factor	Apt #1	Apt #2	Apt #3	Apt #4
Condition of unit				
MAINTENANCE COSTS (include real estate taxes if a condo) Monthly (enter amount)				
Likelihood of special assessments or costs (enter figure if known)				
LOVABILITY Rate your feelings about living in each apartment				
AFFORDABILITY Down payment required				
Special financing such as seller support available				
Mortgaging available (enter any known specifics)				
SOUNDNESS OF CONDO OR CO-OP Financial statements				
Likelihood of special assessments				

COMMENTS [Don't forget to turn to Chapter 9, pages 158–160, to use the forms for an accurate comparison of condo and co-op costs.]

CHAPTER 4

Legal Labyrinths:
Real Estate Law
You Need to Know

Do-it-yourselfing has become almost a national pastime. Around the home, do-it-yourself papering and painting is a pretty sure bet for success. Do-it-yourself plumbing and wiring is somewhat more risky but usually profitable. Practicing do-it-yourself real estate law, however, is like trying to hang-glide in handcuffs. We do not recommend it. The legal aspects of your condo or co-op purchase should be handled by an attorney.

Why, then, are we devoting an entire chapter to condominium and cooperative documents? Because the documents are there. Because you can't buy a condo or a co-op without them. Because they can be overwhelming when presented to you *en masse* as mysterious ''instruments'' in the sale. And because we promised you a complete guide.

To provide you with a sample of every possible document involved in your potential purchase would add a hundred pages or more of fine print to this book, and even if you were to read every word in every sample document, you would still need a lawyer, a real estate agent, and/or a patron saint of real estate investors to explain the entire legal process and its loopholes to you.

We'll introduce you to condominium and cooperative documents, therefore, by naming and describing them, much as a host might introduce you to another guest at his party. You'll shake hands, as it were, and be able to recognize each document and know its purpose and function when it shows up later at your closing table, a unit owners' meeting, or anywhere else.

We'll supply you with some questions to ask your real estate agent or attorney about your particular documents, but we won't (we can't) prepare you to handle them yourself.

Some exceptional buyers read every word in every document involved in their purchases. Reading everything is standard, can't-possibly-be-wrong advice in every legal procedure, but most people get lost among the *wherefores* and *whomsoevers,* glance through the pages, and gladly hand over the responsibility for being sure that all is as it should be to their lawyers, whom they rely on to check that all essentials are included and that all questions are asked and answered. It is for this service that attorneys earn their fees. Whether you choose to read or not to read your documents, however, you should not hesitate to ask questions and to question statements that you don't understand. You are paying for the security of clear answers.

Those of you interested in "pure law" can pursue the documents question further by writing to your state attorney general's office and requesting information on the state's horizontal property acts or real estate cooperative legislation. You can also obtain copies of a model Uniform Condominium Act and a model Uniform Real Estate Cooperative Act by writing to:

National Conference of Commissioners on Uniform State Laws
645 North Michigan Avenue, Suite 510
Chicago, Illinois 60611

Condominium Documents

Condominium documents are somewhat more complex than cooperative documents because each owner's air space must be carefully delineated and separated from its ownership share in the common elements. On your way through a condo purchase you will meet a document that we will call the Declaration, but which may also be called by several other names depending upon where in this country your apartment is located. Master Deed; Enabling Declaration; Plan of Condominium Ownership; and Declaration of Conditions, Covenants, and Restrictions are all essentially this same document. Married to it inseparably, no matter what its name, will be a set of bylaws. The children of this metaphorical couple are the Individual Unit Deeds; without yours you own nothing.

The Declaration

Because it creates the condominium, the Declaration is its principal document. It is the legal instrument that divides an estate into condominium ownership of certain air space and an undivided share in the ownership of the common elements. It must include a plat (a small map) that shows the exact location of all the structures on the land owned by the condominium. It must also include architectural drawings and/or legal descriptions that show the exact location of each unit within those structures.

The Declaration also legally establishes the name of the condominium and its address. It sets out a plan for an association of unit owners and gives that association the powers necessary to govern the condominium. It usually establishes a board of directors (sometimes called a board of managers) to lead that association and direct the day-to-day business of the condominium.

The Declaration also establishes the percentage of undivided interest in the common elements that is assigned to each unit. Ask your attorney to find this clause in the Declaration and check to confirm the percentage that is assigned to your unit. This checkpoint is most important because the percentage assigned in the Declaration usually cannot be changed without unanimous approval of all unit owners and it affects both the value of your unit and your life within it. It will determine the number of votes you hold at meetings of the unit owners' association, the amount you will be assessed for maintenance of the common areas, and the portion of special assessments that you will be required to pay.

Next question for your attorney: How was the percentage of undivided interest in the common elements determined? The answer may be "By a combination of relevant factors" or "By the declarant after a market study" or "By . . . " and the determining factors will be named. Some states specifically require that a certain formula be used in determining the respective value of individual units and their share in the common elements. In other states, any method or combination of methods can be used.

Among the most common methods of determining a unit's percentage of undivided interest in the common elements are:

By fair market value: The appraised original value of the unit is divided by the total value of all the units. For example, the value of the unit 1-E is $50,000. The total value of all the units is $1,000,000. $50,000 ÷ $1,000,000 = .05. Therefore unit 1-E has a 5-percent undivided interest in the common elements. This would probably be translated to five votes at association meetings, and 5 percent of the annual maintenance costs.

By living area: The percentage of undivided interest is determined by dividing the living area of a single unit by the total living area of all the units. For example, Apartment 11-A has 1,400 square feet of living area. The total living area in all the apartments is 210,000 square feet. 1400 ÷ 210,000 = .0066. The owner of apartment 11-A would then have .7 of one percent share in the common elements or seven votes out of roughly 1,000.

In equal shares: The owner of each unit has one vote at association meetings. If there are one hundred units, he has a 1-percent undivided interest. If there are five hundred units, he has a .2 of 1 percent undivided interest, or two votes out of one thousand. The equal shares method is most often used in row houses (attached or detached) where the land and recreational facilities are owned in common.

It is important to understand both the percentage of undivided interest in the common elements attached to a unit *and* how that percentage was determined, for these factors will help you to decide whether or not a particular offering is a good investment. To illustrate: You may be looking to buy a resale unit and discover that construction of a swimming pool and tennis courts has been approved by the unit owners. The cost of these improvements is estimated at $500,000.

"Five hundred thousand dollars!" you say. "Five hundred thousand dollars in added assessment over five years? No, thanks! We can't possibly afford this place."

But you have missed the significance of your unit's percentage in the undivided common estate. Let's say that there are five hundred units in the condominium. The one you are considering is among the smallest and is tucked away on the ground floor in a back corner of the building. Its percentage of the undivided interest was determined by its size and market value. Therefore, it only carries .1 of 1 percent interest in the common elements. As its owner, your share of the special assessment for the recreation facilities would then be $500 to be paid over five years. One hundred dollars a year. That's less than it costs to join a community swimming pool in many parts of the country!

Meanwhile the addition of recreation facilities to the condominium will increase the value of every unit within it. Your least-desirable unit may only appreciate by $3,000 to $5,000 *but* that appreciation cost you only $500.

Regulations regarding condominium construction and conversion have been greatly improved throughout the nation during the past decade. Today the laws of most states are patterned after HUD guidelines and/or the very strict, consumer-oriented condominium statutes of New York, Michigan, and Virginia. Therefore, many of the potential dark crevices of older Declarations have been eliminated and most new Declarations conform rather closely to HUD guidelines. This makes the work of reviewing the Declaration easier for the attorney who will represent you. You may still want to ask some of the following questions, however.

- If you are buying a unit in a condominium not yet built, does the Declaration include a careful description of all streets, parking lots, and recreation facilities and establish the conditions and restrictions of their use?
- Is ownership of areas that are needed or will be used by the unit owners (such as parking lots, swimming pools, laundry facilities) within the common estate of the condominium? In some special instances where two separate condominiums might share certain facilities such as a pool and bathhouse or a golf course, the ownership of those facilities should be held by an association or a corporation in which each unit owner holds membership or shares. Ownership of such shared common facilities should *not* be held by the original owner (the declarant) and leased to the condominium association. HUD-insured loans are not allowed when such facilities are leased.
- Do the Declaration or the bylaws establish the role of a professional management company for the condominium, provide for the purchase of hazard and liability insurance, and perhaps establish a continuing reserve fund?
- Is there a long-term management contract with a company selected by (and sometimes owned by) the declarant? This is a minus point that has cost some condominium owners a great deal of money in the past. Selection of a management company should be in the hands of the unit owners or the board of directors.
- Does the Declaration contain a right-of-first-refusal clause reserved to the association? If it does, you will not be able to sell your unit without first offering it to the association. Such a clause could cause delays in selling of three months or more, and some buyers simply won't wait that long. Right-of-first-refusal clauses, although legal in most states, are prohibited in condominiums financed with HUD-insured funds. FHA-insured mortgages on individual units also will not be permitted when a condominium reserves a right of first refusal.
- Are there restrictions on the use to be made of the units within the condominium? Are they all to be residential? If commercial units are allowed, how are they restricted? How is their share in the common areas determined? Are they paying a substantially higher percentage

of maintenance costs? Do they have more power (votes) in the unit owners' association? How does the presence of commercial units affect life within the condominium?

- Is there any language in the documents that would allow the unit ratios of ownership in the common areas to change at some future date? For example, is the developer permitted to add a new building and therefore more units to share the common areas? You should avoid such arrangements.

Bylaws

The bylaws keep the condominium running. They set forth and control its internal government after the Declaration has established its existence. No condominium community could function without them, for they create and maintain both order and harmony.

Bylaws are so important that everyone who buys a unit in a condominium must agree to abide by them. This agreement is usually secured by a covenant written either into the Declaration or into the bylaws themselves. It states that the mere acquisition, rental, or act of occupancy of any residential unit in the condominium has the effect of signifying that the bylaws of that condominium are accepted and will be complied with. (Which means: When in Rome, you must do as the Romans have decreed!)

So what exactly do the bylaws regulate? Almost everything.

They state how long the Declarant will administer the condominium after the documents have been recorded. They establish when and how the first and all future board of directors will be elected from among the unit owners. They define the responsibilities of the members of the board of directors and provide for certain immunity from legal suit for them. If board members are paid (few are), they establish their salary.

The bylaws will also describe the rules for conducting a meeting of the unit owners' association, the frequency at which the regularly scheduled meetings will be held, the procedure for calling a special meeting, the number or percentage of votes required to resolve an issue, and the form and use of proxies. You may need to know all of this if you are asked to serve on the board or if *you* want to call a special meeting someday.

Because nothing is perfect, especially at its inception, the bylaws should also provide a means by which unit owners can amend the bylaws under which they live. (In contrast to the Declaration, bylaws can usually be changed by a simple-majority vote.) And because no *one* is perfect either, bylaws should also provide a means by which unit owners can remove an incompetent member of the board of directors from office. You might ask your attorney to check to see that these provisions are included in the bylaws of your condominium.

Besides the mechanics of running the condominium, the bylaws govern much of the pattern of life within it. They enable the board of directors to establish a budget and collect funds. They also establish the penalties and the procedures to be followed in the event that a unit owner does not pay maintenance fees or special assessments. Ask what these are in the condominium you are buying. Hopefully, the penalties will never apply to you. And *you* want them stringent and effective enough to discourage deadbeats.

The bylaws establish who may use the common areas, under what conditions, and during what times. Pets, for example, may be allowed in the condominium, but they may be restricted to the freight elevator and the stairs and prohibited from the swimming pool, the tennis courts, and the children's playground. Children may even be restricted from the pool during certain hours in order to give adults a chance to swim undisturbed. In fact, the bylaws may establish any rules which the unit owners decide will facilitate harmonious living in the community. Be sure you can live with these rules *before* you buy.

Individual Unit Deeds

For the most part the deeds to the individual units of a condominium repeat information that is found in the Declaration (which you may remember is also called a Master Deed) and contain a statement naming the location of the Declaration in the county land records office. Legal descriptions of the condominium property and the individual unit are repeated. And the percentage of undivided interest in the common elements assigned to the unit is restated.

All this information is not repeated for the love of words, however. The existence of an Individual Unit Deed enables the owner of that unit to convey title to the property—in other words, to sell his condo apartment.

Cooperative Documents

In most instances, living in a cooperative does not feel much different from living in a condominium. The legal documents that get you there, however, are quite different in name and procedure.

Since a cooperative is a corporation, it must have a Corporate Charter (called a Certificate of Incorporation in some states) and corporate bylaws. In order for shareholders to qualify under Internal Revenue Service code

(Sec. 216) for interest and real estate tax deductions on their federal tax returns, the cooperative corporation must also issue a proprietary lease to each of its shareholders.

At the closing table of a co-op apartment purchase, there is no deed. As a new shareholder in the corporation, the purchaser receives a stock certificate and an executed copy of the proprietary lease for his/her apartment. Like the Individual Unit Deed in a condominium transaction, the proprietary lease entitles him/her to the exclusive use of the specified apartment.

The Corporate Charter

The function of the Corporate Charter is to establish the corporation just as the Declaration established a condomonium. There is no space to be defined and divided up for sale, however, since the property is owned in its entirety by the corporation. Legal title to the property is conveyed to the corporation by deed, just as title to any other property is conveyed.

The Corporate Charter, or Certificate of Incorporation, must include the name of the corporation and its location, and it must identify the state law under which it is being incorporated. It must state the purpose of the cooperative corporation as the acquisition of a particular piece of land and/or building(s) to be used to provide residences for its shareholders.

The charter also establishes the total number of shares authorized in the corporation and assigns a par value to those shares. The life span of the corporation is usually stated as perpetual.

The Corporate Bylaws

Like condominium bylaws, the bylaws of a cooperative corporation establish and describe its administration and working systems. The number of members of the board of directors is named. This figure is almost always an odd number to avoid the difficulties and delays of tie voting on important issues. The various offices on the board are named along with their qualifications, powers, method of selection, and term of office.

Most co-op bylaws or proprietary leases reserve the right of the board of directors (or in some cases a majority of the stockholders) to approve or reject the sale of stock (and therefore the sale of an apartment) to a potential purchaser. This board-approval clause is usually supported by most tenant/shareholders as a means of ensuring the stability and compatibility of the community. It has been tested in court cases and decisions have repeatedly been handed down that it is within the lawful rights of a cooperative corporation to refuse a sale for any reason or no reason, except that a refusal cannot be based upon race, color, creed, or national origin. In most cases, therefore, the board of directors is not required to justify its decision to reject a potential purchaser. If they reject *your* potential purchaser, you are virtually without recourse and cannot sell your apartment to that person (unless you can *prove* that the rejection was discriminatory).

It is important that you understand that the business affairs of a cooperative corporation are managed exclusively by the board of directors. Many tenant/shareholders think that a decision of the board of directors can be overruled by a vote of the shareholders. In the vast majority of cases, this is a misconception. The only real power that the tenant/shareholders have over the board of directors is reelection. When shareholders disapprove of the actions of a board, they can vote its members out of office at the next scheduled meeting.

In the bylaws you will also find explicit information on how to vote at a shareholders' meeting, how to use proxies, how to call a special meeting, and how to challenge at a meeting. These are important points to know, for should you object to the way your board is running the affairs of your cooperative and decide to lead a "palace revolt," you will have to arm yourself with an understanding of procedural requirements for the running of a shareholders' meeting. Many an objecting shareholder has appeared at a meeting with the necessary votes to win his point in hand (by proxies) only to find out that the items in question were not properly put on the agenda. The battle, therefore, was lost for a want of understanding of corporate procedures.

Stock Certificates

The stock certificate of a cooperative corporation looks pretty much like the stock certificate you would receive from any corporation trading on the New York Stock Exchange. It states clearly and exactly how many shares in the corporation you have purchased. This number establishes your voting power in the corporation just as in any other corporation, but it also will determine your share of the corporation's maintenance expenses.

You might want to take a good look at your stock certificate at the closing table. You may never see it again because if you are financing your apartment as most of us do, the stock certificate will be whisked away to the lending institution, where it will be held as collateral for your loan. However, it is much safer in the bank's vault than it would be in your top dresser drawer.

The Proprietary Lease

The legal document that will most often touch your day-to-day life is the proprietary lease. In it are spelled out the respective responsibilities of both the landlord (the corporation) and the tenant (you, the shareholder). It contains the very specifics that will answer the questions "Who pays for what?" and "Who can and will do what, when, and where?"

In most aspects a proprietary lease is similar to any other residential lease. Its term, however, is not spelled out as a one-, two-, or three-year lease on the apartment, but usually runs for ninety-nine years or until you sell your shares in the corporation.

The proprietary lease also does not specify a dollar-amount "rent" to be paid for one, two, or three years. Rather it states that the tenant shareholders will pay the proportionate share of the maintenance fee for his apartment as determined annually by the board of directors.

This determination is made by dividing the projected yearly expenses of the corporation by the number of shares and then allocating each apartment a maintenance fee that is equal to the number of shares it holds times the assessment for one share. (The number of shares allocated to your apartment will be stated in your proprietary lease. Be sure it agrees with the number on your stock certificate.)

The maintenance fee in a cooperative differs from ordinary rent in that the part of it that is allocated for real estate taxes and/or loan interest paid by the cooperative can be deducted from personal income on federal income-tax returns.

The proprietary lease will also state the procedures and penalties that will be followed in the event that a shareholder does not meet his/her financial obligations (that is, pay maintenance fees and/or special assessments). These procedures should be stringent and spelled out clearly, for they protect the investment of every *paying* tenant/shareholder.

While still in the negotiating stage, check to find out if the cooperative uses a flip-tax (the information will be in the proprietary lease). The flip-tax is a kind of transfer fee. Some cooperatives require that a certain portion (10 percent, for example) of the profits on the sale of an apartment be paid to the cooperative. If this clause exists in your lease, you will profit from sales within your building as the flip-tax monies are used for improvements or to defray expenses. Remember, however, that the same tax will cut into *your* profits when you sell your apartment.

The proprietary lease of a cooperative may also allow, regulate, or prohibit subletting. Ask your attorney to check on the wording of the clauses concerning subletting and explain them to you. You may think that you will never sublet your apartment, but one day you may want to when you find yourself holding a winning lottery ticket and decide to take a world cruise. You should, therefore, know all the restrictions on your apartment before you buy it.

Even if you decide to leave the details of the landlord/tenant relationship as defined in your proprietary lease to your lawyer, you should ask your real estate agent or the seller to provide you with a copy of the house rules before you sign a contract to buy. Take these home and read them. You'll go through the regulations for pets, the use of alcohol, the use and placement of major appliances, noise, odors, recreation facilities, children, parking, the use of the roof and basement, special use of common areas, and everything else that your particular community has considered important enough to rule upon. It is house rules on the issues of day-to-day life that keep people living close to one another at peace with one another. Be sure that you can live within the house rules of your co-op without harboring suppressed anger and resentment that might cause you to be very unhappy or unpleasant after the first glow of ownership wears off.

Getting Through the Maze

Don't let the intricate phraseology and the sheer mass of paper of these legal labyrinths deter you from purchasing an apartment that is "right" for you. Leave the *wherefores* and *whomsoevers* to your lawyer. Let him or her protect your legal interests; meanwhile you spend your time protecting your life-style, your happiness, and your financial interests.

If you are not a document reader (or even if you are), ask for the name and phone number of the president of the unit owners' or shareholders' association. Call him or her and ask about life in the condo or co-op. Ask about plans for future improvements, recent maintenance problems, plans for future financing. These will affect *your* living costs. Talk with the superintendent of the building. What does he think are the biggest problems the condo or co-op faces? Talk with an officer of the management company. What problems has he encountered? Talk with other tenant/shareholders. How do they like the co-op or condo community? Do they think their investment is appreciating?

Most important of all, ask for the financial statement of the condominium or cooperative. In it will be stated the exact revenues and expenditures, liabilities and assets of the community. In its pages you will find the most realistic and accurate prediction of what your apartment is going to cost you in the coming years. We'll highlight the most important points to look for in Chapter 7.

CHAPTER 5

Co-op Conversions: Tenant Power and How to Use It

In restaurants, dining rooms, kitchens, and at lunch counters throughout New York City, red herrings are more talked about than Maine lobsters. But it's not a dried and smoked saltwater fish that stimulates these frequent and often ardent conversations. *Red herring* is the New York City nickname for the proposed prospectus tenants get that a co-op plan for their building has been submitted to the state attorney general's office. Conversions occur more frequently in New York City than anywhere else, and every red herring stirs up emotions—most frequently anxiety, anger, disbelief, greed, or the desire to ''fight or flee.''

The process of converting a rental building to a cooperative is more complex in New York City than it is in any other city in the country. Strict state conversion legislation, city rent controls, nationally high interest rates, and a soft economy have currently combined to increase that complexity and to make New York City's conversion process one of the finest examples of real estate negotiation that anyone might witness.

We'd like, therefore, to explain such a conversion. If you live in Fargo, North Dakota, Baton Rouge, Louisiana, or virtually anywhere else, your conversion process will be different in procedure from that of New York City, but it will be strikingly similar in the goals and techniques available to the two parties (seller and buyer) involved. Don't try, therefore, to force your state's procedures to fit the pattern that we describe. Rather, take from this chapter the universal principles of real estate negotiation and apply them to your conversion process or to any real estate deal in your future.

The Idea Is Born

As in business everywhere, profit usually motivates the first action in a real estate conversion. There are two situations that are most common:

(1) The owner of a building realizes that the rental of his apartments is bringing him minimal profit and wants to bail out (sell the property).

(2) The owner is renting profitably but wants to take his cash out of the property in order to invest elsewhere.

Just as in selling a house or a single apartment unit, the seller's first question is, "How much can I get for it?" And at this point, before a single unit is offered for sale, the negotiation process begins. Sellers know that every buyer will ask, "How cheap can I get this?" They know also that they will have to give ground, but resolve to give as little ground as possible. So begins the effort to reach a meeting of the minds. In real estate, this meeting of the minds usually establishes the fair market value of the property— that is, the lowest price at which a ready, willing, and able seller will sell and the highest price at which a ready, willing, and able buyer will buy. In New York City the words *ready, willing,* and *able* are of utmost importance.

Step one in the negotiating process belongs to the sellers, who must set a price that is inviting enough to stimulate an offer and invite negotiation, without giving away their bottom dollar figure. Most New York landlords turn to specialty conversion firms to help them comply with the state's conversion legislation (one of the most demanding in the nation) and get maximum dollars for their properties. But they still must face tenants who are playing a strong hand in the game. Rent control and rent stabilization have spawned a veritable negotiating giant. Watch.

The Professional Evaluation

When a landlord walks into the office of a conversion specialist asking for assistance, he or she is not automatically assured of success. The specialist, whether a lawyer or a management-firm executive, will first determine if the conversion is viable. No one wants to spend weeks or months working on a project that will fall apart and prove unsuccessful in the end. The conversion specialist will therefore study the property to determine if there is a market (demand) for it and *at what price*. Determining the market price is complicated by government controls over housing.

Rent control and rent stabilization in New York allow many tenants to remain in their apartments at rents far below the market as long as they make their monthly payments and do not violate the terms of their leases. Except that there are no tax advantages in renting, rent-stabilized tenants in New York might just as well own their apartments. They have the right to remain there all their lives knowing that the rents will increase only within government-controlled guidelines.

If a building is converted to cooperative ownership, however, even a rent-stabilized tenant may be evicted. (Senior citizens and handicapped persons may *not* be evicted.) *But* conversion is subject to governmental regulations that work with and within rent-control objectives. These regulations make getting tenants out dependent upon getting a certain percentage of tenants to buy. The landlord, therefore, may be ready and willing but *unable* to sell. Here's how it works.

There are currently two options available to the potential sponsor of a conversion: an eviction plan and a noneviction plan. Under the eviction plan, the sponsor must give all tenants the exclusive opportunity to buy their apartments for a period of ninety days after the co-op plan has been approved for filing by the attorney general's office *and* must sell 50 percent of the apartments *to tenants of the building* before the co-op plan can become effective. The need to obtain 50-percent sales puts tremendous pressure on the sponsor to offer the apartments at prices far below market value. If 50 percent of the tenants refuse to buy, sponsors cannot co-op the building under an eviction plan.

Under a noneviction plan, the sponsor must sell only 15 percent of the apartments and can sell them to anyone (tenants or nontenants of the building who intend to occupy the apartment). The tenants who do not choose to buy, however, may remain in their apartments under rent control as long as they meet the terms of their leases. If the apartments are sold to outside buyers, those new owners cannot evict the current tenants except for nonpayment of rent.

The problem, then, in a noneviction plan is not getting 51 percent of the tenants to buy, but getting *anyone* to buy. If all the tenants refuse to buy, the sponsor must sell 15 percent of the apartments to outsiders before he can convert to a cooperative. It is difficult to find such buyers when the law states that purchase will not give the buyer possession of his apartment. The negotiating strength of the tenants in a noneviction plan therefore is just as strong as in an eviction plan, as long as those tenants stand together and act as a unit.

Because of the tremendous negotiating power of tenants who cannot be displaced from their apartments, the professional asked to prepare the offering plan for the co-oping of a building must make two determinations of price. First, it is necessary to determine the fair market value of the property and each apartment within it as though the building were vacant. Then, because the building is not vacant, the professional adviser to the sponsor must determine a price that will induce the tenants to buy. At the same time he must keep in mind the client's desire to get as great a return on his investment in the property as possible.

The Greed Factor

To tenants there are really only two important factors in the decision to buy or not to buy their apartments: price and maintenance costs. Tenants want to know what it will cost them to buy their apartment and what it will cost them to live in it. But no matter what answers they get to these questions, they almost invariably return with the question: "Why or how is *that* better than renting?" In a government-controlled rental housing situation such as that in New York City, tenants feel protected. They need not worry about escalating maintenance costs or interest rates. They know that they can continue to live in their apartments and invest their money elsewhere.

"Look," they say to a sponsor, "my family lives here for $350 a month. We like it. We don't need any more. Now you come along and tell us we should buy the apartment for $40,000. Why? The maintenance fee you've figured out is $350, same as our rent. But how do we know it won't go up faster than the rent would have once the building is co-oped? And tax savings? So we save $100 a month. We could probably earn that much on the $10,000 we have to put down to buy this place. Appreciation, you say. Well, how do we know . . ."

So what will induce these tenants to buy? An offer too good to refuse. Would they buy their apartment for $2,000? Of course. But would the sponsor sell for $2,000? No.

Despite the fact that the sponsor might have bought the building for the equivalent of $1,000 a unit fifteen years ago, he is not going to be satisfied with doubling his money when he knows that market value for one apartment (if it were vacant) is $40,000. He won't hold out for forty times his original investment, but he will hold out for as much as he can get.

But what can he do? If the tenants refuse to buy and refuse to move it might seem that he won't be able to sell for anything, in which case maybe $2,000 a unit would be better than nothing.

Not true. If a sale is completely blocked, a sponsor can and will wait profitably. Even by conservative estimates, in seven years those $40,000 apartments will be worth $80,000. (At 8½ percent, money doubles in seven years.)

So we have a power standoff, or perhaps we should call it a greed standoff. Can the tenants get the seller down below 50 percent of the market value? How much below? They want to be able to count their potential profit with a smile. And the seller wants to count his profit with pride. How much can he get in today's marketplace for these units that only cost him $1,000 each so long ago?

Experience shows that at prices somewhere between 50 and 60 percent *off* the current market value with various incentives through seller financing, reserve funds, and amenities, 95 percent of the tenants in an eviction plan building will buy and 50 percent of the tenants in a non-eviction plan building will buy. The game is to find the price and terms that leave both tenants and sponsor happy with the deal.

Preparing the Prospectus (Offering Plan)

In a city where the vast majority of people rent their housing and have done so for generations, there is a renter attitude that resists buying even when the greed factor becomes appealing. Many tenants do not understand and are fearful of the risks of ownership. Many are also completely unaware of the benefits. The conversion specialist therefore must not only prepare an offering plan, but must prepare it in a way that will help to educate the tenants as to the market value of their apartments and the benefits of ownership.

Basic to both the education of the tenants and the satisfaction of the sponsor is the appraisal of the property. A fair market evaluation must therefore be made by a professional appraiser. The most important factor in this appraisal is the selling price of comparable apartments. Some appraisers get into accounting techniques that use replacement cost evaluations minus depreciation and necessary fix-up costs. Some make projections of potential returns upon capital investment. Essentially, however, these methods are just checks against the comparison of price for comparable apartments. What people in a given city are willing to pay for a certain amount of space in a given area under current market conditions is the best indication of market value.

Early in the preparation work, a real estate agent is sent to inspect and evaluate each apartment and the building as a whole. This evaluation will be a paramount factor in determining the share value assigned to each apartment. It will also be a much-discussed factor in the negotiations over price.

An engineer's report on the structure and working systems of the building is also required by the state of New York in every conversion offering plan. Even if it were not required by the state, however, it would probably be done and included in the prospectus. Every homebuyer fears hidden structural defects in the property he is considering that will destroy his investment or his savings account. The engineer's report ideally should allay buyer fears; in reality it usually establishes negotiating points.

When the sponsor retains the lawyer who will prepare the co-op offering plan, he must provide him or her with information on rent roll, maintenance costs, mortgage costs, and taxes on the building. This information is then used in calculating the projected maintenance costs per month/per apartment in the cooperative.

The proposed conversion plan is then prepared. The insiders' prices for the tenants are established by the sponsor with the knowledge and expectation that there will be further negotiation. All other pertinent information is gathered together and printed in booklet form. A copy is then submitted to the state attorney general's office for review and comments. By law, it must contain full and fair disclosure of all the facts pertinent to the conversion of the building. Then, copies of the proposed offering plan with the red herring stamped in red ink on the front cover are distributed to each tenant in the building.

The red herring reads:

A proposed offering plan relating to conversion to cooperative status of the apartments in this building has been submitted to the department of law of the state of New York bureau of real estate financing, but has not been accepted for filing and has not yet become effective. Information contained herein is subject to completion or amendment. These apartments may not be sold nor may offers to buy be accepted until such time as a completed offering plan has been accepted for filing and a final copy delivered to each purchaser.

Despite the fact that no price negotiations can occur before the plan is accepted for filing (which usually takes from six to twelve months in New York State), there is little quiet in the building once the red herring arrives.

The Tenants Begin to Act

Every tenant suspects that a co-op proposal is imminent long before the red herring arrives. Most people hear the rumor from the doorman or the elevator operator who has watched the real estate agent arrive, and the engineering firm, and the building owners, and the owners' attorney, each to do a careful inspection of the property. And most important, the tenants have noticed that the owner has stopped renting vacant apartments. Some people are elated and tell their friends to try to rent apartments in the building so that they too might be able to get in on the insiders' prices. Other people begin to read the *Apartments for Rent* advertisements in the newspapers.

The day the red herring actually arrives, however, everyone turns immediately to Schedule A, which lists the prices of the individual apartments and their share allocations, and finds his/her apartment. And *no one* believes that the prices are fair. Even though the sponsor avows that these prices represent a discount of 40 percent off the fair market value, all tenants are sure that the sponsor is trying to "make a killing" at their expense.

"How can there be such a discrepancy in opinion on the value of an apartment?" you ask. "Forty percent off should look like the bargain it is to everyone if the fair market value analysis is a true and accurate picture."

Not necessarily so. Tenants who have lived in one apartment for years are rarely in touch with the real estate market. They have little or no conception of the market value of the rooms they have taken for granted.

So the war is on. Every tenant is certain that the apartments are overpriced. The engineer's report is branded "totally inaccurate"; every tenant can attest to at least three things wrong with his or her apartment or the common areas that do not appear in the report. And of course the reserve fund is totally inadequate.

"Tenants' meeting! Tenants' meeting!" The cry goes out through the building, prompting almost 100-percent attendance. "We're going to fight this!" goes the conversation. Unification and power are the predominant thoughts of the evening.

That first meeting is usually organizational. A steering committee of twelve to fifteen persons is elected with one member named as chairperson. The tenants' group then exists as an unincorporated association. There is no need for further paperwork. The association should agree upon an assessment (usually $50 to $100 per tenant at the outset) in order to establish a working fund. A bank account should be opened with two signatories required.

There may be much venting of opinions at the first meeting and perhaps the speaking and listening is therapeutic and beneficial in binding together the group as a working entity. *No Buy* pledges, such as the pledge agreement below, may be collected as another means of assuring unified action.

Pledge Agreement

I am a tenant or subtenant at _____ , New York, New York (the "Building"), and reside in Apartment   .

1. The term *Tenants' Steering Committee* means a committee composed of certain tenants residing in the building whose names are attached hereto on a list marked "Exhibit A." The term *Tenants' Committee* shall mean those tenants in the building who have executed this Pledge Agreement.

2. I agree that the purpose of the Tenants' Committee is to negotiate with the Sponsor modifications and improvements in a Plan of Cooperative Organization with respect to the building for the benefit of all the tenants in the building. Each of the tenants who has executed this Pledge agreement is a member of the Tenants' Committee and has designated the Tenants' Steering Committee and the attorneys for the Tenants' Committee to act as his exclusive representative for that purpose. The Tenants' Steering Committee and the attorneys may circulate and distribute this Agreement which I have executed and may prepare and circulate statements embodying the terms set forth in this Pledge Agreement, together with a list of the signatories hereof.

3. I will not purchase or agree to purchase any apartment in the building pursuant to any plan to convert the building to cooperative ownership during the term of this Pledge Agreement, until an amendment to such Plan is accepted for filing by the Attorney General's Office which incorporates the recommendations that shall be set forth in a report of the Tenants' Steering Committee, signed by a majority of that Steering Committee and countersigned by the Attorney for the Tenants' Committee.

4. The other tenants and subtenants who are signing identical Pledge Agreements may rely upon the statements contained herein, and this Pledge Agreement shall be binding on me and shall be enforceable by any and all of the other tenants and subtenants in the building signing identical Pledge Agreements. I am relying upon the Pledge Agreements signed by the other tenants and subtenants in the building in signing this Pledge Agreement.

5. I consent to the jurisdiction of the Supreme Court of the State of New York, County of New York, in any action to enforce this Pledge Agreement, and to the service of process in any action for that purpose

by certified mail, and to the granting of injunctive relief as a matter of right without notice in the event of a breach or threatened breach of this Pledge Agreement.

6. IRRESPECTIVE OF ANY RECOMMENDATION MADE BY THE TENANTS' STEERING COMMITTEE, NOTHING IN THIS AGREEMENT SHALL BIND ME TO PURCHASE MY APARTMENT.

7. This Pledge Agreement shall terminate automatically and without further notice on a day 15 months and one day after the red herring prospectus which has heretofore been served is accepted for filing by the Attorney General's Office.

8. This Pledge Agreement shall not be effective unless the Tenants' Committee receives identical Pledge Agreements signed by 51 percent tenants or subtenants (having the right to purchase under the terms of the Plan) in the building and the Tenants' Committee gives notice of that fact to all signers of this Pledge Agreement no later than 60 days after such Plan has been accepted for filing by the Attorney General's Office.

_____

Dated:
_____, 19   .

The real work of the tenants' association begins at the first meeting of the steering committee. Finding a legal counsel to represent the tenants' association in negotiations with the sponsor and his attorney is their first task. Unfortunately the counsel is sometimes chosen because someone knows someone who . . . This is a risky path to follow, for the person chosen to represent the tenants will be the most important single factor in determining how much the deal described in the original offering plan is improved.

Tenants should interview from six to eight lawyers before deciding upon their representative. The three most important qualifications of these lawyers should be experience in co-op conversions, negotiating skill, and knowledge of financing (both the marketplace and the so-called creative methods).

Testing for experience is the easiest of the three. Ask them how many buildings they've converted for a sponsor, and how many tenants they've represented. It is important that an attorney know the goals and tactics commonly used on both sides of the negotiating table in order to advise either side most effectively. Beyond familiarity with both sponsors' and tenants' positions, however, experience is a matter of numbers.

The attorney who has done the largest number of conversions, however, may *not* be the best person to represent a particular tenants' group, for excellence does not necessarily follow experience. If a group is especially interested in arranging advantageous financing or in negotiating for some renovation work along with lowered prices, they may need a lawyer with special skills. Finding one takes judgment. It's a more difficult assignment than finding an "experienced" lawyer.

When members of the steering committee interview a lawyer they should ask how the final price and terms of purchase for insiders on a conversion that he handled differed from the terms of the original offering. Where did the tenants make gains? Was special financing arranged? What role did he play in its structure? How did the financing save the tenants money?

After choosing an attorney to represent them, the tenants will want to get their own engineer's report to be used later in the negotiating. Usually the attorney will have worked with several firms and will be able to make suggestions to the tenants. Tenants will also want to get their own fair market value appraisal of the property, again to be used as a negotiating tool.

Tenants need not rely entirely on an appraiser's report for a sense of property value, however. Much information can be gathered by going out to look at other apartments and by reading newspaper reports on area housing conditions. Is there a shortage? Are apartments selling? Is the area subject to change in the next few years? Will a highway come through nearby? Is revitalization money being spent in the area? Is the economy about to turn? Up or down? Are real estate sales slowing or picking up? Have any prices on similar apartments *decreased* recently? (If they have, the fair market appraisal based on prior sales may be very inaccurate!)

If there is anything that tenants can do to strengthen their negotiating power besides getting the best possible representation, it is to become informed on the conditions of the real estate market in their area and knowledgeable about financing procedures and options. Sometimes a question thrown out to a lawyer can stimulate an entirely new approach to a deadlock.

As the time for negotiating approaches, the tenants' association may find it necessary to collect additional assessments. They will need funds for the engineer's report, the real estate agent's appraisal, and the lawyer's fee, for starters. If a better purchase price and terms result, however, the money will be well spent and bring a return many times itself.

At the Negotiating Table

Once the plan for the conversion of a building has been accepted for filing by the attorney general's office, each tenant will receive a revised copy of it, without the red herring legend on the front cover. This second distribution of the co-op offering plan is nicknamed the Black Book. It now specifies the ninety-day period during which the tenants will have an exclusive right to buy their apartments.

Once the Black Book is distributed, negotiation begins between the sponsor's attorney and the tenants' attorney. The sponsor (sponsors, if the property is owned by a group) and members of the tenants' steering committee are also present at these meetings.

Because the sale of the units in a conversion involves a great deal of money and many people, there are usually a good number of negotiating sessions before a meeting of the minds is reached. It is a good idea to list the items to be negotiated before meetings even begin. Here's a sample list:

Recommended Items to Be Negotiated
Regarding Cooperative Conversions

1. Reduction of purchase price.
2. Increase in working capital fund net of adjustments.
3. Review of mortgage, including term, interest rate, refinancing.
4. Financing for tenants.
5. Interior repairs to apartments and appliances.
6. Restriction on reserve fund application if noneviction plan.
7. Right to assign subscription agreements prior to closing.
8. Amendment of bylaws and Proprietary Lease to eliminate sponsor control, number of board members necessary at the first meeting, cumulative voting.
9. Right to select the management company.
10. Tenants' rights to exchange apartments versus tenants' rights to purchase vacant apartments versus co-op's rights to purchase apartments and unsold shares.
11. Contracts that survive the closing; leases that survive the closing; real estate tax implications.
12. Use of space in the building reserved for Sponsor or Tenant.
13. Use of roof, basement, or other facilities.
14. Assignment fee, flip-tax fee, fee on unsold shares.
15. Possible change from eviction plan to noneviction plan.
16. Violations on property to be cured at closing. Violations on individual apartments; painting to be done on individual apartments.
17. Use of professional space on ground floor. Is it being sold or rented?
18. Use and occupancy of apartments limited to residential use.
19. Right to sublet apartment. Restrictions on sales of apartments by the board of directors.

It is also a good idea to keep a status sheet like the following memorandum on each meeting so that a written record of progress is always on hand for discussion.

Negotiations Memorandum

Date and Location_____

Present: For Tenants_____

_____

For Landlord_____

_____

	Demand	Offer

Purchase Price
_____

Reserve Fund
_____

Guarantee of Maintenance
_____

Financing
_____

Other items

The first negotiating sessions are usually feelers. Neither party wants to show too much of their hand. Idealized demands are set out and reasons for the demands are made known. Information is considered. Sometimes the points of negotiation are singled out—for example, are the tenants looking for better financing? More money for maintenance and fix-up costs? Are the offering prices considered too high to even open negotiations?

Occasionally a tenants' association takes a hard-line kill-the-plan approach and simply deposits the Black Book in the wastebasket. The strategy usually is "If we ignore him [the sponsor], he'll either lower the prices considerably because he can't sell without us or forget the whole thing." Unfortunately this approach is a dead end as a negotiating device.

Negotiation means a willingness to give as well as get, and few sponsors will negotiate with a kill-the-plan group. These tenants therefore slam the door on the conversion of their building before examining the potential investment that is being offered to them. They seldom get another chance at a similar windfall to real estate profit.

When tenants do sit down with the sponsor to negotiate, pressure gradually builds at each session. The intensity of that pressure, however, is very dependent upon market conditions. In a soft market (a recession) when real estate is selling poorly, the tenants have tremendous power, for apartments are not easily or quickly sold to outsiders. In a good market, however, the sponsor has the greater power since there are buyers literally waiting outside the door and many tenants are eager to buy in order to sell again at tremendous profits.

As the gulf between seller and buyer is narrowed at the negotiating table, attorneys begin to trade and juggle. One of the most important focal points of negotiations is the reserve fund. Tenants usually ask that more money remain in it. What they often do not realize, however, is that the size of the reserve fund bears upon the price of their apartment. The sponsor is interested in the bottom line. How much money is he going to get out of this sale? If $100,000 can be trimmed from the reserve fund, it can often be used to reduce the price of the individual units. So a fine judgment line develops between what is absolutely necessary fix-up in the building and what should be trimmed to lower the prices of the apartments.

Improvement of sponsor financing terms is another common request from the tenants. Three-year financing at three percentage points below the prevailing interest rate (10 percent rather than 13 percent) will induce many tenants to buy. Few, however, realize that the offer of below-market financing is expensive to the sponsor. He might well be willing to reduce the price of the apartments by 10 percent for an all-cash deal. This is appealing to some tenants who would prefer to get long-term financing from a conventional lender than take the risk of refinancing in three years.

Since the real cost to the lender of below-market interest rates for a specified number of years can be determined in dollars, some skilled attorneys are negotiating compromise agreements wherein tenants may choose between two prices upon their apartments; one (the higher price) with a short-term low-interest-rate loan and the other (the lower price) for an all-cash deal (the buyer gets his own financing).

Don't forget that the terms of the underlying mortgage are negotiable. Every tenants' attorney should also argue adamantly for the right of every tenant to assign his subscription agreement. By getting this right, the tenant who thinks he wants to move out of the building can sell his apartment before closing and make a handy profit while putting up a very minimal amount of cash.

Most negotiations usually arrive at a price that is mutually agreeable. But how good a deal the tenants really got is not always apparent in that price. How much reserve money remained for the tenants' use at the end of negotiations? What kind of financing arrangements were made? How beneficial were these to the tenants? These are questions every bit as important as, What did your apartment cost you? Why? Because their answers markedly affect the monthly maintenance costs of living in that apartment.

Co-op and Condominium Conversions Around the Country

Because of its strict consumer-protection legislation, the conversion process in New York State is one of the most complicated in the country. As conversions become more common, however, more states are modeling or will model their legislation after these careful and extensive laws, or the laws of Michigan or Virginia. Eventually, the conversion process across the country will be similar from one state to another.

Today in some states tenants are given only sixty days' notice that their building will be converted to a condominium or cooperative. There is no minimum percentage of apartments that must be sold before that conversion can be accomplished and all tenants can eventually be evicted. (Some states have protection plans that allow tenants to remain for a number of years after the conversion.) These laws leave the tenants without power to block a conversion.

What to do in such a situation? It looks as though you have to buy or move. And, yes, those are the options. But even in areas with little governmental control, tenants have more negotiating power than they realize.

Why? It is a general rule in real estate that the first houses in a development and the first apartments in a building are the hardest to sell. Few people are genuinely adventurous with their money, and in real estate, being first is something of a risk. On tracts, therefore, the first few houses are sold at the cheapest prices. Once the development is populated by a few families who have put in their grass and landscaping and are "living happily ever after," other people are attracted to the area and the builder raises his prices. By the time the last house on the tract is sold an increase of 30 percent in price is not unusual.

In the conversion of an apartment building or complex, the sponsor or declarant also wants to ''get the building moving.'' It is therefore advantageous in both time and money to sell to the tenants at a discount price. The tenants' strength lies in working as a group and in knowing what to negotiate.

Just as in New York City conversions, knowledge of the local real estate market is essential. Tenants should send delegates out to look at other apartments and report back to a steering committee. They should compare asking prices and selling prices of units in nearby buildings and complexes. And if the tenants' association is willing to spend a little money, they should hire a real estate agent to give them a fair market value evaluation of their apartments, and an engineering firm to evaluate the condition of the building and its working systems. Then the tenants should negotiate for price, reserve fund, and most important, financing.

Generally speaking, 85 percent of fair market value is the best price that tenants in a non-rent-controlled area can do. If you are getting a discount greater than 15 percent, you are doing well indeed. In a very slow real estate market, however, tenants can sometimes negotiate especially good terms and financing as an inducement to buy. The secret of their success is usually in their willingness to act as a group. The sponsor or declarant profits when he can pick off the tenants one by one.

A recent survey by the National Association of Realtors showed that 75 percent of converted unit buyers were first-home buyers. This fact indicates an extra burden on the tenant in a conversion. Because he is a first-time buyer, he is usually unfamiliar with the purchasing process. He may also have fears about the risks and responsibilities of owning property. But help is available and well worth its cost. Hiring an attorney to represent a tenants' group even where there are minimal rent or conversion controls can provide a knowledgeable person to advise on the real costs of ownership and to negotiate on an equal footing with the building's owner. Costs for representing a group are usually considerably less than the costs for representing the same number of tenants individually, and the tenants have the added advantage of negotiating from the strength of numbers.

CHAPTER 6

Paper Castles: How to Buy an Apartment Before It's Been Built

Nancy Stevens had been divorced just over a year and was struggling with the maintenance chores on her large suburban home. On a rainy Monday morning after a weekend of raking, she complained about her aches and pains to a co-worker whose wife happened to be a real estate agent, and he suggested that she look at a new townhouse condominium community just opening less than five miles from the office.

There were four models built along Route 202. The remainder of what was to be a 220-unit complex was a hilly, heavily wooded tract. Rolls of blueprints and architectural drawings stood propped in corners of the sales office. Spread about on the center table and on every end table were booklets explaining the condominium concept, copies of the offering plan for Deer Haven, drawings of the pool, the tennis courts, the clubhouse, and various apartment models, data sheets, and real estate agents' cards.

Nancy was impressed by the carefully decorated models, especially the cathedral-ceiling unit with its sliding glass doors to a fenced and trellised deck. This townhouse was smaller and less gracious than the home she now owned, but she was tired of the ever-present and ever-changing demands that her property was putting upon her time. It was time she wanted, and the agent's promise that "Here at Deer Haven you can own a home of your own and never worry about outdoor maintenance chores" lured her into signing a contract to purchase.

She chose a corner unit, telling herself that it would be "quieter" but knowing that she was choosing the unit that most resembled the detached home she was accustomed to. She never considered heating costs. She chose a building in the center of the complex because she didn't want to be near the highway. She never considered the time it would take the builder to work his way to the center of the tract. And she never considered the lay of the land.

In fact, Nancy Stevens never even walked the land. Looking from the top of the hill where the models stood, she could see only woods and brambles. The plat showed roads and parking lots and greens and gardens, a swimming pool and tennis courts. Everything looked lovely on paper, and from the top of the hill, the woods looked lovely in their springtime laciness. For all she knew, however, her building may have been sited upon the winding stream that ran through the property or in the boggy marsh that was not indicated on any map.

Nancy's contract said her unit would be complete in six months. She left a 10-percent deposit with the builder ($9,500) and signed a listing contract on her house with the wife of the co-worker who had steered her to her purchase. Interest rates soared and Nancy's house sat on the market, no offers. She began to chain-smoke; she couldn't sleep at night. How would she pay for the condominium if her house didn't sell? Feeling a little like a criminal returning to the scene of the crime, she paid a visit to the tract. It was now four months after she had signed her purchase contract.

Nancy expected to see a child's picture-book scene of roads, machines, and the skeletons of buildings. Men would be hammering nails into wood. She expected to see her building, her apartment, nearing completion.

What she saw rarely appears in books. Two more four-unit buildings near the highway were at stages nearing completion. Standing on the last bit of pavement near the second building, Nancy looked down the hill. Virtually all the trees had been cut down. Three more foundations filled with muddy water, floating food wrappers, and beer cans stood near the gravel trails used by the heavy equipment. The rest was gulleys and rocks and mud. Nancy could not even imagine where in this rutted, lifeless landscape her "home" was scheduled to stand.

She never bothered to talk to the builder that day; she knew there was no chance that she would be asked to close on the purchase of a completed townhouse in two months.

It was eighteen months after she signed the contract that Nancy Stevens finally moved into her condominium. But even then only after much pleading with the builder. Her house was sold and the buyers were demanding a closing. So Nancy had her furniture set down upon subfloors with taped and spackled wallboard as a decorating backdrop. She began "the condominium life-style" without kitchen appliances and, worst of all, without a paved parking area or grass over the mud that surrounded her building.

The builder told her he was doing her a favor. He had made a special effort, he said, to get a Certificate of Occupancy (CO) for her unit so that she could move in. But he refused to close with money held in escrow to guarantee the completion of the unit.

"If she wants to take possession, I want all my money," he said to her lawyer. "If she doesn't like it that way, she can wait until I get finished. Or she can have her deposit back and walk out of the deal."

Nancy had no viable options. The lawyer for her buyers had sent a formal notice that "Time is of the essence." Those buyers would wait no longer for possession of her house. She didn't want to put her furniture in storage and move into a motel; the cost was too great and the inconvenience overwhelming. And most important, she did *not* want out of her deal.

Her $9,500 had been held without interest by the builder for eighteen months. In that time the prices of the units in the complex had been raised $20,000. She wanted her unit at her contracted price and she wanted to move in *now*. The best her lawyer could do for her was a signed promise from the builder listing the unfinished or missing elements of the apartment and stating that they would be completed in two weeks.

"I'm a man of my word," he said as he extended his hand across the table. Nancy shook it, but she remembered the original closing date on the original contract.

Fortunately, the builder did keep his promise. Not exactly in two weeks, but relatively quickly. Today Nancy Stevens is happy in her townhouse condominium. She showed us around with pride and mentioned several times how little it costs to be freed from the demanding work of homeownership.

But she has a few regrets: She wishes she had seen her lawyer before she signed the contract so that he might have told her that she could have gotten interest on that $9,500 for the eighteen months she waited. She wishes she had walked the land to get a feeling of where she would live. Her location near the foot of the hill exposes her deck and back windows to the view of all the apartments above her. And she looks longingly at the units on the outer perimeter of the complex whose patios face the wooded buffer zone that surrounds the tract. She wishes her heating bills were not so high. Not only does the corner unit that she chose expose more wall surface to the weather, but that long wall faces north. And she wishes she were closer to the pool.

But all in all, Nancy Stevens was lucky. Buying anything, but especially buying real estate from paper drawings, is risky. You are putting your money down upon a promise. More often than not the investment is very profitable in the end, but usually at the cost of multiple migraines and sometimes a good deal of unanticipated money. If you want to take the risk of buying from paper, however, there are some safeguards to help you. Most will save you money on both aspirin and lawyer's fees.

The First Decision

Even if there is not a single building on the tract, you can judge the location of the condominium, and location is still and always will be the most important factor in the value of your investment. Just as though you were judging a house or a resale apartment, evaluate the town, the neighborhood, and the land. Does the town have a reputation as a desirable place to live? What are similar living units selling for in the immediate neighborhood? What is the zoning? Could office buildings, a factory, a school, or a sewage-processing plant be built upon land immediately adjacent to the tract where your unit will be built? How close are the major highways? Are any new highways proposed nearby?

Walk the land! How will the removal of trees and the paving of roads and parking areas affect drainage? What provisions have been made for this? Is the tract in a flood plain area? Is federal flood insurance available?

If you are considering new construction in a major metropolitan area, what is happening around the site of your building? Are government rehabilitation funds or restoration monies being allocated to the area? Is the area primarily residential or primarily commercial? Are there plans for other new buildings in the immediate neighborhood? What transportation facilities are nearby?

Every one of these questions can be answered and evaluated before a shovel ever breaks the earth to start construction on an apartment building. And you should ask and answer the questions carefully, for your first decision should not be whether or not you want to buy a particular apartment but whether or not you want to live on that particular piece of the earth.

Who Is the Builder?

Any parent will tell you that the state certificate saying that a person is qualified to teach in the public schools has little to do with the quality of his or her teaching. The art of teaching depends upon the skill, talent, and dedication of the individual. So it is also with builders. Calling oneself a builder, even a builder with a great deal of experience, does not guarantee quality. The best way, perhaps the only way, to judge quality in the building trade is to judge work already completed.

If you have basically decided to buy a new apartment from paper plans, ask where else the builder has built. Go there. If you're lucky enough to see people walking about the grounds, stop and talk with them. Some are sure to be social enough, or angry enough, to want to talk about their experiences with the builder. You may even get a tour of an apartment. Ask about how well he kept to his due dates. Did he return to repair flaws? How soon? How many flaws *were* there? Were there any major structural problems? Were there any money problems? Were extras added onto the cost of the apartment that were not indicated in the original plans? Were changes made for these? How accurate were estimates of the monthly maintenance costs?

If you will be getting financing through a conventional lending institution, they may also be able to help you check out the builder. For a fee some banks will run a credit check if you explain why you want one done. It's worth the fee. You don't want a builder who has gone bankrupt recently. (It could happen again and this time with *your* money!) And you don't want a builder so deeply in debt that his creditors are clamoring to be paid; such a situation could influence too directly the quality of the materials chosen for *your* home.

Who Is the Architect?

You may never see the person who most influences the comfort or discomfort of life in your apartment. Architects are responsible not only for the floor plan within which you live, but also for the structural soundness of a new building, the outside appearance, and the layout of the entire complex. But architects are harder to track down than builders.

Ask the real estate agent who the architects are for the condominium you are considering. Ask what other buildings they have designed. (The agent probably won't know. But insist that he or she find out for you before you sign a contract.) Then snoop about a bit. Can you find any of the buildings that the firm has designed? Have they been involved in renovation work? If so, try to go to a renovated building and talk to the co-op or condo owners there about their satisfaction or dissatisfaction with the work.

If you're particularly careful or particularly discriminating in your taste, call the architectural firm and ask for the architect who designed the condominium you are considering. Ask what his goals and plans were for this complex. What were his problems? Land? Space for the money? How did he solve them? What does the architect feel is the outstanding feature of the condominium? How many condominiums has he designed? Any awards? (You probably won't have to ask about awards; if the firm has won any, the architect will probably volunteer the information.)

Get Yourself a Lawyer

Because you are buying a paper castle, you will need a lawyer more when buying a to-be-built condominium or co-op than in any other kind of real estate transaction. And it is important that you make contact with a lawyer before you begin negotiating for the apartment of your choice. The real estate agent will be able to handle offers and counteroffers, but it will most likely be your lawyer who will save and protect your money.

Deposits are just one example. Ten percent of the purchase price is the amount that every real estate agent will request as an escrow deposit. Yet every lawyer will tell you that there is no set required amount of deposit. If you're five thousand dollars short of ready cash, negotiate!

Most builders also like to have the deposit money turned over to them once the mortgage commitment and other contingencies in the contract are met; and most real estate agents and unknowing buyers simply turn the money over. But it is not necessarily so, and it is much to the buyer's advantage that it *not* be so. Ideally, the deposit money should be held in escrow by the seller's attorney until closing. In this way, the buyer is protected in the event that the builder should go bankrupt before completion of the project. What's the protection? You'll get your money back.

Since most deposits are substantial and most building takes many, many months, there is also a question of interest on that deposit money. No law states who should get that interest. As a buyer, however, you should ask your lawyer to argue adamantly that the money does not belong to the builder until closing and the interest therefore should be credited to your account. (You may not get this request, but it is worth fighting for. If you must give it up, negotiate some other concession in return for it.)

A good lawyer will also help you to write a tight contract. What happens, for example, if the builder does not or cannot deliver the unit on time? Sometimes specific penalties can be written into a contract. (You'd be surprised at how much those penalties can stimulate construction.) On the other hand, you may wish to leave space in your contract so that a situation like Nancy Stevens' will not put undue pressure upon you. There are no easy sets of rules that we can list for you regarding contracts for the purchase of yet-to-be-built apartments. Each situation is truly unique. But a good co-op or condo lawyer will examine *your* needs and try to tailor the contract to fit and support as many of them as possible.

Your lawyer will also make certain that your contract complies with the standard real estate contractual procedures in your state. More important, he or she will know you and your contract when and if problems arise at any point between the time you sign the contract and the time you take possession of your unit and title to the property. Be certain, however, that you choose a lawyer who is well experienced in condominium or cooperative sales. The finest divorce or criminal lawyer in the county might well be the weakest advocate in the county when it comes to negotiating a contract or navigating a closing.

The Right to Assign Your Purchase Contract

Among the most important concessions that a lawyer can win for you in a contract to purchase a yet-to-be-built co-op or condo is the right to assign the purchase agreement at its original price. Assigning a purchase agreement means selling to another person the right to buy the property referred to in the contract as it was signed by you.

Such a clause will protect you against the possibility that some event in your life (a company transfer, a divorce, a death in the family) may make the purchase of your apartment impossible or inconvenient. Should such a situation occur, the right to assign your contract might save you a great deal of trouble and could possibly result in a windfall profit.

For example if, as is usually the case, the prices of the units are raised as construction and sales proceed, six months after your contract is signed but still six months more before the unit will be complete, you will hold a ticket to a bargain purchase. Anyone interested in buying the apartment in your building or complex at that point will have to pay, let's say $9,000 more than the price you agreed to pay. You may therefore sell your right to purchase your apartment at your price for, let's say $4,500. You make $4,500 and the buyer saves $4,500. Everyone is happy. Everyone, that is, except the builder who lost a sale at the higher price!

And even if prices have only gone up $1,000 while you held your contract, you can assign that contract for $1, using the $1,000 discount as an incentive to a quick sale and a quick exit out of a deal you no longer want or need.

Getting Your Money's Worth

Most paper-castle condo and co-op units are sold by constructing, equipping, decorating, and furnishing anywhere from one to four "model apartments" and promising that your apartment will be "just like" the model you choose but, of course, in a different location. This is a lovely thought, but what does "just like" mean?

Almost everything in the world comes in a wide variety and range of quality and price. How can you know that your apartment will be "just like" the model? You can't. But you can specify in writing as many "just likes" as you can think of. When your attorney draws your contract, it should be full of specifics. Is the carpeting included in the purchase price? What is the name brand and style of the carpet installed in the model? Is that the brand and style that will be in your apartment? What plumbing fixtures will be used? Name brands? Styles? Models? Colors? How much allowance is made for lighting fixtures? Or exactly what lighting fixtures will be used where? Catalog pages from manufacturers can be Xeroxed with special notations as to where certain fixtures are to be installed. These pages should be initialed by both the buyers and the builder and then attached to the contract.

What about windows? Name brands? Insulating glass? Are storm windows and screens included? And appliances also should be specified by name brand and model number. Again catalog pages and pictures can be attached to the contract. We could go on and on: doorbell chimes, intercoms, kitchen cabinets, countertops, insulation, soundproofing, flooring material, even the quality of the paint and wallpaper should be specified as explicitly as possible.

In states that have had high quality condominium and co-op legislation, most of these specifications will be in the prospectus. You and your attorney need only check to see that they are complete and accurate.

Choosing a Place on the Paper

Choosing the location of an apartment within the building or complex is one of the most important decisions that the buyer of a yet-to-be-built unit will be asked to make. If you are among the first buyers, you will have a wide choice, and few stars to steer by. It is difficult to imagine the view from the seventeenth floor of a building that is now a half-finished one-story structure containing three models and closed off at the back by heavy plastic sheeting. Or like Nancy Stevens, it is difficult to imagine how it will feel to live in the middle of a townhouse condominium community, when all that can be seen at the moment are treetops. There are some guide-posts to choosing, however.

Let's start with geography. Look at the plat or the architectural renderings of the building and determine which way is north. If you were building a house, this procedure would be called siting, and whole bookshelves have been filled with writing on its importance. In choosing the location of your apartment within its building or complex, you are indeed siting it.

If you live in the northern part of the country, having a long wall or a great many windows facing north may significantly increase your heating bills or the necessity of heavy blankets at night and sweaters in the daytime during the winter months. If you happen to be an artist, however, it might provide excellent light. Facing east means morning sunlight; west catches the sunsets. South is warmer, brighter.

After you choose your siting, you should consider views and amenities. What will you see from the windows of your high-rise? How high do you have to go to escape the street noise? Would you like the use of the roof or the opportunity to cut skylights into your ceiling? Is there a chance that your ground-floor unit might open onto a courtyard that might be transformed into a garden?

If you are concerned with height and view, try to find a way to go up into a neighboring building. You might have a friend who lives in the area; or perhaps you are good at talking a doorman into arranging a short tour of an existing building for you; or sometimes a real estate agent can help you to get a feeling for views and exposures by showing you through some area apartments that are currently for sale or for rent.

In a townhouse community or patio-plan condominium community, try to look at the traffic plan of the whole. Do you want to be near the pool, or the clubhouse, or the golf course? Or would you rather be away from everything? How much traffic will pass your doorway in various locations?

How convenient is parking? Would you prefer the security of being in the center of the community or the privacy of the perimeter? What will you see from your windows? Are you to be higher or lower than surrounding apartments? Drive through some nearby communities and try to get a feeling for being in different parts of each one.

Paper Floor Plans

Model apartments decorated by professionals are both appealing and deceptive. They are designed to make people want to live in them, and almost everyone who considers buying one thinks that his/her apartment will be just as appealing (subconsciously at least) once the furniture is moved in and appropriately arranged. But just as the "model family" rarely exists, so the model apartment rarely represents real living patterns. As you walk through the models displayed by the builders in your area, therefore, try to think of youself and your family living within the space and its partitions.

When you are seriously considering an apartment, ask the builder to lend you a set of blueprints overnight. Spread them out on your kitchen table and try out a little imaginative living. With a pointer, trace your way through a typical day. Start with waking in the bedroom, showering, dressing, having breakfast, and getting your things together to leave for work. How many family members would you bump into while navigating hallways? Where would the things you need be kept? Are the closets conveniently located? Large enough?

How about the kitchen? Is there enough working space and are the appliances well arranged? Imagine cooking a meal for the family. A meal for dinner guests. Can two people work in the kitchen at the same time? What would happen to traffic flow during a cocktail party?

And your furniture. If you really want to try out your paper apartment before you buy it, measure your major pieces of furniture and cut out pieces of paper to represent them to the scale of the blueprints. Then try arranging your furnishings within the apartment.

All this trying out of an apartment that is not yet built should not dissuade you from buying in a building or complex that appeals to you. It may, however, help you to eliminate a floor plan that is inappropriate to your life-style, or to choose among several that seem equally appealing.

The Spec Apartment

Buying a new apartment that is already completed is somewhat less risky than buying from a paper plan. These completed units are often referred to as "spec" apartments because the builder put them up on speculation that he would sell them at a profit. Their purchase is less risky because you can see, touch, and smell exactly what you are buying.

With diminished risk, however, you also have diminished choices. You cannot choose the location of your apartment within the building or complex because it is already built. Often you cannot choose the paint, fixtures, appliances, or carpeting because they are already installed.

On the other hand, you can check out the view and the exposure. You can walk through the rooms, try out the water pressure, test the appliances, and try out the fireplace, if the unit has one. (A new fireplace should be tested for its draw. Don't be embarrassed to ask the real estate agent to light a fire if you are seriously considering an apartment. If the fireplace has been incorrectly built and you don't notice the fault when you buy in May, you will have a room full of smoke when you want to sit by a glowing hearth in December.)

If you are planning to buy a spec apartment, be sure that you evaluate the workmanship. Check the moldings to see that they are even with the floors and meet without inappropriate angles and spaces. Are the doors properly hung? Do they close tightly without sticking? Are the kitchen cabinets well made? Are the walls finished so that the taping does not show? Open and close the windows. Do they move smoothly? Be sure that nails are not popping out of green lumber in the walls and ceilings. Do all the lights work? The sockets? The switches? The outdoor lights? The doorbell? The intercom? Where are the phone jacks? And don't forget to place your hand at the window closure to see if there is a draft.

Negotiating

In his novel *1984*, George Orwell said, "All animals are equal, but some animals are more equal than others." In the real estate game, everything is negotiable, but some things are more negotiable than others. The price tag on a yet-to-be-built or spec apartment is one of those less-negotiable items. But don't be fooled by the printed price in the prospectus. That prospectus permits negotiation of price and all other items.

There is sometimes a little more room for negotiating on a spec apartment, especially if the market is slow or the builder in need of money (which you can find out by making a low offer and sticking to it for a while). With this kind of negotiating, however, you run the risk that someone will come along, do just a little better than you on their offer, and take the unit out from under you.

On new construction, it is never wrong to make an offer under the asking price, but don't be surprised if the builder holds fast to the exact penny of that asking price. It happens more often than not.

The real place to negotiate on new construction is on the terms of the contract and the financing. If you can persuade the builder to finance your apartment for three to five years at below-market rates, you have in reality shaved thousands off the purchase price. Some builders can be talked into financing with buy-downs on mortgages obtained through conventional lenders. In a buy-down situation, the builder pays the lender a certain sum up front in order to induce him to give the buyer a reduced interest rate for a specified period of time (usually two or three years). Sometimes, after negotiating a buy-down, you can persuade a builder to give you the equivalent of the buy-down in a cash discount off the price and then obtain your own financing at market rates. (See Chapter 9 under the heading Bargain Interest Rates.)

Closing costs are another point of negotiation. A builder eager to get sales rolling may be willing to take on the closing costs and thus save the buyers a good deal of out-of-pocket expense. Some early buyers in garden-type condominiums where there is a large tract to be developed have negotiated the suspension of all maintenance fees (they are to be paid by the builder) until a certain date or a certain percentage of the apartments are completed and occupied together with completion of the roads and recreational facilities.

And finally interiors are often very negotiable. Try for a better grade of carpet, more expensive models of the appliances, finer lighting and plumbing fixtures, storm windows and screens, even wallpapering, without increasing the list price of the unit. These items cost the builder less than they would cost you, which means that he may be willing to throw them (or some of them) into the deal in order to consummate the sale. And you may walk away with a bargain, not in the list price of the unit, but in its quality.

Maintenance Fees

Go over the projected maintenance fees for a new building or complex carefully with a professional (*your* lawyer or accountant). Do not accept the assurances of your real estate agent that there'll be no problem meeting these figures. If possible, find out what owners of similar apartments in similar buildings or complexes near you are paying in monthly fees. Be suspicious if the figures for your unit are appealingly low.

And get some guarantees in writing from the builder. If you are one of the first to move into a condominium community, and the pool is yet a dream, the grass but handfuls of seed upon the mud, and the landscaping nonexistent, your maintenance fee should be negligible. In fact, many builders set minimal fees for the first occupants and guarantee that they will remain constant until the condominium or cooperative is complete or until a certain number of apartments has been sold and the unit owners' association takes over management of the condominium.

The Builder's Warranty

New residences are customarily guaranteed by the builder for one year after closing. *Get it in writing*. There are always things left undone, or poorly done, and there are always things that go wrong in that first year. Again if you are one of the first occupants and other units are still being built (in other words, if the builder is still around), you shouldn't have too much trouble getting workmen to come back to your apartment to fix what should have been done properly in the first place. If, however, you are one of the last to move into a building or complex and the builder is leaving for another project in another location, you may have problems getting things fixed. This is when the guarantee in writing takes on maximum importance.

Some builders, members of the National Association of Home Builders, offer a program called HOW (Home Owners Warranty). This is a warranty backed by insurance coverage that protects a new condominium or house for a period of ten years.

During the first year, the builder warrants against defects caused by faulty workmanship or materials because of noncompliance with HOW's standards. The second year the builder is responsible for malfunctioning of wiring, piping, ductwork, and any major structural defects. In condominiums, the common elements are covered by the same warranties as the individual units.

The HOW insurance during these two years also protects the buyers and condominium association against the failure of the builder to meet his obligations. For the last eight years of the insurance program, HOW protects against major structural defects regardless of how many times the ownership changes.

Since the number of new cooperatives being built is very small (most co-ops are conversions), the warranties offered by their builders are less structured and nationally uniform than those offered by HOW. This creates another job for your attorney if you are buying into a *new* cooperative. What is guaranteed by the builder? For how long? And with what assurance? (Is a certain amount of money being held in escrow? Is there insurance company backing as in the HOW program?) These questions can also be applicable to exensive renovation and restoration work done by a builder for a conversion.

The Closing

At the closing table you will pay your money and take title to your property or receive your shares in the cooperative corporation. One of the most important parts of closing day, however, takes place *before* you enter the closing room. It starts in your new apartment.

Take a pencil and paper with you on the morning of the closing and go to your apartment. Go through it room by room. Write down *everything* you see that is not finished, imperfect, or missing. Even if it happens to be a lock on the window of the spare room or a chip in the plasterboard behind the light switch in the kitchen. Be that specific. Try out the appliances again. Open and close the windows. Everything!

Take your list to the closing and show it to your attorney. He will ask the builder to sign it together with a statement saying that the items will be repaired or replaced within a certain period of time. Depending upon the extent and contents of the list, the lawyer may suggest that some of the purchase money be held in escrow until the flaws are corrected.

After the closing, put a plant in the living room of your new apartment. It may be a while before the squeaky newness wears off and the place feels like home. But it will.

CHAPTER 7

The Right Resale: Finding and Negotiating a Good Deal

We've already warned you to beware the grinning sales agent who assures you, "It's just like buying a house," as he hands you a pen. Buying a condo or co-op apartment is not "just like" buying a house. Hunting for the right resale apartment, however, *is* just like hunting for the right resale house. Both require time, patience, skill, knowledge, the help of a real estate agent, and an awareness of the roles of head and heart in your decision.

Time and patience are yours to give, and we've been working on the skill and knowledge part in the last six chapters. Which leaves "the help of a real estate agent" and "an awareness of the roles of head and heart in your decision" for this chapter.

We can hear you thinking: "Real estate agents! I think I'll skip this part." *Don't.*

An agent can literally save days of your time by taking you to the apartments most likely to appeal to you within the price range that you can afford. And yes, we know, an agent can also drive you in seemingly endless circles and can get you entwined in a purchase that cannot possibly end successfully. An agent can make negotiations work. Or break down. An agent can sometimes pull financing out of the clouds. Or direct you into a financial maze where all the alleys end in brick walls.

Few other professions seem to have so wide a breadth in the competence, working methods, ethics, and knowledge of the individuals who call themselves members. In what other profession do 50 percent of the new licensees drop out in the first year? But that's not all. Another 30 to 40 percent drop out within three years. Which leaves a survival rate of 10 to 20 percent per year who go on to become experienced real estate agents. And the sad part of that statistic is that a large number of those "experienced" agents leave sales to manage offices as brokers.

So how do you find a "good" agent? In fact, what makes an agent "good"? And even more important, how can you use an agent's skill and knowledge to your advantage? Let's talk first about what to look for.

Evaluating the Real Estate Agent

Experience

"Twenty years in the business!" does not mean that you are working with a great agent. What if those twenty years were spent in commercial leasing? Or selling estates in Arizona from behind a desk in Maryland? Or even selling single-family detached houses? Does your agent *really* know condominiums and/or cooperatives?

In any real estate purchase, the agent that you work with should be experienced in handling the type of real estate that you want to buy. If you're looking for a high-rise co-op in Washington, D.C., the woman who sold single-family houses in Dallas for ten years but just got her license in the District of Columbia is virtually worthless as an adviser. And even the agent familiar with condo sales in Atlanta would have a difficult time being effective in New York City, where there is no Multiple Listing Service and the apartment market is primarily in co-ops.

So it is not only in the type of real estate where experience counts, but also in the location. To repeat: real estate is a local business. Your agent should live in the area where he or she sells and should know it intimately. A personal stake in the market is the best motivation to keep in touch with trends and events that will effect its future.

Probably most important: twenty years of holding a license does not always mean twenty years' experience in selling real estate. Many part-timers' licenses hang on the walls of real estate firms. More often than not when a salesperson who holds one of them happens to walk in, the full-time people think he or she is a customer! *You* want to work with a full-time agent who is making his or her living at selling real estate.

Two years' experience in a residential sales office where a good portion of the business has been in apartment sales is sufficient to give most agents a good grasp on their job. Much less than that and you are working with an apprentice.

Training

Training and experience are not exactly the same thing. First of all, a person who has just passed the state real estate exam has neither experience nor training. The required study to pass that exam is focused almost exclusively upon state real estate law. How to show apartments, qualify customers, negotiate, and obtain financing are rarely even mentioned.

Excellent training can be accomplished on the job when a broker is willing to work with his salespeople carefully. More often today, however, teaching the nuts and bolts of the job is being turned over to franchise training programs or to traveling sales seminars.

Both of these training programs focus upon the "art" of selling. Much time is spent in teaching agents lead words and phrases and tricks of getting signatures or manipulating the attitudes of the customer. Because an agent is associated with a nationally advertised franchise and has graduated their training program does not make him or her a good agent. It may have made him or her a good *salesperson,* but a salesperson is not necessarily the agent you need.

Besides the careful one-to-one teaching of an experienced and ethical broker, probably the best training and teaching program currently available is the one sponsored by the National Association of Realtors. The GRI (Graduate Realtor Institute) designation of this program is proudly displayed by those who have received it. And justifiably so. The program is a lengthy one: three separate courses, each approximately equal to a college semester. When completed, however, the graduate knows something about zoning, tax laws, effective showing and scheduling, negotiating, shared-space housing, and the effects of Planned Unit Developments, to name but a few topics. The Realtor Institute has a core curriculum that leaves room in each course of study for local Realtor groups to include issues and problems indigenous to their area.

Professionalism

Real estate sales is a very competitive business. Some agents, eager to "get" customers, will take them from apartment to apartment day after day, never knowing what their "people" can afford or even what they really want. These agents are afraid or unable to ask, "How much do you make? How much down payment do you have? How many outstanding debts do you pay on monthly?" for fear of offending their new customers. And thus they do them the real estate profession's greatest disservice.

Qualifying a customer (determining how much he can afford to pay for property) is one of the most important functions of a real estate agent. It is also the service most often avoided by incompetent agents.

To qualify a customer, the agent must spend some time in the office taking down essential financial information and adding up the figures. Then he must come up with an accurate estimate of how much that customer can afford to pay monthly for housing. More homework still follows, since finding the right apartments to show to this customer might well be a balancing out of down-payment requirements, maintenance fees, mortgage or loan interest rates, local taxes, and insurance costs.

An agent who takes your quick-guess approximation of what you can afford as a true and accurate statement without working up any figures and then begins showing you lovely apartments is not working efficiently for you or for himself. You may be flattered that the agent thinks you can swing a $150,000 apartment, but you won't feel quite so heady when the bank turns down your loan application. So shy away from the agent who avoids asking ''personal'' questions about your financial status. Even if you know exactly what you can afford, the incompetence of an agent who is afraid or unwilling to ask you about it may well show up again when he or she is negotiating.

It is almost as important to spend some time in the agent's office establishing ''needs and wants.'' The agent should list these carefully and show you apartments that fit most of your established criteria. If, for example, you have specified a patio-type condo complex with a garage and three bedrooms, and you are being shown high-rises and mid-rises with dining rooms that could easily be ''converted'' into that third bedroom, change agents!

Often you can save a great deal of in-office time by compiling your own family profile and need-and-want list. Write out the important facts about your family: how many members, ages and sexes of the children, pets, hobbies, and interests. Then make a two-column list headed: MUST HAVE and WOULD LIKE. List your requirements or desires in order of importance. Xerox your list and give it to every real estate agent you work with.

Organization

The real estate agent who pulls the car to the side of the road and takes out his/her map in order to decide which way to turn next is not for you. First, the agent should *know* the areas in which he sells, and second, he or she should have the route mapped out in advance. In fact, the very best agents under the best circumstances drive each route and inspect each apartment before taking customers out.

Listing information on all the apartments to be shown on a particular day should be arranged and gathered for your inspection in advance of your getting into the agent's car. (Don't be afraid to eliminate an apartment that you have already seen or that you know you will not consider.) Appointments for showings should allow adequate time without rushing you.

When you find an agent who is organized, efficient, and sincerely trying to find an apartment that will meet your needs, you should try to stay with that person throughout your apartment-hunting in the area that he or she serves. If you decide to look in a town twenty-five miles away (or in a major city twenty-five blocks away), however, you should get another agent who is familiar with *that* local area.

And don't stop reading the real estate section of your newspaper even if you have found a good agent, or several good agents. You still know best what appeals to you. If you should see an apartment advertised that you think sounds good, ask your agent to "check it out" for you. Even in areas that do not use a Multiple Listing Service, most brokers will cooperate with each other. Your agent will call the listing agent, get permission to inspect the apartment advertised, then report back to you. If the place still sounds interesting, you can inspect it with your agent and work any offers or negotiations through him/her.

Negotiating Skill

How good is your agent at getting two parties (buyer and seller) to come to a meeting of the minds? That's a difficult question to answer since there are no certificates of competence in negotiating. Yet negotiating skill can save you thousands of dollars or its equivalent in better terms and financing. And good negotiating skills have kept more than a few faltering deals together.

But again: How can you tell how your agent will perform? There is no right way to negotiate. Every situation is different and what works for one individual does not necessarily work for another, and vice versa. So *you* must judge how effective your agent is with people. Do you feel that you trust him/her? Are his answers honest? Consistent? Knowledgeable? Does he hold your attention and respect without being arrogant or dominating? Can he point out the other side of questions you ask or objections you raise without antagonizing you? Ideally, he should be able to show you another way to look at something or think about something so that you say "Ahh-haa" instead of "Not for me!" He should avoid clichés, yes-buts, and changing a topic when the question is uncomfortable.

Knowledge of the Financial Marketplace

Ask your agent as many questions about financing as you can think of. The next chapter will give you a rundown on the different types of financing currently available in this country. Ask your agent what is being used in your local area. At what rates? Under what current conditions? Who is lending money? Insurance companies? Pension funds? Ask his or her opinion on which methods are best and why. Ask him if he or his firm have been successful in getting seller financing.

In Chapter 9, we'll go through some actual figures for you, using various types of financing. Using those figures as models, ask your agent to help you work out the figures for your potential or possible deal. This should be done before you make an offer (or even find the right apartment) so that you can judge how effectively the agent will work for you.

There! The profile is complete. Your ideal agent will be experienced in condo and co-op sales, well trained and knowledgeable, and a full-time professional. He or she will know the local area, take time to qualify your buying potential, define at the outset a profile of your needs and wants, and handle showings in an organized and responsible way. He or she will be personable and honest, at ease with people, persuasive, quick thinking, and will know the ins and outs (and some of the in-betweens) of financing. Now, how do you find this paragon?

Finding a Good Agent

The worst way to find an agent is the way most commonly used. Prospective buyers read an ad in the newspaper, think the apartment sounds appealing, and call the real estate office number listed at the end of the ad.

In most offices the privilege of answering the phone is assigned to the agent with "floor time." In this way that agent picks up all the inquiries on ads that come into the office during his/her assigned time. The object is to get the people who call in on an ad to make an appointment to go out and look at the apartment (and half a dozen others).

The odds of getting a good agent by this method are not good. Floor time is *not* assigned preferentially in most offices. The hardworking agent does not get any more time than the inefficient agent; the experienced agent rarely gets more time than the rookie. But prospective buyers who insist upon taking their chances with whoever answers the phone can increase their odds on finding a competent person by calling offices with an excellent reputation in residential sales. Office managers there tend to be very selective in their hiring in order to keep that reputation.

The best way to find a good agent is the referral. Ask friends who have recently bought or sold apartments or houses about the agents who worked with and for them. Run through the criteria of a good agent that we gave you point by point and ask how your friends would evaluate their agents. When you find one who scores high, go out to look at apartments with him/her. But if *you* don't feel comfortable and satisfied, change. The chemistry and rapport between buyer and agent is just as important as the agent's references.

Referrals are best, but what if you're new in the area or you don't happen to have any friends or associates who have recently bought or sold real estate? What should you do then?

You can watch your local newspapers. Frequently photos of agents who have made the million-dollar-sales club or achieved other notable success are published in the business or real estate sections. These people have won the recognition of their peers, and it's difficult to argue with success. When you see such a photo, don't call the real estate office and ask about an apartment, ask *for* that agent. Then ask the agent about the apartment. It may take a few tries before you meet an agent that you like personally, but at least you will have eliminated the deadbeats.

If you enjoy going out on a Sunday afternoon to look at apartments, you might try going to open houses. There are always one or two agents assigned to each open house, and your walk through the apartments will give you a chance to talk with them. They will be asking you questions about what type of apartment you are looking for; you should ask them questions about themselves, their working hours, the financial marketplace, and the real estate market in general. You'll be surprised at how good you'll become at evaluating agents in five-minute conversations!

And don't worry that you'll be hounded by phone calls once an agent has your name. If you decide that you don't want to work with a particular person, simply reply to his call by saying that you have chosen to work with another agent or that you are not ready to look seriously for an apartment at this time. No one wants to spin his wheels for people who will not buy and you won't be bothered by very many return phone calls.

For Sale by Owner

Working with an agent does not preclude running down the FOR SALE BY OWNER advertisements in the newspaper. Don't begin this chore, however, until you have been out several times with an agent and have formulated an idea of the market value in your area. Most owners selling their own apartments overprice the units, and it often takes a good many days on the market before they come to a realistic appreciation of the worth of their property.

If you should find a for-sale-by-owner apartment that you want to purchase, your most difficult task will be in negotiating. In order to convince the owner of fair market value, try to get the selling prices of as many recently sold properties in the area as possible. And use a lawyer. Do not sign any papers or make any commitments on financing or terms without allowing him or her to review everything.

Offering by Prospectus Only

A varient of for-sale-by-owner is the offering by prospectus only. Here real bargains are available because *everything* is negotiable by you as an individual buyer while at the same time the tenants occupying the building are negotiating for the best possible deal on the conversion itself.

The Right Apartment

Given the knowledge you now have about condominium and cooperative ownership and the importance of weighing variables in real estate, you may wonder how you will know when you have found the right apartment for you. The answer may surprise you. You will fall in love.

Your feeling upon meeting the right apartment is a little like the electricity between a man and a woman. You'll walk into a living room, and something, you're not sure what, will make you want to stay. This feeling grows into wanting to own it. (A near relation to wanting to own it is being afraid that someone else will buy it!)

We believe you should love an apartment at least a little to choose it as your residence. Without that spark of attraction, you will probably be unhappy even with the best of financial deals. *But* do not let your heart rule your head completely. Fall in love, say "This is it!" but don't let the agent talk you into making an offer the first day you see the apartment. Buying a place to live in is too large an investment to be left entirely to the heart. Follow your heart, yes, but judge with your head.

Testing Your Love

When you are very excited about an apartment and begin to feel that you *must* have it, *go home*. Tell the real estate agent that you will call him in the morning. Have a good dinner and then test your love for that apartment. (This procedure works best when two people have seen the property, but you can do it even if you are buying alone.)

Take several sheets of paper and a pencil and go into separate rooms. Give yourselves a time limit (twenty to thirty minutes) and agree to get together at the end of it. Now try to draw the floor plan of the apartment that you love *from memory*. Put in doorways, windows, closets, the kitchen appliances, fireplaces, bookcases or other built-ins, everything!

When you have finished drawing, look at your floor plan and think through a year in the apartment. Where would you keep your golf clubs, your bike, your skis? Where would you store your photography equipment or oil paints and easel? Where would you find a quiet place to read? Where would you entertain friends? Write out any questions that come to mind as you draw the plan or think through ordinary days or holidays in the apartment.

Then get together with your spouse, or roommate, or just a friend who has seen the property with you and compare your floor plans. Don't argue about who is right. Unless you are both very unusual people, the floor plans will be different. No person can notice and record every detail of a residence accurately on a first viewing. Much of what we think we see is actually colored by what we *want* to see. (Which is why we urge you not to buy anything the first time you see it.)

As you compare the two floor plans (or go over the one you have drawn if you are alone) list the additional questions that come up in your conversation. Did the fireplace have a mantel? Were there really four feet of uninterrupted working space in the kitchen or was the sink in the middle of that span? Were there two windows or three in the master bedroom?

Once you have your floor plans and your list of questions, get a good night's sleep. The next morning call the agent and make an appointment to reinspect the apartment. Take your floor plans and your questions with you and a twenty-foot tape measure if you have one. (The tape measure will settle disputes about the size of things.)

When you inspect the apartment for the second time, you will see it differently. Compile a corrected floor plan. Answer the questions on your list based on what you see on this second visit or from information that the agent can give you. And note flaws or faults that you missed on your first visit.

Do you still love the apartment? If yes, you are ready for the next step. But that step is still not a signature on anything, nor even a verbal offer to buy. You have tested your love for the apartment, now you want to test its price and monthly cost to you. Here's where your head takes over.

Fair Market Value

We have explained to you the use of real estate comparables in determining market value (Chapter 3). Now is the time to ask your agent to get them out for you. Listen to what he or she says is the probable value of the apartment, *but make your own judgment*. And do *not* tell the agent the figure that you arrive at. In order to give yourself the greatest latitude in negotiating, it is important that you do not reveal the numbers you are negotiating toward. Your agent will work harder to get an agreement at the price you have offered at each stage of the game if he or she does not know *if* or *at what price* you'll make another offer. So despite your friendship and trust for your agent, keep your goals and evaluations to yourself until you decide to present them as steps in the negotiating process.

Even when you are certain that you want an apartment and quite sure that you know its fair market value, there is still one more checkpoint before you are ready to make a buying commitment. You will want to know what it will cost you each month to live there and you will want to be sure that those costs will not escalate out of hand in the coming years. Your best checks against the possibility of special assessments or huge jumps in the maintenance fees are in examining the financial statement of the cooperative or condominium and in talking with a member of the board of directors.

The Financial Statement

Unless you have some accounting experience, the columns and numbers of a financial statement, especially those figures in brackets [ ], which indicate losses or shortages, may well send you running to a rental agent or out to look for a nice vine-covered (cheap) cottage. But stop, a little time and knowledge can change a monster into a friendly pet. Let's look at the financial statement of a fictitious apartment cooperative, Olympus Towers, Inc. We've selected a co-op since co-op statements include mortgages on the building and are considerably more complicated than condominium statements. If you can get through a co-op statement, however, you will have no trouble with a condo statement.

After you get through the introductory amenities of the financial statement, you come upon Exhibit A. It lists both the assets and the liabilities. "Why are both totals the same?" you ask.

To accountants, a zero is ideal: everything balances out just right. Total assets minus total liabilities in a corporation ideally equal zero. How that can be is explained by the share value; the shares that the stockholders own are a liability against the assets of the corporation. But balancing numbers is not the important factor for you at this moment. You are looking at the financial statement to help you determine if there are likely to be any major jumps in the maintenance fee that you must pay in the foreseeable future. So don't waste your time trying to understand how each and every entry balances out.

First, focus upon the liabilities section of Exhibit A. In a cooperative the item to look for is financing. At Olympus Towers a second mortgage of $500,000 will come due in the next fiscal year (1983) and a first mortgage of $1,501,203 will come due in 1993. (See the accountant's notes at the end of the financial statement for the dates of these mortgages.) Interest on these mortgages is now being paid in the maintenance fee for your apartment. You know what that figure is, but you want to know how changes in the mortgages will affect you later.

The first mortgage for $1,500,000+ will not change (need refinancing) until 1993, so you as a buyer in 1983 have ten years before that 8½-percent-per-year interest rate will be changed and therefore have any effect upon your current monthly payment.* The second mortgage for $500,000, however, matures in the year that you are buying your apartment. How will that affect your payment? Let's see.

(Remember, you'll be able to calculate the probable increases in payment due to the refinancing of the first mortgage in 1993 by these same procedures.)

---

*It is very important to check that the first mortgage does not prohibit the renewal of secondary financing or that the second mortgage is so large that it requires a refinancing of both first and second mortgages at the same time. If either of these two possibilities exists, it may mean a significant jump in your maintenance costs.

OLYMPUS TOWERS, INC.
FINANCIAL STATEMENT
DECEMBER 31, 1982 AND 1981

STANLEY STRAIT, C.P.A.
JOHN NARROW, C.P.A.

TELEPHONE
(212) 555-0001

To the Board of Directors
Olympus Towers, Inc.

We have examined the balance sheet of Olympus Towers, Inc. (a co-operative housing corporation), at December 31, 1982 and 1981, and the related statements of operations and accumulated deficit and changes in financial position for the years then ended. Our examination was made in accordance with generally accepted auditing standards and accordingly included such tests of the accounting records and such other auditing procedures as we considered necessary in the circumstances.

Included in the accompanying financial statements are projections which were prepared by the board of directors. The accuracy of the projections are contingent on various controllable and uncontrollable circumstances. Our opinion does not include the projections included in the accompanying financial statements.

In our opinion, the accompanying financial statements present fairly the financial position of Olympus Towers, Inc. (a co-operative housing corporation) at December 31, 1982 and 1981, and the results of its operations and changes in financial position for the years then ended, in conformity with generally accepted accounting principles applied on a consistent basis.

Certified Public Accountants

New York, New York
March 10, 1983

OLYMPUS TOWERS, INC.
INDEX
DECEMBER 31, 1982

STRAIT & NARROW
CERTIFIED PUBLIC ACCOUNTANTS

OLYMPUS TOWERS, INC.
(A Co-operative Housing Corporation)
BALANCE SHEET
DECEMBER 31, 1982 and 1981

ASSETS

	1982	1981
Current Assets:		
Cash (Note 1)	$ 54,790	$ 21,815
Real Estate Taxes—Escrow Account	77,970	80,304
Rentals Receivable	10,293	26,677
Prepaid Expenses	15,608	21,626
Total Current Assets	158,661	150,422
Land, Building, and Improvements (Note 2):		
Land	1,311,416	1,311,416
Building	2,988,309	2,988,309
Building Improvements	286,520	200,593
	4,586,245	4,500,318
Less Accumulated Depreciation	658,776	585,308
Total	3,927,469	3,915,010
TOTAL ASSETS	$ 4,086,130	$ 4,065,432

LIABILITIES AND STOCKHOLDERS' EQUITY

	1982	1981
Current Liabilities:		
2nd Mortgage Payable (Note 3)	$ 500,000	$ —
Accounts Payable and Accrued Expense	64,660	37,256
Due Management Agent	11,860	1,295
Total Current Liabilities	576,520	38,551
Long-term Liabilities (Note 3):		
1st Mortgage Payable	1,501,203	1,501,203
2nd Mortgage Payable (Note 3)	—	500,000
Total Long-term Liabilities	1,501,203	2,001,203
Total Liabilities	2,077,723	2,039,754
Contingencies (Note 6):		
Stockholders' Equity:		
Capital Stock—$1 Par Value		
29,805 Issued and Outstanding	29,805	29,805
Paid-in Capital	2,516,914	2,516,914
Additional Assessments for Building		
Improvements (Note 4)	102,313	48,807
Accumulated Deficit	(632,625)	(561,848)
Treasury Stock—75 Shares	(8,000)	(8,000)
Total Stockholders' Equity	2,008,407	2,025,678
TOTAL LIABILITIES AND STOCKHOLDERS' EQUITY	$ 4,086,130	$ 4,065,432

See Notes to Financial Statements.

STRAIT & NARROW
CERTIFIED PUBLIC ACCOUNTANTS

OLYMPUS TOWERS, INC.
(A Co-operative Housing Corporation)
STATEMENT OF OPERATIONS AND ACCUMULATED DEFICIT
FOR THE YEARS ENDED DECEMBER 31, 1982 and 1981

| | Year Ended December 31, 1982 | | | Year Ended December 31, 1981 |
	Actual	Budget	Increase (Decrease)	Actual
Income—Schedule B-1	$ 750,265	$ 749,000	$ 1,265	$ 709,191
Expenses:				
Operating Expenses				
Wages and Payroll Taxes	162,972	163,000	(28)	151,773
Welfare Benefits and Pension Fund	5,715	6,000	(285)	7,572
Uniforms, Laundry, Valet	423	2,000	(1,577)	829
Total Labor Costs	169,110	171,000	(1,890)	106,174
Telephone	680	1,000	(320)	675
Heating	70,224	103,500	(33,276)	91,957
Electricity and Gas	33,061	28,000	5,061	25,391
Water and Sewer	9,290	10,000	(710)	9,371
Miscellaneous	5,155	4,000	1,155	4,258
Repairs and Maintenance	23,668	27,000	(3,332)	30,501
Other Insurance	16,340	17,000	(660)	15,042
Management	12,000	12,000	—	12,000
Total Operating Expenses	339,528	373,500	(33,972)	349,369
Interest on Mortgage	156,352	156,000	352	156,352
Real Estate Taxes	215,769	218,500	(2,731)	204,218
Franchise Tax	3,210	3,000	210	3,806
Professional Fees and Other Costs	32,715	5,000	27,715	14,600
Total Expenses	747,574	756,000	(8,426)	728,345
Operating Surplus (Loss)	2,691	$(7,000)	$ 9,691	(19,154)
Depreciation	73,468			65,157
Net Loss	(70,777)			(84,311)
Accumulated Deficit				
Beginning of Year	(561,848)			(477,537)
End of year	$(632,625)			$(561,848)

See Notes to Financial Statements.

STRAIT & NARROW
CERTIFIED PUBLIC ACCOUNTANTS

OLYMPUS TOWERS, INC.
(A Co-operative Housing Corporation)
SUMMARY OF INCOME
FOR THE YEARS ENDED DECEMBER 31, 1982 and 1981

	Year Ended December 31, 1982			Year Ended December 31, 1981
	Actual	Budget	Increase (Decrease)	Actual
Maintenance Income	$644,251	$644,000	$ 251	$585,682
Rental Income:				
Stores and Professional Offices	91,884	89,500	2,384	86,740
Total Rental Income	91,884	89,500	2,384	86,740
Total Income	736,135	733,500	2,635	672,422
Interest and Dividends	5,312	2,500	2,812	19,397
Other	8,818	13,000	(4,182)	17,372
TOTAL INCOME	$750,265	$749,000	$ 1,265	$709,191

See Notes to Financial Statements.

STRAIT & NARROW
CERTIFIED PUBLIC ACCOUNTANTS

EXHIBIT C

OLYMPUS TOWERS, INC.
(A Co-operative Housing Corporation)
STATEMENT OF CHANGES IN FINANCIAL POSITION
FOR THE YEARS ENDED DECEMBER 31, 1982 and 1981

	1982	1981
Source of Funds:		
Net Loss for the Period	$(70,777)	$(84,311)
Item of Expense Not Requiring Outlay of Working Capital—Depreciation	73,468	65,157
Funds Provided (Used) by Operations	2,691	(19,154)
Funds Received for Capital Improvements	53,506	48,807
Total Funds Provided	56,197	29,653
Application of Funds:		
Expenditures for Building Improvements	85,927	152,277
Mortgage Maturing in Current Year	500,000	—
Total Application of Funds	585,927	152,277
(Decrease) Increase in Working Capital	$(529,730)	$(122,624)
Changes in Working Capital—(Decrease) Increase:		
Current Assets		
Cash	$ 32,975	$(157,864)
Rentals Receivable	(16,384)	22,052
Real Estate Taxes Escrow Account	(2,334)	1,244
Prepaid Expenses	(6,018)	9,846
	8,239	(124,722)
Current Liabilities		
Mortgage Payable	500,000	—
Accounts Payable and Accrued Expenses	27,404	592
Due Management Agent	10,565	(2,690)
	537,969	(2,098)
(Decrease) Increase in Working Capital	$(529,730)	$(122,624)

See Notes to Financial Statements.

STRAIT & NARROW
CERTIFIED PUBLIC ACCOUNTANTS

OLYMPUS TOWERS, INC.
(A Co-operative Housing Corporation)
NOTES TO FINANCIAL STATEMENTS
DECEMBER 31, 1982

Note 1—Cash:

Cash includes funds on deposit in a savings account of $12,077 and funds invested in a money market fund of $42,713.

Note 2—Building and Improvements:

Depreciation is provided on the straight-line method on the building over an estimated useful life of 50 years. Building improvements are being depreciated on the straight-line method over an estimated useful life of 5 to 15 years. During the year, capital improvements amounting to $85,927 were made. Miscellaneous equipment purchases are charged to expense.

Note 3—Mortgage Payable:

The Corporation has an outstanding mortgage with the Dime Savings Bank amounting to $1,501,203. Interest is payable at 8½% per annum with the principal due in 1993.

The second mortgage held by The Earthworks Realty Corporation is due on August 31, 1983. Interest only at the rate of 5¾% per annum is due quarterly.

Note 4—Additional Assessments for Building Improvements:

This represents funds received from tenant shareholders for expenditures for building improvements as follows:

Year	Per Share
1982	2.89
1981	5.12
1974	.81
1973	.82

Note 5—Contingencies:

There are two lawsuits pending against the Corporation. The principal lawsuit alleges the Corporation refused to sell an apartment to a divorced and disabled woman. The plaintiff seeks damages of $2,000,000. The Board of Directors believes there are various meritorious defenses and this lawsuit is covered by insurance. The second lawsuit does not involve monetary liability.

STRAIT & NARROW
CERTIFIED PUBLIC ACCOUNTANTS

113

We'll assume that the $500,000 second mortgage will be refinanced and at the current market rate. (It virtually always is.) Your current maintenance fee has been partially based upon your percentage contribution to the interest-only payment at 5¾ percent per year on $500,000, which is $28,750 a year. Now if the $500,000 is refinanced through a similar interest-only mortgage at 18 percent the payments will increase to $90,000 a year.

"Wow!" you say. "The payment is going up $61,250 a year. Let's find someplace else!"

Wait. That number is *not* important. What is important is how it will affect your maintenance payment. You'll need your calculator.

The interest payment on the second mortgage will increase 213 percent (divide $61,250 by $28,750, which equals 2.1304). *This does not mean that your monthly payment will more than double.* To determine the effect of the new financing upon *your* payment, you must determine what portion of the total maintenance fee is represented by this second-mortgage interest payment. To do this turn to Exhibit B. There you will find the total expense of the corporation for 1982 listed as $747,574. (The entry for Interest on Mortgage represents both the first- and second-mortgage payments, but you know from the accountant's note that the annual payment on the second mortgage is 5¾ percent of $500,000 which is $28,750.) To determine the second mortgage's percentage of the total annual expense divide $28,750 by $747,574 which equals .0384577, just under 4 percent of the total expenses. This calculation means that just under 4 percent of your monthly maintenance fee goes toward paying the interest on the second mortgage.

Now take the monthly maintenance fee for your apartment—let's say it's $900. Four percent of that is $36 a month. That number ($36) will increase by 213 percent if the second mortgage is refinanced at the current market rate of 18 percent. So 2.13 × $36 = $76.68. Your $36 payment will increase to $76.68, a total increase in your maintenance fee of $40.68 a month due to the increased interest payment on the second mortgage. Not nearly so staggering a figure as $61,250 a year, is it?

And if your total monthly maintenance fee on the apartment were $325 instead of $900, your increase under exactly the same circumstances would be $14.69, a figure manageable by virtually every budget.

To Determine How Cooperative Refinancing Will Affect
Monthly Maintenance Fee:

1. Look at the financing listed under Liabilities in the Financial Statement of the Corporation.
2. Note when mortgages will come due.
3. Calculate the probable rate and cost of refinancing (yearly payment).
4. Calculate the *percentage increase* over the current yearly payment for that financing.
5. Calculate the percentage of the total operating expenses of the corporation represented by the payment on that mortgage.
6. Take the percentage determined in step 5 and multiply it times your monthly maintenance fee.
7. Multiply the dollar amount determined in step 6 by the percentage increase determined in step 4.
8. This amount will pay your percentage of the new cost of financing. Subtract the original dollar amount of your percentage payment toward the old financing (step 6) from it and you will have your total increase in monthly payment due to the refinancing.

A word of caution here about accounting entries that do not really require cash and are therefore deceptive. Exhibit B reads Statement of Operations and Accumulated Deficit and lists a net loss of $70,777. Even with all those lucky sevens, this is a figure large enough to frighten off most buyers. Who wants to live in a place where they are losing $70,000 a year! A closer look, however, reveals that $73,468 of that deficit was an entry for *depreciation,* which cost the shareholders nothing. (In fact, it probably saved them a few dollars in taxes.) The building actually showed an operating surplus of $2,691. These paper deficits will continue to accumulate as the building is depreciated for tax purposes. Don't worry about them.

Another somewhat frightening entry in this particular financial statement occurs on Exhibit C, which shows a decrease in working capital of $529,730. Does that mean that the corporation will have to make up over half a million dollars by increasing maintenance fees next year? Not in this case. If you'll notice, $500,000 of that figure is the amount of the second mortgage, which will come due in the coming year. Assuming that the mortgage will be refinanced, the decrease in working capital is $29,730. This shortage occurs after a deficit of $122,624 in the previous year, which resulted in a special assessment to the shareholders of $2.89 a share.

A large deficit in the Changes in Working Capital section in a financial statement will often result in a special assessment whether you are examining a cooperative or a condominium. At Olympus Towers, it appears to be the result of some capital improvements in the building. Hopefully these have been completed and will not result in further special fees. (Ask about this from an officer of the board.) If the deficit is the result of mismanagement, however, you may want to reconsider your purchase.

Small deficits such as the $29,000 showing on this year's schedule are often the result of spiraling maintenance costs. You can generally expect increases of from 6 to 10 percent a year in the cost of running a building and these increases will usually be reflected in the maintenance-fee schedule for the following year. It is better, of course, if there is no deficit and if the change in working capital is a positive one. But too great a positive change indicates that you paid too *high* a maintenance fee the previous year!

The section titled Changes in Working Capital in any financial statement will tell you how efficiently the building is being managed; how major improvements were handled; how accurately the board estimated the expenses for the previous year; and how likely is an increase in the maintenance fee for the coming year.

In examining the financial statement of a condominium, the element of financing is nonexistent since a condominium cannot mortgage the common elements. The main focus of your examination before buying a condo apartment, therefore, should be upon the Changes in Working Capital. Is there any money in reserve? Is the condominium being efficiently managed? Is there a growing deficit? A growing surplus? Has there been a recent special assessment?

If all this is hopelessly confusing to you, take the financial statement for the condominium or cooperative that you are considering to a professional managing agent or property manager and pay the fee necessary to have it explained and evaluated for you. You will sleep much better; you will have a good idea of where your maintenance fees are going; and you will feel that both your investment and your life-style are a little more secure.

Someone on the Board

After you finish examining the facts and figures, you'll probably have some questions. For example, what caused the special assessment of $2.89 a share in 1982? Are the repairs, renovations, complete? Do you anticipate any further need for special assessments?

Now is the time to talk to a member of the board of directors. Ask the real estate agent to get you names and phone numbers. Call and talk. You can get not only the answers to your questions from the board member but also information on any new developments that have occurred since the financial statement was issued. For example: The financial statement ends on December 31, 1982. What if you are buying in April 1983? How would you know that the furnace blew up in January 1983 and the corporation had to spend $10,000 for repairs and replacement parts? You would know if you asked the president of the board if there had been any unusual expenses since the first of the year. And you could probably find out what that expense will mean in terms of added maintenance costs.

You can ask a board member about plans for refinancing the building; changes in the income from commercial leases; any liens that have been placed on the property; are any tenant/shareholders in default; are the tenant/shareholders satisfied with the management company; and anything else that bothers you even a little.

Making the Offer

You still love the apartment and you are now sure that you can afford to live in it. It's time to make your first offer on the property. During the past few days while you were checking on your heart and head responses to the apartment, you should also have been trying to ascertain as much information as possible about the motivations, needs, and expectations of the sellers. Ask your agent: ''How long has the apartment been on the market?'' (The longer on the market, the more likely the sellers are to negotiate.) ''Have there been any price reductions?'' (Price reductions indicate a growing eagerness to sell, especially if there have been several.) ''How soon can the owners vacate?'' (You can't always get the answer to this question, but if you do, you'll be able to use the information effectively in getting both a better price and terms.) ''Have there been any other offers on the apartment? When? For how much?'' (Your agent can call the listing agent on the apartment for the answers to these quesions. If an offer near what you want to pay for the apartment was refused several months ago, do not hesitate to make your offer still lower. People often change their minds about price after several months on the market or several low offers from different buyers.)

When you are ready, tell your agent that you want to make an offer on the apartment. Make that offer several thousand dollars *less* than what you have determined is the fair market value of the apartment and/or what you have determined is your ideal purchase price. All sellers price their properties above what they want to get for them, and those same sellers do not believe that the first offer of a buyer is his highest possible price. If you bid your ideal price, you will be squeezed up several thousand dollars before you holler "Ouch!" and refuse to go higher.

And *never* tell your real estate agent what your real top-dollar figure is on a particular apartment. If you say, "We're offering $94,000 but we can go to $100,000 on this one if we absolutely *have* to," you will end up at $100,000. It may be conscious or subconscious on the part of the agent, but negotiations invariably end up at the buyer's top dollar.

With your first offer do not ask for extras (appliances, carpeting) or concessions on the closing date. Save these as negotiating points as you are forced to come up in price. In other words, if you come up $3,000 on your offer, you also want the custom draperies in the living room and the wall-to-wall carpet, right? And if you must come up another $2,000 on another counteroffer, you could ask that the closing date be postponed two months. The sellers will then have to weigh closing two months later against $2,000. If you had found out before negotiations started that they had already placed a deposit on an apartment in Arizona, you may be gambling that an early closing date is preferred to the extra cash. Or you might come to a compromise in which the closing is postponed one month and you increase your offer by only $1,000. The possibilities are limitless. Just be sure that *you*, not the real estate agent, control the negotiating, and be sure that you do not reveal your next move before the one in process is played out.

Signing in Safety

Do not make your first offer—or any offer, for that matter—through an executed contract that awaits only the signatures of the sellers. They may surprise you by accepting that offer and then you will be bound by the terms of that contract, fine print and all.

Give your real estate agent an earnest money check—$500 or $1,000 is the customary and usual amount, but any amount can be agreed upon—and give him/her the information he needs about the amount of your down payment, financing, closing dates requested, and so forth. Don't sign anything. Have contracts drawn by an attorney after everyone comes to an agreement on everything.

If your real estate agent insists that an offer cannot be made without a written (signed) offer to purchase, use a "binder" or "short offer form" and be absolutely sure it contains a statement to the effect of:

This agreement is subject to contracts for purchase to be drawn by the buyers' attorney and executed by all parties concerned in the sale within five (5) business days.

If the office offer form does not contain such a statement, have it typed in and above your signature.

Your contract to purchase your apartment should be subject to your being able to obtain financing and subject to board of directors' approval of your purchase if that is required in the particular co-op or condo community. It can also be subject to a satisfactory report by a home inspection service.

The contract should specify the amount of money to be held in escrow and who is to hold it. This money should be placed in an interest-bearing account and you should try to get the interest credited to yourself. (Who gets the interest is sometimes a point of negotiation.)

Your contract should also include a list of all the personal-property items (rugs, appliances, lighting fixtures) that remain with the apartment and a list of those that do not remain. It is a good idea to have this page initialed by all parties concerned.

Once your contract is signed, no one else can sneak in and buy the apartment out from under you. *But* your work is not yet done. Now you must find a way to pay for your purchase. Financing is so big an issue today that we've had to devote not one but two chapters to it.

CHAPTER 8

Alphabet Soup:
The Language and Principles
of Financing

Financing is the most difficult and complicated aspect of real estate today. Neither of us can remember another time of so many knotty problems, so much uncertainty, and so much "creativity." A new mortgage type pops up almost before an old one can be explained.

It's tempting to acknowledge the complexity of the topic, advise you to consult your lawyer or banker, and go on. But then you would have no choice but to rely almost blindly upon the advice of the professionals you chose. If, on the other hand, we explain the basics of the mortgage market, you might (and should) still seek that advice, but you would seek it knowing the language and principles of home financing. We've decided, therefore, to risk boring or confusing you with the hope that, in the end, we will have armed you with questions to ask and alternative options to propose.

We'll start with a classical overview of concepts and mortgage instruments that have been around for decades. Then we'll go on to the new "alphabet soup" mortgages, those strange combinations of initials that bankers and real estate agents are dipping into more and more in an effort to make buying a home a realistic possibility.

What's a Mortgage?

Let's consider the word. *Mortgage* comes from the Old French and it means "dead pledge." Don't laugh, we know. That start is a little like giving a friend who is departing on a cruise a copy of *A Night to Remember* (the story of the *Titanic*). But you may as well begin knowing the worst. When you mortgage your home, you pledge it as security that you will repay a loan. If you don't pay, the lender can take that home in place of the money you owe him.

But the word *mortgage* is often used incorrectly, and its incorrect use results in confusion. You, the homeowner, mortgage your home—that is, you give the lender a mortgage on your home. The lender gives you a mortgage *loan,* or to say it another way, a loan secured by the mortgage you have given. You therefore are the *mortgagor,* the one who gives the mortgage. The lender of the money is the *mortgagee,* the one to whom the mortgage is given.

These words are especially confusing because homebuyers, real estate agents, and even lawyers routinely talk about *getting a mortgage*. What they really mean is getting a mortgage *loan*.

More confusion: In some southern and southwestern states, people don't talk about getting a mortgage. They talk about a "trust deed." The names are different; the principles are the same. If you take out a trust deed, you are the *trustor* and the lending institution or lender is the *beneficiary*. Another party who actually holds the title to your property is called the *trustee*. Rather than foreclosure proceedings if you default on payments for your trust deed, the trustee is empowered to use an auction of your property to repay the loan.

Just a few more basic terms: The amount you borrow is called the *principal*. The charge levied for borrowing that principal is called *interest*. The number of years for which you borrow the money is called the *term* of the mortgage (or trust deed).

Financing a Co-op

Next point of popular confusion: If you are buying a co-op apartment, you cannot get a mortgage loan. Why? Because your apartment is not a separate piece of real estate and you don't own it. As we've said, you own shares of stock in the corporation that owns the building and all the apartments within it, and you hold a proprietary lease on the apartment that is tied to those shares. The loan you take out from a lending institution to "buy" your co-op apartment, therefore, is a loan to buy stock in a corporation. You apply not for a mortgage, but for a personal loan. Your stock in the corporation is offered as security for that personal loan. Recent legislation allows the lender to assume those shares of stock and the proprietary lease attached to them in the event that you should default on your payments.

"That doesn't sound much different from a mortgage to me," you say. And you're right. Many of the principles, conditions, and words of mortgaging apply to co-op loans, which is exactly why, even though your head and heart may be committed to buying a co-op, you can't stop reading at this point. Co-ops *are* a part of the financing game. So pass GO, collect your stipend, and continue around the board.

You may in fact *need* that extra stipend if you choose a co-op over a condo because most lending institutions (but not all lenders) charge a slightly higher interest rate for co-op loans than they are charging for mortgages. The banks will tell you that the higher rate is due to the greater risk involved in the loan and to the fact that there is no secondary mortgage market for co-op loans. The second statement is true.

The secondary mortgage market, by the way, is the term used for the lenders and/or investors across the country that buy home mortgages from the banks and lending institutions, thus freeing up the bank's cash flow. Your life insurance company might be one of them, or you may have heard or read the name Fannie Mae. Fannie Mae is the nickname given the Federal National Mortgage Association, the big boy (or perhaps "girl" is more appropriate) in the secondary mortgage marketplace. It is a shareholder-owned corporation, not a federal agency.

The traditional lending institutions, however, are not the only source of co-op purchase loans. Sometimes financing can be obtained from the sponsor of a converted building at very attractive rates. These loans can be written with an almost limitless number of variables, but most are similar in essence to currently prevalent practices in the mortgage marketplace.

Among the newest and perhaps the most controversial means of financing co-op apartments are shared-equity loans that pair a tenant-would-be-shareholder who cannot afford the purchase price of an apartment with a small investor as co-owners of the shares assigned to a particular apartment. More about this under SAM (shared-appreciation mortgage) and partnership mortgage further along in this chapter.

Financing a Condo

When you buy a condominium apartment, you do own a piece of real estate, even if that real estate is only air space. Because you own it, you can mortgage it. Virtually all the financing options available to single-family homebuyers are open also to condominium buyers.

Let's start then with what used to be the tried-and-true, most common mortgaging method, the conventional mortgage. A conventional mortgage is an amortizing loan issued by a lender at a fixed rate of interest for a fixed term. It is an endangered species.

Amortizing or amortization is the gradual paying out of a loan through regular fixed payments over a period of time. Early in the term the payments are almost all interest; late in the term, almost all principal. But at the end of the term, you the borrower owe the lender nothing. The mortgage papers can be burned, and your home is yours to have and to hold. Amortizing mortgages are sometimes called self-liquidating mortgages.

Today, conventional mortgages are more often referred to as fixed-rate mortgages in order to distinguish them from the variety of fluctuating-rate mortgages available. But before we get into this electronic age of mortgages, let's look at the unconventional mortgages of the good old days . . . FHA and VA.

*FHA Mortgages*___

In the real estate world, FHA stands for Federal Housing Authority, and FHA loans are a large part of that world. Contrary to popular misconception, however, the FHA does *not* give mortgage loans; it insures them.

This all started in the 1930s as a government brainstorm that was to inspire banks to lend more money to prospective homebuyers with small down payments by offering the lender the security of government-sponsored insurance. The increased lending was supposed to help the economy. (It did.)

The insurance offered by the government, however, is not free. It costs the buyer ½ of 1 percent in additional interest. The extra fee is added to and paid with the monthly principal and interest payment. FHA mortgages can be cast (loans made) only by an FHA-approved lending institution. There is a 1-point fee to the buyer. (We'll do points in just a bit.)

FHA loans are available on most condominiums, with some restrictions generally intended for consumer protection. Maximum loan amounts are periodically revised, but if your condo costs more than the FHA maximum loan, *you* must come up with the additional cash (and without using a second-mortgage loan to do it). The amount of FHA-insured financing that you can get is also dependent upon an FHA appraisal. This can take several weeks and a lot of paperwork.

The FHA appraiser checks your condo apartment and the building against the FHA Manual of Minimum Standards. If there are deviations from the standards, a list is often sent to the seller requiring repair before the mortgage loan will be approved by the FHA.

As of this writing, all FHA loans are assumable and for long terms (usually thirty years). The assumable part makes them a premium loan in today's market because it guarantees that a buyer for your home five years or more from now can take over the payments on your mortgage at the original interest rate. The long-term, fixed-rate nature of FHA mortgages, however, has also prompted most lenders to add a heavy point penalty to the seller's side of the closing costs.

FHA Graduated Payment Mortgage

Believe it or not even before interest rates tried to reach the ozone layer of this planet, young people were finding it difficult to buy and finance their first homes. In response to their need, the FHA introduced a mortgage plan (FHA 245 program) designed to help first-homebuyers who were trying to get started on incomes that were relatively low but likely to move upward over the years. The interest on these fixed-term (usually thirty-year) mortgages are also fixed, but the payments are arranged so that they will be lower at the outset and rise by 7.5 percent per year for the first five years. (Note: The dollar amount of the *payment* goes up by 7.5 percent, not the interest rate.) The monthly payment would then remain fixed from the sixth year through the remaining term of the mortgage. The amount of this monthly payment is higher than it would be in a conventional mortgage loan at the fixed rate named in the agreement because the homebuyer was in effect borrowing extra money to make lower payments in the early years of the loan.

VA Mortgages

The VA is the Veterans Administration. With some exceptions in times of tight money or in areas where financing is generally unavailable, the VA also does not give mortgage loans; it guarantees them. You must be an eligible veteran to qualify for a loan, which means you must have served in the armed forces for a certain length of time during certain designated periods of time. If you are unsure about your eligibility, call the VA office nearest you and request Form 26-1880: "Request for Determination of Eligibility and Available Loan Guaranty Entitlement." You may have to wait several weeks, but you will receive notice of your status.

With a VA loan, you can sometimes buy a condominium apartment with no down payment, depending upon the price of the unit, the VA appraisal, and your ability to carry the loan. Like the FHA, the VA does its own appraisal, and issues a Certificate of Reasonable Value. They also carefully check your employment history and credit references before agreeing to guarantee your loan. There is no additional fee for insurance on VA loans, but the point situation is exactly the same as the FHA loan system. And like FHA loans, VA loans are assumable by a new buyer.

The VA operates a free home counseling service at most of its regional offices. You can obtain more information by writing to:

Veterans Benefits Office
Veterans Administration
2033 M Street NW
Washington, DC 20421

VA Graduated Payment Mortgage

At this time the structure of the VA graduated payment mortgage is the same as the FHA graduated payment mortgage, but subject to review as conditions warrant. VA-GPMs are limited to one-family owner-occupied homes (new or existing) and VA-approved condos. The minimum term is thirty years and the mortgage is fully amortizing.

Points

Points are often called "discount points" and this is one of the most deceptive misnomers in the English language. Discount points are actually a fee charged by a lender to make the mortgage more profitable. Points are due and paid in cash at the closing; in other words, they are up-front money.

Each point equals 1 percent of the face amount of the mortgage loan (principal). For example, if you are borrowing $50,000 and must pay 5 points to get your loan, you will need $2,500 in cash (or certified check) at the closing table.

When the points a lender attaches to a loan are clearly stated as being a part of the cost of obtaining that loan (whether it be a mortgage or a co-op loan), they can be tax-deductible as interest in the tax year in which they were paid. For points to qualify as a tax deduction, however, the charging of points must be a common practice in your local area, and the number of points charged must not exceed that being commonly charged by other local lenders.

Both FHA and VA mortgages have a 1-point limit to the buyer, but no limit on the number of points that can be charged the seller. Since both government agencies set maximum interest rates for the mortgages they will insure or guarantee, there are often times when FHA or VA loans carry lower interest rates than other types of financing. The lending institutions, however, are not required to cast FHA or VA loans, and if the maximum interest rates on those loans are too far below the going rates for other types of mortgages, the banks effectively shut the programs down. When the difference in interest rates is within workable limits, most banks simply tag on points to be paid by the seller in order to make the loans profitable.

"Great!" says the buyer. "The government finally did something for me." Not quite. It looks lovely on paper, but the overwhelming majority of sellers simply figure out the cost of the points and add it to the price they would have settled for on a contract that didn't involve points. So who pays the points?

Actually in times of very tight money and few homebuyers (what is traditionally called a buyers' market), the scene is not quite so simple. Many sellers *can* be negotiated into paying at least part of the points and closing costs without increasing their selling price. It is painful for them, however, since the amount *they* pay in points cannot be directly deducted as interest paid out on a loan on their federal income-tax return; it can be deducted only from the profit on the sale of the property. From the buyer's point of view, however, it is always better to have the price reduced rather than have the seller pay the points, since the points are tax deductible to the buyer.

Second Mortgages

A second mortgage is a mortgage that is second in line to be paid off in the event that the borrower should default. In a foreclosure sale, the first-mortgage lien is paid first; what is left goes toward paying off the second mortgage. This situation, of course, means higher risk to the second mortgage lender, and because of the higher risks, second mortgage interest rates are usually higher than first mortgage rates.

Second mortgages are also usually written for shorter terms and therefore require relatively high monthly payments. Some more "creative" lenders, however, are now offering many of the new financing options available for first mortgages on their second mortgage loans also. For example, you might be able to get a three-year renewable balloon second mortgage with a thirty-year pay-out and private mortgage insurance. Or you might choose a ten-year straight, adjustable rate.*

---

*Most conventional loans on condos and co-ops today prohibit secondary financing. So have your lawyer check your first mortgage loan documents carefully before you commit to a second mortgage.

Sounds complicated? It is, but keep reading. By the time you finish this chapter, you should be able to understand those options. Remember, the interest that you pay on a second mortgage is tax-deductible just as the interest on a first mortgage. In areas of the country where trust deeds are used instead of mortgages, a second mortgage is called a second trust deed or a second deed of trust.

Straight Mortgages

These have been around a long time but were almost never used by lending institutions to finance residential real estate. The name is therefore not familiar.

In a straight-mortgage situation, a certain amount of money is borrowed for a certain period of time. Periodic payments are made for interest only. At the end of the mortgage term, the full original loan (the principal) is due and payable.

This kind of financing agreement is sometimes being called a nonamortizing or an interest-only mortgage in today's financial jargon.

Straight mortgages are commonly used by sellers or private (noncommercial) lenders. Most are written for relatively short terms: sometimes as few as three years, rarely longer than ten years. Of course, you can plan to refinance when a straight mortgage comes due, but remember that refinancing can cost almost as much as a closing.

The Balloon Mortgage

This is a little more complicated. It starts out as an amortizing conventional mortgage—that is, a mortgage at a fixed rate that would be completely paid out over its term. The payments that you make to the lender are exactly the dollar amount that they would be on a conventional thirty- or even forty-year loan, and you are paying out the same portion of the principal in each payment that you would be on that conventional loan. *But* at some point that was mutually agreed upon when the mortgage was cast— let's say five or ten years from the date it all began—the entire unpaid principal becomes due. (That's the balloon, or to some, the burst balloon!)

Since amortizing mortgage payments are mostly interest in the early years and mostly principal in the last years, the borrower with a balloon mortgage for ten years on a forty-year pay-out schedule has repaid very little of the principal when the balloon becomes due.

Needless to say, there is some risk in this kind of borrowing. It does make for lower monthly payments and high interest deductions on federal tax forms, however. It's also relatively safe if the buyer is fairly certain of a corporate transfer during the term of the balloon.

The roll-over mortgage and the adjustable rate balloon are related options we'll describe later.

The Call

To call a mortgage means to demand payment in full. In the past some lenders have skirted the problem of fixed-rate long-term conventional mortgages by including a clause in their lending agreements specifying call periods. These are named dates at three-, five-, or seven-year intervals (or actually any interval) on which the lender may legally demand that the entire remaining principal be paid. Some mortgages written in the tight money times of the mid-1970s contain call clauses. An option to allow the borrower the chance to renew the loan at the prevailing interest rate without refinancing charges may or may not be included with a call clause.

If a conventional mortgage contains a call clause, it is really a potential balloon mortgage in disguise (a wolf in sheep's clothing).

Assumable Mortgages

The term *assumable mortgage* is another point of popular confusion. There is no particular mortgage called an assumable mortgage. Any mortgage theoretically can be assumed by a buyer if it does not contain a due-on-sale clause or if its due-on-sale clause is invalidated by law.

To assume a mortgage, the buyer must give the seller the amount of equity that he (the seller) has accumulated in the property. For example, if a condo that was originally mortgaged for $50,000 were sold for $70,000, the buyer would have to pay the seller $20,000 plus whatever portion of the principal had been repaid to the lender. Let's say in the course of three years, $1,326 had been applied toward repayment of the loan's principal. The buyer would therefore pay the seller $21,326 and take over responsibility for the remaining balance due under the terms of the original loan agreement (usually lower interest).

A due-on-sale clause written into a mortgage, however, states that if the property is sold the entire unpaid principal becomes immediately due and must be paid to the lender. It usually forces the buyer to get a new mortgage.

There is currently considerable controversy over due-on-sale clauses across the nation. Consumers and real estate agents are opposed to them; they want all mortgages to be assumable. Lending institutions say that they cannot stay in business without due-on-sale clauses as a means of dumping outmoded long-term mortgages written at low and now painfully unprofitable fixed interest rates.

California (and several other states) took a stand against the clauses in favor of assumptions. Lenders there protested and the question of a state's right to rule upon the policies of a federally chartered lender finally found its way to the Supreme Court. In the summer of 1982, the court ruled that a state may *not* regulate a federally chartered lending institution and the due-on-sale clause became valid at all federally chartered institutions. State laws still pertain to state-chartered lenders, however.

Private Mortgage Insurance

Private mortgage insurance is an option that allows buyers to purchase property with very small down payments. Similar to the FHA program, but not associated with the government in any way, it is available from a number of private mortgage insurance firms throughout the country. Like FHA loans, the private-mortgage-insurance borrower may have as little as 5 percent of the purchase price to use as a down payment. Also like FHA loans, there is a fee for the mortgage insurance, sometimes including a lump-sum payment at the outset. The fee for the insurance may decrease as equity in the property increases and some lenders will allow the buyers to drop the mortgage insurance completely after a certain period of time and/or a certain amount of accumulated equity.

So-called "magic" mortgages are mortgages insured by Mortgage Guaranty Insurance Corporation, the largest private mortgage insurance company in the United States. The firm's initials MGIC make the name obvious. Insurance is also available from the PMI Group, whose name does *not* stand for "private mortgage insurance" but rather the initials of the founder's name!

Five years ago another page or two would have concluded this chapter; today we have just begun. Now we stir our alphabet soup.

AMI (Alternative Mortgage Instruments)

Alternative mortgage instruments is a collective term meaning the "new" mortgages. Essentially that includes almost anything that is different from the old-fashioned fixed-rate deal. Most of the initials that follow focus upon the primary or most important aspect in a particular financing scheme's structure, but some are nicknames and some, we think, just sounded good.

AML (Adjustable Mortgage Loan)

AML covers the most widespread and varied category of alternative mortgage instruments. Like conventional mortgages, the term of these loans is usually long, giving the borrower some security. But the interest rate on the loan is adjusted according to a named national public index that is beyond the lender's control. Besides the movable (up, more often than down) interest rate, other variables may also be adjusted in some AMLs. The amount of the monthly payments might fluctuate because of interest rate changes. If interest rates were to rise sharply, the amount of the principal owed might be adjusted (increased) in order to keep monthly payments more nearly stable. Or the term of the loan might be changed (lengthened). AMLs are available through savings banks and savings and loan associations.

Considering that monthly payment, interest rate, principal, and term are all adjustable in an AML, the possible number of different combinations that might be written into *your* mortgage and the possible effects on *your* future spendable income after housing costs are staggering. We urge you, therefore, to get the advice of a competent attorney or financial adviser before signing any commitment for an adjustable loan.

ARM (Adjustable Rate Mortgage)

Authorized by the Office of the Comptroller of the Currency for national banks, this loan program is similar to the AML but with certain restrictions (see chart on pages 132–133). Currently it may contain a due-on-sale clause or it may be assumable at the bank's option.

Regulations and Regulators

Though tedious, it is important before we go further that you understand that loans from federally chartered "thrift institutions" (savings banks and savings & loan associations) and loans from federally chartered banks are regulated by different federal agencies. The lenders therefore operate under slightly different rules and restrictions. The Comptroller of the Currency regulates banks; the Federal Home Loan Bank Board regulates savings banks and savings & loan associations. The following chart compares the regulations on adjustable loans.

Parity Laws

To complicate matters yet a little more, state-chartered banks, savings banks, and savings & loan associations operate under the regulations of their respective states. Some states, however, have parity laws that allow state-chartered lenders the same lending policy guidelines that apply to certain federally chartered lenders. These laws vary considerably from one state to another, but you can obtain information on banking regulations in your state by writing to your State Banking Commission.

VRM (Variable Rate Mortgage)

Once called the VIR, the variable interest rate mortgage was one of the earliest forms of fluctuating rate mortgage allowed in this country. There was an attempt to introduce it nationally during the 1974–75 mortgage closedown, but consumer opposition prompted Congress to pass a resolution against the VIR at all federally chartered savings institutions. The VIR did become available at some state-chartered institutions at that time, however.

By 1980, VRMs were approved for national use, and today they are considered almost as outmoded as conventional mortgages. The VRM (or VIR) is a long-term mortgage (again usually thirty years) whose interest rate and therefore monthly payments may be increased or decreased at six-month intervals. When the plan was conceived, increases were limited to ½ percent per year or 2½ percent over the entire life of the loan, which made it obsolete almost before it could be appropriately admired.

Some Federal Regulations for Adjustable Mortgages

Mortgage Variable	Federally Chartered Banks (ARMs)	Federally Chartered Savings Institutions (AMLs)
Time interval of rate changes	Regular adjustment intervals must be established in writing. Minimum interval is 6 months.	No restrictions. Adjustments may be made whenever necessary or intervals may be set by mutual agreement.
Rate changes	Must be linked to one of several specified indexes.	Can be linked to almost any chosen index.
Rate increases	Not more than 1 percent increase in any 6-month period. Any change greater than 1 percent may be carried into the next 6-month period. Cumulative rate increase may not exceed	No ceilings on rate increases. (Ceilings can be written into individual mortgages by mutual agreement.)

Rate decreases	5 percent in any established adjustment interval. Mandatory and linked to the index specified.	Optional (Linkage to an index can be negotiated and written into the agreement.)
Amount of monthly installment payment	Changes are allowed within set limitations; ceiling on maximum increase allowed.	Unlimited changes allowed; no ceiling on increases. (Caps may be negotiated for each mortgage.)
Amount of loan (principal)	Changes allowed within specified limits. Ceiling on maximum amount increase.	Unlimited changes allowed. No ceiling on maximum amount of loan increase.
Term of loan	No change allowed in the original term.	Loan maturity can be increased up to 40 years.

VRMs were no longer issued by federally chartered lenders after July 31, 1981. If you can find an assumable VRM (and many were written) on a property that you want to buy, grab it! In the present financial marketplace, it's a good deal.

RRM (Renegotiable Rate Mortgage)

The renegotiable rate mortgage is similar to the VRM and was introduced and accepted nationally at almost the same time. It's interest rate, however, is renegotiated at three- or five-year intervals rather than six-month intervals, and that rate remains stable during the negotiated period. In the original RRMs, the increases could not exceed ½ percent per year with a maximum of 5-percent increase over the life of the loan, but if you can find a lender who will adhere to these original limitations, camp on that doorstep.

Most RRMs actually become due and payable at the end of each three- or five-year rate-adjustment period but are automatically renewed upon acceptance of the new interest rate. There is no additional fee for refinancing at the new rate, but you as borrower are caught between a rock and a hard place. If you don't accept the new mortgage rate, you must pay off the balance of your loan or the bank can foreclose. If you decide that another lender has a better deal, you will be forced to pay origination, application, and appraisal fees, and other costs such as surveys, which may well bring your expenses close to those of a traditional closing. Not so good for consumers.

GPM (Graduated Payment Mortgage)

A private-sector mortgage plan that is like the FHA plan except that the frequency and rate at which the early payments increase can be negotiated between the lender and the borrower. The period of increasing payments, however, may not exceed ten years, after which point the payment must remain fixed until the end of the mortgage term. The graduated payment mortgage is approved by the Federal Home Loan Bank Board for use by the thrift institutions, but it is hard to get because it is a fixed-rate, fixed-term loan. Its younger sister, GPAML, is much more popular with lenders.

GPAML (Graduated Payment Adjustable Mortgage Loan)

A combination of an adjustable mortgage loan and a graduated payment mortgage. The payments must be adjusted within ten years and at least every five years thereafter. When you get into playing with this many numbers, you simply have to trust the bank's computers and believe that things are indeed working out mathematically (and fairly).

GEM (Growing Equity Mortgage)

This is a mortgaging plan for homebuyers who want the security of a fixed rate loan even if it means higher monthly payments. The interest rate is fixed but the amount of the mortgage payment increases year after year (a 3-percent increase each year is a typical figure) with all the extra payment being applied toward repayment of the loan's principal. This arrangement results in the homebuyer amortizing his loan early, often within fifteen years. For obvious reasons, these loans are sometimes referred to as early ownership mortgages.

FLIP (Flexible Loan Insurance Program)

This is an *insured* graduated payment mortgage program *without* FHA sponsorship or involvement. It uses complex calculations that enable payments to start lower and gradually increase for a specified term within the mortgage term by using the interest on a down-payment account to supplement the borrower's monthly payment. Although it sounds horrendously involved, the bottom line effectively is similar to the GPM, but you will pay extra for the insurance.

PAM (Pledged Account Mortgage)

The same program as FLIP but without insurance from a source or company outside the lending institution that is granting the mortgage loan. It saves you the insurance fee, but it is not available through all lenders.

Roll-over Mortgages

The basic difference between a balloon mortgage and a roll-over mortgage is at the end of the term, when the entire unpaid principal becomes due. In a roll-over, the lender guarantees to renew the loan, usually without additional charges or fees. The new loan, however, is written at the prevailing interest rate. It can be any number of percentage points higher or lower than the original interest rate. Some savings and loan institutions volunteer to put a cap on the potential interest rate escalation; others will include a cap clause if asked to do so. It's a good idea to get one if you can. Who would have thought that interest rates would go from 9 to 18 percent between 1979 and 1981?

ARB (Adjustable Rate Balloon Mortgage)

A balloon mortgage whose interest rate may be adjusted in response to prevailing conditions in the financial marketplace. The principal remains fixed, as does its due date, but the dollar amount of the payments that must be made will fluctuate with interest-rate changes.

Negative Amortization

Now here's something truly creative. You take out a loan and you make monthly payments for, let's say, five years. Then one day you look at the annual statement that the bank sends you and you discover that you now owe the bank more than you borrowed.

Actually it's not as bad as it sounds. Negative amortization is being used with both fixed-rate and adjustable mortgages to help keep the monthly payment either low or more stable. In an AML or ARM situation, for example, if the interest rate goes up significantly, the agreed-upon monthly payment may not cover the interest due. Rather than raise the payment, the shortage is added to the balance of the original loan, thus the negative amortization. In ARMs written by national banks, the negative amortization is limited by regulations depending on the conditions and terms of the loan.

If rates were to come back down again, a negative-amortization adjustable rate loan may return to positive amortization. In other words, you will be paying off the principal again, rather than adding to it.

RAM (Reverse Annuity Mortgage)

Let's say you're sixty-five and want to buy a retirement condo. You pay cash for it, using the profit from the sale of your house. Then you realize that paying both the maintenance fees and the normal costs of daily living leaves you very little money for fun. And you want some fun in your life. You can help solve the problem by getting a RAM.

The RAM is a negative-amortization plan in which the lender pays *you* a set amount monthly. The payments gradually build up a larger and larger mortgage on the property. The debt is payable upon the sale of the property, the death of the borrower, or a specified date, whichever comes first. Federal Home Loan Bank Board regulations prohibit lump-sum disbursements— that is, the paying of the entire remaining annuity at one time. The lender must continue to distribute funds during the entire term of the agreement.

RAMs may be written with adjustable rates. The lender is not required to guarantee refinancing, but a refinancing agreement can be negotiated and written into the loan agreement.

SAM (Shared Appreciation Mortgage)

If RAMs are for seniors, SAMs are for starters. Because high prices and interest rates are keeping most first-home buyers out of the real estate marketplace and because lenders are always open to new paths to profit, SAMs are here.

In a SAM situation, homebuyers get a lower mortgage rate, perhaps 10 percent rather than 14 percent. In return for the favor, those buyers pledge a part of the profits from their home when they sell it *or* refinance it. The percentage or portion that the lender gets is mutually agreed upon when the mortgage is written, but Federal Home Loan Bank Board regulations will not allow the lender's share to exceed 40 percent. Improvement expenses are deducted from the gross profit before the division is made between homeowner and lender, so if you're in a SAM, be sure to keep careful records.

Sometimes a balloon-type arrangement is made in SAM loans whereby the borrower pays on a thirty- or forty-year pay-out schedule, but must have the property appraised after five or ten years and settle with the lender through a cash payment, refinancing, or the sale of the property.

As a buyer, a SAM may give you a chance to get into the real estate marketplace, but your net cash gain when you sell will *not* equal the appreciation of your property. Upon selling, therefore, you may still find your-self short the cash necessary to buy an equal or nicer apartment.

SAMs also hold some risk to the lender, however. If you buy in an area of high appreciation, he will do extremely well in return for his few points' leeway in the interest rate. If, however, your condo does *not* appreciate or goes down in value between the time you buy and the time you sell, the lender gets nothing. Meanwhile, you have benefited from the lower interest rate for whatever number of years you owned the property.

The fact that lenders are writing SAMs in today's market says a lot about their opinion of the future of real estate in this country.

Partnership Mortgages (Shared-equity Mortgages)

This is SAM among private investors. The plan is being touted by some of the largest real estate franchises in the nation who are pairing small-scale individual investors with cash and/or income short potential homebuyers.

Often no down-payment money is required from the homebuyer; it is put up by the investor. He also provides some portion of the monthly principal and interest payments. In return the investor gets tax-shelter benefits and a good-sized chunk of the long-term capital appreciation of the property. (The actual percentage is negotiated in each and every deal individually, as are interest rate and mortgaging terms.) A word of caution, however; as of this writing the Internal Revenue Service is still reviewing guidelines for tax deductions. So check with a competent tax attorney before taking on a partnership mortgage whether you're the homebuyer or the investor.

Meanwhile the homeowner/occupant has the right to live in the house/ apartment, the right to sell the property whenever he wants, and the right to buy out the investor at any time (based on fair market value appraisals).

Is it a good deal? If you're the owner/occupant, it can provide a place to live, some tax benefits, and the hope of some cash appreciation when you sell, but you won't get rich on the plan. If you're the investor, you may get richer, but you may also buy some rather large-sized headaches.

Several specialized real estate firms are working this plan successfully in condominium and co-operative conversions, thus allowing tenants to remain in their apartments as part owners without increased costs. In fact, sometimes the homeowner/occupant's costs go down from the rental amount that was being paid.

These private-enterprise equity- or appreciation-sharing plans are varied, unregulated, and brand new. For some people (both investors and tenants-who-would-be-owner/occupants) they may be an ideal solution to problems and investment plans, but we advise anyone entering into such an arrangement in either capacity to seek a well-qualified attorney for a careful review of the agreement.

WAM (Wrap-around Mortgage)

Also called All-inclusive Trust Deeds. Born in California, the concept of the wrap-around is spreading across the country. Its newness is much talked of, but actually it is as old as assumable mortgages and second mortgages. In fact, a wrap-around *is* an assumable mortgage with a second mortgage blanketed over it.

Let's look at a specific example. If a property that sold for $70,000 had a balance of $30,000 on its 8-percent fixed-rate assumable first mortgage, an avant-garde lender might accept a $20,000 down payment from the buyer and write a $50,000 WAM at 13 percent. The buyer would make payments to the WAM lender, who would use part of that cash to continue the payments on the $30,000 first mortgage until it was paid out. Needless to say, this is a very profitable situation for the WAM lender, which accounts for its popularity among sellers willing to help with financing.

Buy-downs

Not a mortgage plan at all, but a promotional device offered by some developers, sellers, and/or large real estate firms. They agree to pay the lender a lump sum in return for reducing the interest rate anywhere from 2 to 5 points for a given period of time, commonly two to three years. This kind of subsidy might reduce the interest rate that a buyer would pay on his condo loan from say 14 percent to 10 percent. That would lower monthly payments and thus give the buyer some extra cash to settle into his apartment and meet early payments while hoping that his income increases during the buy-down period. At the end of that period, however, the unsubsidized interest rate will take effect and that buyer will have to come to terms with a substantial jump in housing costs.

Zero Interest Rate Mortgages

Some builders are offering to finance their properties for short terms (three to five years) at zero interest. They usually require at least 50-percent down payment and then rather large periodic payments that will pay out the remainder of the purchase price within the specified time. Sounds good?

Watch out that the price of the condo is not elevated to cover carrying costs. Be aware that some of these "builder/financeers" charge hefty origination fees that cannot be deducted from federal income taxes as interest. And be *sure* you can make those large payments.

Disclosure Requirements

In an attempt to help homebuyers sort out loan complexities, federal regulations require that every lending institution provide loan applicants with disclosure information about the *real* costs of borrowing money. These costs can include interest rates, points, insurance fees, loan application fees, appraisal fees, and loan origination fees (simply another name for an extra cash charge for the loan).

The picture becomes very complicated when AMLs or ARMs are used. Probably the most important piece of disclosure information in an adjustable mortgage is the name and description of the index being used to adjust the interest rate. The law requires that the lender explain this index to you and show you evidence of how that index has performed in relation to interest rates over a period of time.

The disclosure information must also include a statement setting forth the frequency at which rate changes will occur and how and when the rate changes will affect your monthly payment. Some statement and/or concrete examples of how the financing plan being offered you would work under a variety of circumstances over a period of years must also be included.

If you are confused or uncertain about what you read in the mortgage agreement or the disclosure statement, see your attorney or a financial adviser before you sign anything. It's also a good idea to compare the disclosure statements of several lenders. *And* it's a good idea to do all of this before you find the condo or co-op that you just love and just have to buy, so that you can make your financing decisions with a cool head and plenty of thinking time.

The New Marketplace

Once upon a time, as far back as 1979, you went to a savings bank, a savings & loan association, or perhaps a mortgage broker for your home mortgage. It was easy. Essentially, those were the only options available; those lenders were the only ones interested in making home mortgage loans.

Not so today. Loans of every type are being written by every kind of financial institution, by private investment groups, by individuals, and even by pension funds in some states. Money lending is one of the growing-est industries this country has. And it is growing more competitive at the same rate.

Home financing is a marketplace to shop in very carefully—a market-place where knowledge is your most precious possession. We've pointed out types and varieties and turned over the products (mortgages and loan agreements) so that you might examine all sides, but we still haven't dis-cussed what this new marketplace will mean to *you*, the consumer, and to your pocketbook. That's the subject of the next chapter.

CHAPTER 9

Interest, Dollars, and Sense: Choosing Your Best Financial Strategy

How does a homebuyer go about shopping for the best mortgage, trust deed, or co-op loan? What are the new risks in home financing? How do the risks and costs of various plans compare? What does owning an apartment really cost? And when is it more profitable to rent than to buy?

These are questions that hit home, if you'll pardon the pun. We don't have all the answers (no one does), but we'll give you some good examples and a program of attack that should help you to evaluate your unique financing questions.

Loan Shopping

Contrary to popular rumor, you need *not* appear in person at a lending institution with a signed purchase contract in hand in order to obtain information on the lender's policies and guidelines. Yes, you do need a contract in order to *apply* for a loan, since the amount and perhaps even the terms of that loan will depend upon the lender's appraisal of the property. But before you fill out a loan application, you should be certain that your lender of choice is offering the best deal in town or at least the best deal for you.

How to be sure? Use your phone and ask questions. The first place to call is the bank where you have a savings or checking account. Then look in the

Yellow Pages of your phone directory under BANKS, MORTGAGES, and/or HOME FINANCING. Then call every lender within a reasonable distance of the area in which you intend or hope to buy. (*Reasonable* varies depending on where in the country you live. A fifty-mile radius may be reasonable in rural Texas or Iowa; the city limits or even ten city blocks may be reasonable in Boston, Chicago, St. Louis, Miami, New York, or any other major city; something in between would probably be reasonable for suburban areas.)

When you call the lenders tell the switchboard person that you would like information about home financing. When you have reached someone in the home loan department, begin your questions. Those questions should fall into roughly four categories: 1. What percentage of the appraised value of an apartment will the lender finance? (You are asking how much down payment you will need.) 2. What are the lender's guidelines as to the ratio of loan to income? (You are asking how much loan you can qualify for.) 3. What types of financing are you offering? (Fixed rate, adjustable rate, rollovers, FHA, and so forth.) 4. What are the initial costs of obtaining a loan? (You are asking about up-front fees. Interest rates are not the only factor in determining the cost of a loan. Fees to be paid at the closing table can wipe out the advantage of a whole point in lower interest rate for a period of ten years or more.)

We're sure you're thinking that all this is beginning to sound complicated. How can anyone ever remember who is giving what and come out with an accurate evaluation of the best deal? No one can, so don't try to remember. Write your information down on prepared fact sheets. We've included a model with sample entries on pages 146–147 that you may want to copy (or improve upon). Run off a dozen or so sheets at the nearest public copy machine. Be sure that you have enough copies to allow one per lender.

As you look at our fictitious survey of Security Savings & Loan Association, you will notice that some of the blanks contain numbers that have no dollar value with parentheses beneath them. For example, under *Costs at Closing* we have written 3 points (   ). The parentheses are necessary because you will not know exactly how much 3 points will cost you until you know how much you will need to borrow. So don't make a final decision about your lender until you have an apartment in mind.

When you do (and you know the price you will have to pay for that apartment), fill in the dollar amounts in red on the sheets of your most promising lenders. Then do the calculations necessary to determine a dollar figure for the cash needed at the closing and the monthly carrying costs for your loan.

The numbers will tell you which bank is giving the best financial deal.

THE PENNY SAVINGS BANK

COOPERATIVE APARTMENT LOAN PROGRAM

PLAN #1   *3 Year Rollover* — Based on 30 year term
     *Interest Rate — **Penny Customers — 14¾%
                     Non-Customers — 15¼%

Loans are rolled over at the end of each three year period at the prevailing rate to over-the-counter customers, at the customer's option. Interest rate and monthly payment amount are fixed for each period.

PLAN #2   *3 Year Constant Payment/Variable Rate* (C.P.V.R.) — Based on 30 year term
     *Interest Rate — **Penny Customers — 14¾%
                     Non-Customers — 15¼%

Monthly payment amount is fixed for each three year period. The interest rate, however, is adjusted every six (6) months based on the higher of the following indexes —
    (a) 26 week T-Bill plus 200 basis points
    (b) F.N.M.A. Conventional Auction plus 50 basis points

PLAN #3   *5 Year Balloon*
Monthly payment based on 30 year payout
     *Interest Rate — **Penny Customers — 16%
                     Non-Customers — 16½%

Unpaid (Balloon) balance is paid in full after five (5) years. No obligation on the Bank to renegotiate.

PLAN #4   *6 Month Adjustable Rate Loan* (A.R.L.) — Based on 30 year term
     *Interest Rate — **Penny Customers — 11¾%
                     Non-Customers — 12¼%

Monthly payment amount is fixed for each two year period. The interest rate is adjusted every six (6) months based on 125% of the change in the most recent 26 week T-Bill Auction — No limitation in the amount of change.

*Loans in excess of $150,000. are 1% higher than above.

**A minimum deposit of $500. in a N.O.W. (interest bearing

144

checking) account is suggested to commence a depository relationship at the Penny. The Penny also offers a range of other deposit products to satisfy the needs of any borrower — i.e. IRA, KEOGH, CD's, MONEY MANAGEMENT ACCOUNTS, etc.

LOAN AMOUNTS

Under plans 1, 2 and 3 purchasers may borrow up to 75% of the purchase price. Tenants-in-residence may borrow to 90% of the "insider" price on rental conversions.

Under plan 4, the maximum loan cannot exceed 75% of the purchase price *under any circumstances*.

On refinances, the maximum loan cannot exceed 75% of the appraised value. Appraisal to be performed by qualified appraiser at customer expense.

FEE SCHEDULE

*Application Fee ——— $150. (Non-Refundable)
  Origination Fee ———
     Plans 1, 2 and 3   — 3.75 points on loans to 75%
                    5.00 points on loans over 75%
     Plan 4 ————— 4.00 points
  Attorneys Fees   ——— Under $50,000. — $200.
                      — $50,000. and over — $225.
  Lien Search Fee ——— $100. all loans
*Payable at time of application. All other fees are payable at loan closing.

LOAN PREPAYMENT

Penny co-op loans may be prepaid, without penalty, as follows:
    Plan #1 — After First Anniversary
    Plan #2 — After First Interest Change Date
    Plan #3 — After First Anniversary
    Plan #4 — After First Interest Change Date

LIFE INSURANCE

Life Insurance of up to $75,000. is available under our low cost S.B.L.I. Group Mortgage Protection Plan at additional cost, but is not required.

Model Fact Sheet for Lender Survey

Lender: Security S & L

Address: Charter Oak Plaza Hartford   Phone: 555-0751

Questions	Data	Costs at Closing	Cost per Month
What percentage of the appraised value of the apt. will the lender finance?	80%	20% of price of apt. down payment ( )	
What are the lender's guidelines as to the ratio of loan to income?	up to 30% of gross income ( )	—	We can afford $960 a month
What types of loans are being written?	adj.-rate fixed term	3 pts. ( )	17% interest 30-yr. pay-out schedule ( )
	constant payment adj.-rate & term	4 pts. ( )	17% interest 30-yr. pay-out schedule ( )
	roll-over (3 year)	3 pts. ( )	16% interest 40-yr. pay-out schedule ( )

What are the initial costs of obtaining a loan?		½% interest for 10 years
application fee	$150	
search & filing fee	$100	
bank atty. fee	$200	
appraisal fee	$125	
mortgage insurance	1 point ( )	
title insurance	1% of first $50,000 .5% over ( )	
Totals:		
What will it cost to get the loan?		
What will it cost to carry the loan?		

After filling in the above chart for all your potential lenders, make yourself fill out the following sample disclosure statement so that you will know exactly what your loan is going to cost.

Cooperative Loan Disclosure Statement

GOLDSTICK, WEINBERGER, FELDMAN, ALPERSTEIN & TAISHOFF, P.C.

Premises: _____

Apartment No. _____ Shares _____   Date _____

Borrowers' Names and Addresses

_____

_____

In this disclosure statement the words, *I*, *me* and *my* refer to the borrower(s) named above. *You* and *your* refer to

1. Loan Proceeds	$ _____
2. Additional charges (which are not being financed)	
a. filing fee	$ _____ 0
b. Other (itemize)	$ _____
attorney's fees	$ _____
	$ _____
Total	$ _____
3. Prepaid FINANCE CHARGE	$ _____
4. Amount Financed	$ _____
5. Interest	$ _____
6. FINANCE CHARGE (3 + 5)	$ _____
7. Total of Payments (4 + 6)	$ _____
ANNUAL PERCENTAGE RATE	_____ %

Payments

One payment of $ _____ (estimate) due

on _____ (estimate) and

thereafter _____ consecutive

equal payments of $ _____ payable

on the _____ day of each month and one final irregular

payment of $ _____ (estimate)

due on _____ (estimate)

148

SECURITY:

This loan is secured by an assignment of the proprietary lease on the above apartment, and for a certificate of stock for the above number of shares issued by _____

The terms of the assignment are described in a separate assignment that I will sign. The security interest in the shares of stock is governed by the Uniform Commercial Code and by the terms of a security agreement I will sign.

PREPAYMENT:

If I am not in default I can prepay my loan in full or in part at any time. If I decide to prepay I will give you written notice at least 30 and no more than 90 days in advance. The notice must set forth the amount of the prepayment and the date on which it is to be paid.

CHARGES FOR LATE PAYMENTS AND DEFAULT:

If any installment under the terms of the Cooperative Loan Note is not paid within 15 days of the date it is due I will pay a late charge equal to 4% of each unpaid installment except for any installment which has become due earlier than scheduled because of my default. If you use an attorney who is not your salaried employee to collect or enforce the note I will pay you, in addition to all other sums due, a sum equal to the actual expenditures for any such action, including reasonable attorney's fees.

ESTIMATED INFORMATION:

This statement is based upon an approximate closing date of _____. The amounts and dates appearing above as estimates will vary depending on the actual closing date. In no event, however, will the dollar amounts be greater than those disclosed herein.

ACKNOWLEDGEMENT:

By signing this statement below I acknowledge receipt of the above fully completed loan disclosure statement.

_____   _____
                                              DATE

_____   _____
                                              DATE

149

You will still have to determine who is offering the mortgage or loan type most appealing to you and most suited to your needs. (If you are offered seller financing, fill out a sheet just as though the seller were a bank. Be sure to calculate the dollar value of the lower interest rate. We'll tell you how later in this chapter.)

You can get the help of your lawyer, real estate agent, or financial adviser at this point, and you should listen to their advice. But *you* must decide what you need and feel comfortable with. Is the security of a fixed-rate, fixed-term mortgage worth an extra $900 in up-front money to you? Does the seller's interest-only purchase money mortgage look as appealing when you consider that you will have to find financing again at market rates two years down the road? Which is more important to you, the assurance that your mortgage or trust deed will be paid off in thirty years or the assurance that your monthly loan payment will not increase significantly while you live in your apartment?

The Risks in Home Financing

During the past fifty years, Americans who worked hard all day at middle-level jobs and then returned to their homes to mow lawns and build basement family rooms rarely got rich. But they did get comfortable. As promotions and/or cost-of-living pay increases raised their salaries, they found themselves with more and more spendable income. A large part of that growing financial security could be credited to their home mortgages.

Monthly payments were fixed for twenty, twenty-five, or thirty years; only real estate tax increases would occasionally nudge them upward a bit. In inflationary times (most of the time any of us remember), this arrangement guaranteed that even the family that had begun homeownership eating beans and pasta and paying only their most clamoring creditors would find themselves in the enviable position of paying less than 10 percent of their income for shelter by the time they were ten years into their mortgage term.

Virtually all the risk in home financing fell to the lender. That risk was not "Will the homeowner make his payments?" but "Will the money be profitably loaned ten or twenty years from now?" In most instances the answer to the first question has been "Yes, people have paid on their mortgages"; and the answer to the second question has been overwhelmingly "No, money loaned ten years ago is no longer profitable." For example, a loan made at 5½ percent in 1960 might have a balance of $10,000 in 1980, with another ten years needed to repay that balance. That $10,000, if it were available to lend in 1980, would command 17 or 18 percent per year! The money therefore is out at a loss.

Given the spiraling interest rates prevalent since 1980, lenders are no longer willing to assume such risks. They are asking the homebuyer to take his chances in the financial marketplace, while they assure themselves that their loans will continue to command a rate of return at or near market rates. Homeowners can still be secure in knowing that the financing on their properties will be written for long terms, but like renters, they can no longer be immune from periodic increases in shelter costs when their mortgages are cast with the new adjustable rates.

Juggling Risk and Cost

Let's assume that you are buying an apartment at $100,000 and that you have $35,000 to use as a down payment. You need financing, therefore, for $65,000 of the purchase price. Which of the currently available loan arrangements can you best afford? Which risks are you most willing to take? Let's look at some of the most common situations.

Fixed-rate, Fixed-term, Self-liquidating Mortgage

Despite rumors to the contrary, there are still some of these around! You can still find a mortgage broker that will lend you the $65,000 at 17 percent for thirty years. At the end of the term, your loan will be completely paid out and you will own your apartment free and clear. Your monthly payment for principal and interest will be $927 a month for the entire thirty years.

If your income increases during the thirty-year term, you will find yourself with more and more spendable cash and you will have your growing equity in your apartment as a retirement nest egg. If interest rates go to 19 percent soon after you close on your property and stay at that rate or continue to climb, you will be feeling pretty smug indeed.

But: What if interest rates drop to 14 percent and stay more or less at that level? The payment on a thirty-year fixed-rate loan at 14 percent is approximately $770 a month. *Now,* you do not like paying $157 a month ($1,884 a year) more in interest than your neighbor who happened to borrow the same amount of money but six months later. So what do you do?

"Refinance, of course!" you say.

It's not quite that simple.

When you took out that fixed-rate loan, you were charged a 5-point mortgage origination fee ($3,200), a $150 mortgage application fee, a $100 search-and-filing fee, and a $200 bank attorney's fee, a total of $3,650. Refinancing will cost you these same fees again.

"Well, I'll make it up in two years at the new rate" you say. And you're right. With a drop of three full points, you should spend the money to refinance.

But (again): What if the rates drop to 16 percent and stay there? Your payment at 16 percent would be $874 a month, $53 less than your current payment. It would be almost six years before the change in interest payment would cover your expenses in refinancing. And what if the rate dropped another 1 percent two years into *that* new loan?

If interest rates continue to climb steadily throughout the next two to three decades, the fixed-rate, fixed-term, self-liquidating loan is definitely your best deal. If they fluctuate, however (which is more likely to happen), it may not be the financing option of choice, despite the security it offers.

Adjustable-rate, Fixed-term, Self-liquidating Mortgage (ARM)

Let's assume that you want to pay off your mortgage in thirty years. You can afford the $927-a-month payment now and you see potential for increased income over the course of your career. The adjustable-rate, fixed-term, self-liquidating loan is a viable choice for you.

If mortgage interest rates go to 18 percent your monthly payments will increase to $980; at 19 percent to $1,033. If on the other hand, interest rates drop to 16 percent, your payment will decrease to $874 without the burden of refinancing fees. (These figures are approximate, based upon fixed-rate, fixed-term tables. Actual dollar amounts will vary somewhat as adjustments are calculated and made.) At the end of the thirty-year term, you will own your apartment free and clear.

Constant Payment, Adjustable Rate and/or Adjustable Term Loan (AML)

This time let's assume that you are married and have managed to save the $35,000 down payment by putting aside one of your two salaries. You qualify for the $65,000 loan based upon your combined income, but you don't tell the bank that your wife is pregnant and plans to stop working when the baby is born. You would not qualify for the loan based upon your salary alone, but you think you can make it (with careful budgeting). A jump in interest rates equal to $100 a month, however, would probably put you under.

You opt, therefore, for a fixed-rate, fixed-term loan but you discover that the only lender in your area willing to write such a loan is charging 6 points mortgage origination fee, and $3,900 seems like too big a chunk of cash for the security it buys. Therefore you select the next best bet, the constant payment, adjustable loan. If interest rates go up, your monthly payment will remain exactly the same, but you will enter upon a negative-amortization situation and may still owe part of the $65,000 you borrowed when your thirty-year term is up.

However thirty years is a long time and your apartment should be appreciating in value, not to mention the effects of inflation. Meanwhile, you do not have to worry that an increase in mortgage payments will make it impossible for you to go to an occasional movie or eat out once in a while.

Some lenders are adding an adjustable term to their constant payment, adjustable rate loans. If you choose this option, your term can be extended from thirty years up to forty years before you begin negative amortization.

The Wrap-around (WAM) and the Second Mortgage

The wrap-around is a type of second mortgaging situation that is very profitable for the lender. Given our $100,000 apartment again and assuming that it has a first mortgage on it at 9 percent with no due-on-sale clause, we can create the story of a WAM.

The wrap-around becomes a viable option when the seller does not need to take all of his equity out of his property. He owes a balance of $35,000 on his first mortgage. The payments of $377 a month on that original mortgage will liquidate it in fifteen years. The seller's current equity in the property is $65,000.

If you, the buyer, had $65,000 ($100,000 sales price minus the $35,000 mortgage balance = $65,000 equity), you could give the seller cash for his equity and assume his mortgage payments. You would own the apartment free and clear in fifteen years. But you have only $35,000 in cash to use as a down payment. There is a difference of $30,000, therefore, between your ready cash and the seller's equity. To compensate for this shortage (in other words, to lend you $30,000) and to make a handsome profit, the seller offers to take back a wrap-around mortgage.

This WAM will include the $35,000 balance on the first mortgage and the $30,000 that the seller is willing to lend. It is mutually agreeable between you and the seller that the $65,000 WAM will be a straight mortgage (interest-only) at 13-percent interest with a term of fifteen years.

So what happens? First the seller takes your $35,000 down payment. Then you sign the WAM papers and agree to pay the seller $8,450 a year (13 percent of $65,000) for fifteen years. At the end of fifteen years, you will pay the seller the $65,000 you owe (the difference between your down payment and the agreed-upon selling price of the apartment). Meanwhile the seller continues to make the regular monthly mortgage payments of $377 on the first mortgage.

Each year, then, you pay the seller $8,450 in interest. He pays the original lender $4,524 in principal and interest payments on the first mortgage loan. And then he pockets the remaining $3,926.

At the end of fifteen years, the seller owes nothing on his original mortgage. You owe the seller $65,000. And the seller has collected $58,890 in additional interest above the amount needed to make the payments that liquidated his first mortgage loan.

If the seller had chosen not to use the WAM, he could have allowed you to assume the original mortgage by lending you the $30,000 written as a second mortgage note. If this note were written under the same terms as the WAM (13 percent interest-only for fifteen years), the seller would collect $58,500 in interest on that second mortgage, while you would make payments on the first mortgage.

"For the seller that $58,500 is just about the same amount in interest that he gets on the WAM ($58,890). Why should he bother with the WAM at all?" you ask.

Because with the WAM the seller made $35,390 *more* than he would have made with a second mortgage loan of $30,000 at 13 percent.

"How?"

Look at these figures:

	$65,000 WAM	$30,000 Second
Down Payment	$ 35,000	$ 35,000
Interest Income	58,890	58,500
Principal Payment	65,000	30,000
Total Income	$158,890	$123,500

The secret of the extra income for the seller who uses a WAM is the self-liquidating low interest first mortgage that he continues to pay out during the term of the WAM. Through it the $35,000 that he still owed when he sold the apartment has been repaid without cost to himself. So the seller made $35,390 extra for the bother of writing a monthly check to his first mortgage lender.

"Well, I guess I'll stay away from wrap-arounds!" say you, as a buyer.

Not always a good idea. These figures are based upon the premise that the seller would have accepted a second mortgage at 13 percent. As second mortgages go, that is an extremely low rate. At a lending institution you would expect to pay a full point or more above the going first mortgage rate.

So if the seller offers you a wrap-around or nothing, is it worth going to a second mortgage lender for the extra cash you need to assume his mortgage? A $30,000 fifteen-year interest-only second mortgage at 18 percent would cost you $450 a month ($5,400 a year, $81,000 over fifteen years) and you would still owe the original $30,000 borrowed. A $30,000 self-liquidating fifteen-year second mortgage at 18 percent would cost you $482.70 a month ($5,792.40 a year, $86,886 over fifteen years), but you would owe nothing at the end of its term.

As an overview: The wrap-around would cost you $704.17 a month; the assumption with an interest-only second mortgage would cost you $827 a month ($450 on the second, $377 on the first); and the assumption with a self-liquidating second mortgage would cost you $859.70 a month ($482.70 on the second, $377 on the first).

Here's how it all comes out in chart form:

	Monthly Payment	Total of Monthly Payments	Balance Due at 15 years	Total Payment
Wrap-around at 13%	$704.17	$126,750	$65,000	$191,750
Assumption with interest-only second at 18%	$827	$148,860	$30,000	$178,860
Assumption with self-liquidating second at 18%	$859.70	$154,746	0	$154,746

Obviously, the assumption of the seller's existing mortgage by taking out a fifteen-year self-liquidating second mortgage leaves you in the best position fifteen years after you buy the apartment. But if $700 a month is all you can afford to pay at the time you buy, is the wrap-around a good deal? Think about it.

Bargain Interest Rates

Many sellers are willing to give short-term financing at below market rates in order to sell their properties at or near the original asking price. Few calculate the real financial loss of lending money at below market rates. With a prevailing rate of 17 or 18 percent, buyers often find themselves being offered financing at 12 percent for three, four, or even five years. When such short-term bargain financing is offered, it is important that you "cost it out"—that is, calculate its value in present-day market prices.

To do this you need some insider's information (available through your local banker) about the key numbers being used to calculate the present-day value of money. (These are the figures used in calculating the charge that a lender would make to a seller who wanted to arrange a buy-down loan for his buyers.) A working example is the clearest way to explain the calculation.

Let's keep our $100,000 apartment, but let's assume that as an incentive to buy the seller is offering you financing for five years at 12 percent while requiring only a $20,000 down payment. An $80,000 mortgage at only 12 percent for five years! Sounds like a fabulous deal, right? Maybe.

First of all, is the apartment *worth* $100,000? (You already know how to test this.) Second, remember that at the end of five years you will have to refinance $80,000 at market rates or you could lose your apartment to a foreclosure. And third, what is the bargain interest rate really worth in today's dollars? (This is the cost-it-out part.)

To calculate the real worth of short-term bargain financing you must use the bank's key numbers for the present value of money. These numbers change with movements in the financial marketplace; for our example we'll use figures prevalent in 1982. You must ask your banker for the figures that are current when you are ready to buy.

On a three-year loan use 2.36
On a four-year loan use 3.2
On a five-year loan use 3.7

Now take the interest rate being offered by the seller (12 percent) and the current market interest rate (17 percent) and subtract. You are getting a 5-point discount from the prevailing rate. Take this 5 points and multiply it by the key number for the term of financing being offered; in this example, four years, which means the key number is 3.2. Thus 5 (points discount) × 3.2 = 16.

Sixteen percent of your *loan* (not the purchase price) is the total dollar value of the discount being offered you by the seller. So .16 × $80,000 = $12,800 is the present-day worth of the discount in financing. Any price on the apartment below $87,200 represents an additional saving for you.

Now if you could get the seller to accept $84,000 all cash (or even $85,000, or $86,000) you would be getting a real bargain that would be worth financing through a conventional lender at prevailing market rates. (You should do this by offering $83,000 all cash and then negotiating up to 84, 85, or 86.)

Let's see how this works out on monthly payments: The seller's offer will cost you .12 × $80,000 = $9,600 a year or $800 a month. And you will still owe him $80,000 at the end of four years.

At a negotiated price of $85,000 you would use your $20,000 for a down payment. You would finance therefore $65,000 at 17 percent for a thirty-year-term self-liquidating mortgage which will cost you $927 a month. The security of not having to refinance at market rates in five years will cost you $127 a month. (If you are in the 50-percent tax bracket, this is a real cost of $63.50 a month, since the extra interest cost is tax deductible.)

"Why pay $127 (or even $63.50) a month extra?" you ask. "I'll take my chances with the market five years downstream and enjoy my 12-percent interest-only mortgage while I can."

A fair retort. Especially if you believe the financial marketplace will show lower interest rates in five years and you are just a bit of a gambler. But what if you plan to sell the apartment at or near the end of that five-year term?

Assuming appreciation of 10 percent per year, your apartment will be worth approximately $160,000 at the end of five years. If you had accepted the seller's financing, you would have a gross profit (before the expenses of selling) of approximately $60,000 since you would have to repay the seller's $80,000 and deduct the $20,000 you originally put down. If you had negotiated an all-cash price of $85,000 on the apartment and financed it through a lender, you would have a gross profit of $75,000. The extra $15,000 profit would have cost you $7,620 in additional monthly loan payments to the bank (before taxes). So you would have a clear profit of over $7,500 just because you refused the seller's bargain rate and talked him into accepting all cash.

And this is the *least* profitable situation if you plan to sell the apartment. If you sold after one year, the appreciation would put its value at $110,000. You would make a gross profit of $10,000 with seller financing. You would make a gross profit of $25,000 with bank financing at the prevailing rate minus one year times the extra carrying cost. $127 × 12 = $1,524. Thus $25,000 − $1,524 = $23,476. Almost $13,500 more than you would have made if you had accepted the seller's bargain financing.

What should you do? What's the "right" answer in this situation? In each of these stories? There is none. In judging the right financing for you, you must combine the numbers with your needs and plans.

Obviously, we could go on creating "let's assume" situations for you for many more pages, but that would serve no useful purpose. None of these situations is your situation. We have spent these pages with them because we wanted to impress you with the importance of exploring various financing options *on paper*. Numbers are not evaluated well intuitively even if you are the most sophisticated buyer that ever signed a contract. Use your calculator, make up your own hypothetical situations for what you think might happen to you in the next "x" number of years, and see how the figures work out.

There is always some risk in buying property and today there is always some risk in financing. But you should know what these risks are in each possible situation and then choose which path you want to follow.

Better to Rent

Much has been written about the advantages of owning property: a home of your own, potential appreciation in value, tax benefits, security, and so forth. Yet the question remains: Is buying always preferable to renting? And you may be surprised to hear that our answer is, No, not always. When the real cost of owning your apartment is greater by more than 120 percent of the cost of renting, you should consider renting (if only for the short term) and investing your down-payment money elsewhere. To give you an example: you can rent a two-bedroom 1,400-square-foot apartment for $600 a month. To make your investment profitable, your real monthly cost of owning a comparable apartment should not exceed 1.20 × $600, which equals $720.

Before you go off to find a rental agent, remember we said the *real* cost of owning. The following is a step-by-step procedure for calculating the real cost of owning a cooperative apartment or a condominium apartment.

Calculation of net cost of ownership—Cooperative apartments

Purchase price $ _____   Monthly maintenance fee $ _____

A. Estimated annual amount of the maintenance fee that is deductible for income tax $ _____ divided by 12 (months) equals $ _____ .
                         (1)
B. Entry (1) $ _____ times your federal tax bracket equals $ _____ , which is your net after-tax savings per month on
        (2)
your maintenance charges.
C. Monthly maintenance $ _____ less No. (2) equals $ _____ , your net after-tax monthly maintenance cost.
        (3)

D. Cost of the apartment $ _____ times X% (prevailing interest rates) equals $ _____ , which is the annual interest cost if you
                            (4)
borrow 100 percent of the cost of your apartment.

E. No. (4) $ _____ times your tax bracket equals
$ _____ , which is your after-tax savings on the cost of
      (5)
borrowing.

F. No. (4) $ _____ minus No. (5) equals $ _____ , which
                                                    (6)
is your after-tax loan cost.

G. No. (6) $ _____ divided by 12 (months) equals $ _____ ,
                                                          (7)
which is your after-tax monthly loan cost.

H. No. (3) $ _____ plus No. (7) $ _____ equals
$ _____ , your after-tax monthly cost of ownership.
    (8)

Note: Since you will not be borrowing 100 percent of the cost of the apartment, the calculation in step E takes into account opportunity costs of the balance of the purchase price. (Opportunity costs are the investment potential of your down payment.)

Calculation of the net cost of ownership—Condominium apartments

Purchase price $ _____   Monthly maintenance fee $ _____

A. Annual real estate taxes $ _____ , which is a tax deductible
                                (1)
expense per year.

B. No. (1) $ _____ divided by 12 (months) equals
$ _____ , which is your monthly tax-deductible payment.
    (2)

C. No. (2) $ _____ times your federal tax bracket $ _____ ,
                                                            (3)
which is your net monthly tax savings on your real estate tax payment.

D. No. (2) minus No. (3) equals $ _____ which is your net
                                    (4)

after-tax real estate tax monthly payment.

E. Cost of the apartment $ _____ times percentage (prevailing interest rate) equals $ _____ which is the annual interest cost
$$(5)$$
if you were to borrow 100% of the cost of your apartment.

F. No. (5) times your federal tax bracket equals $ _____
$$(6)$$
which is your after-tax savings on the cost to borrower.

G. No. (5) minus No. (6) equals $ _____ which is your
$$(7)$$
after-tax loan cost.

H. No. (7) divided by twelve months equals No. 8, which is your after-tax monthly loan cost.

I. No. (4) plus your monthly maintenance fee $ _____ plus No. (8) equals your total after-tax monthly cost of ownership.

Note: Since you will not be borrowing 100 percent of the cost of the apartment, the calculation in step F takes into account opportunity costs of the balance of the purchase price. (Opportunity costs are the investment potential of your down payment.)

In areas that have governmental rent control you rarely will find that your after-tax costs of ownership make sense to buy. For this reason, tenants should demand substantial discounts off the market price to compensate for the fact that the after-tax costs of ownership will be more than 120 percent of their rental costs.

CHAPTER 10

Selling Your Apartment: Success Tips (with and without a Broker)

Selling one's home is an unfamiliar and high-risk game for most people, yet most play it without a thought to strategies, without even knowing all the rules. And very few play rationally. Homesellers do not ask, "What do I do?" and "How do I do it?" They ask, "How much can I get for this place?" And they seek the answer to their question in the most unlikely places.

In a major metropolitan center, for example, a young executive stops at the doorway of his high-rise.

Mr. Climber: Hiya, Peter! How's it going?

Peter: Just fine, Mr. Climber. How are you doing with that washing-machine problem? Got it running yet?

Mr. C: O.K. It's running smooth as silk. No more jumping. We've got another problem now, though. We're moving. Company transfer.

Peter: Oh, gee. Sorry to lose you and Mrs. Climber. Where are you going?

Mr. C: Alabama.

Peter: Nice and warm down there. You'll like it.

Mr. C: Yeah, I think we will, but we have to sell this apartment before we can go anywhere.

Peter: Oh, you'll make a mint, Mr. Climber.

Mr. C: Think so, Peter? I'm a little nervous about the market.

Peter: Oh, no, the market's great around here. I have a friend who works at 245 Riverside Drive. He said one of the places in his building just went for

three-quarters of a million dollars! We're only a few blocks from there.
You could probably get that for yours too. I been in that building. It's not
so great. Not any better than here.

Mr. C: Really, Peter? Have you seen the apartment that was sold?

Peter: No, but my buddy told me it wasn't much. It's just that a lot of rich
people, they want to live in that building, especially them foreigners.
My buddy said there were people crawling around like ants after it went
on the market. Sold it in two weeks!

Mr. C: Is that so, Peter? Three-quarters of a million, huh?

Peter: Yeah, Mr. Climber. And I'm sure that's right. My buddy heard it
from the guy's next door neighbor.

Mr. Climber lists his apartment for sale at $799,000.

Meanwhile at a barbecue in a garden-apartment complex more than half-
way across the country, a guest approaches her host.

Muffy: John darling, we heard you and Sara were moving. We're going to
miss you terribly! Where are you going, dear?

John: Colorado.

Muffy: Colorado? Oh, how lovely. And you both enjoy skiing so much.
When are you leaving?

John: Don't know, Muffy. It'll depend on how soon we can sell this
apartment.

Muffy: Oh, that's right! Well, you won't have any trouble. My cousin's
wife is in real estate in Plainston (that's about thirty miles east of here) and
she's doing a great business in condos.

John: Really? I thought the market was pretty slow right now.

Muffy: Oh, no, darling. *Houses* are slow! Apartments are in tremendous
demand. Everyone wants an apartment now.

John: They may want it, but what about financing?

Muffy: Well, my cousin says not to worry about it. His wife's office always
arranges financing for people. You'd be amazed at how creative they get.
People are willing to pay almost anything when they know they're getting a
good deal on the financing. What are you going to ask for your place?

John: $90,000 I guess.

More people start to gather around the two speakers.

Another guest: Oh, John, that's not enough! My brother just sold his place
for $110 and I don't think it's as nice as this.

John: Really, where is it?

Guest 2: It's in Kensington.

John: That's a pretty ritzy town. Stuff is probably worth more there.

Guest 3: I don't think so. This is just as good a town and our schools are better than theirs. Once the state finishes the highway the commute will be just as easy as it is from Kensington. The real estate agents will tell people about the highway, you know. I think you could get more than $110,000. You should put it up at $115.

John's wife joins the discussion group.

Sara: See, I told you it was worth more than you thought, John. You never see the value of our things. You have to think more positively. Think of the money we've spent decorating this place.

John: Honestly, Sara, I don't think we can get $115. That's almost double what we paid.

Guest 4: So what, John? *Everyone* is doubling their money nowadays. Why don't you put it on the market at $115,900 and see what happens. I'll bet you get it sold in a week.

Muffy: Wait, John. I have an idea. Let me call my cousin's wife. I'll find out what this place is really worth for you. Can I use your phone?

John: Sure, Muffy. Why don't you use the one in the bedroom? It's quieter.

Muffy returns a few minutes later.

Muffy: John darling, I have the best news for you. My cousin's wife says double your purchase price is very realistic. She's had some clients who have made more than double this year. You've got a really good thing going here.

Sara: Oh, Muffy! How nice of you to help us out!

John: Yes, Muffy. Thanks a lot. After all, what can we lose? If other people are doing it, we might as well give it a shot.

John and Sara list their apartment for sale at $115,900.

How Much Is It Really Worth?

Are these apartments overpriced? Underpriced? Will they sell quickly? Eventually? Not at all? What effect will the asking price have upon the negotiations and the ultimate sales price? And to take our questions to their outer limit: Will selling their apartment be a contributing factor in John and Sara's divorce?

That may sound like a soap opera to you, but the last question is every bit as realistic as the others and its outcome about as predictable. No one could answer these questions with the information we have been given. In listing their apartments, Mr. Climber and John and Sara have given the asking price less care and consideration than they might give to the movement of a queen in a chess game. And unfortunately these sellers that we have created are typical. Despite the fact that the original asking price of a piece of property will affect the entire selling experience and its outcome, few people take the time to approach it logically or carefully.

The logical way to do it is so simple that people frequently just don't see it. If you were buying, you'd go out and comparison shop before making an offer on an apartment, right? So you should comparison shop before setting your asking price as a seller.

How? One method is to go out with an agent and look at half a dozen apartments in the price range you guess is applicable to your apartment. By comparing these on-the-market apartments to each other and then to your apartment, you will be able to evaluate your property as better or worse, more expensive or less expensive. But there is a disadvantage in the comparison shopping method. These apartments are for sale, not yet sold. Therefore they are only testing the market, not indicating its present state. The actual selling prices of the apartments can be many thousands of dollars lower than their asking prices.

Relying on professional evaluations is a much more accurate and less bothersome method of establishing the value of your property. Call three to five (or more) different real estate agencies. Tell the salesperson who answers the phone that you are planning to sell your apartment and that you would like a competitive market analysis. *This is not an appraisal*. An appraisal is a formal fair market value estimate of the property done by an appraiser for a fee. A competitive market analysis is a service offered without charge by most real estate firms. It is done by a salesperson using information available within the real estate office.

You're probably wondering what to expect. Is this akin to a complete physical? More or less. To do a competitive market analysis an agent will come to your apartment, inspect it, and compare it to the comparables he or she brings along for that purpose. (Comparables are listing sheets for apartments that have been sold in the past year. The apartments will be similar to yours in size and location and each listing sheet will contain the exact actual selling price along with original asking price, price-reduction information, and length of time on the market.) After comparing your apartment to those that have already sold, the agent will come up with a probable selling price and a suggested asking price. Ask him or her how he arrived at the figures.

When three agents have each done a competitive market analysis, you can begin to evaluate their work. If they all cluster about the same price, it is probably accurate. If the probable selling prices differ by many thousands of dollars, call in another agent or two or more until you begin to see some pattern develop. And don't forget, you yourself should carefully read and evaluate the comparables that are brought to your apartment and make your own evaluation of worth.

While each agent is in your living room, you should ask him/her questions about the market. Local patterns may be different from the national picture. Ask: What is the average time on the market before selling? How much negotiating room should you allow? What is the usual commission? How does the real estate agency help in obtaining financing? Ask the same questions of each agent and note how their answers compare.

Remember there is no obligation to list with the agents who visit your apartment. The competitive market analysis is a service offered by brokers as a means of selling you the agency's services. Listen to what the agents promise you. Compare each one to the other. But most of all, use the competitive market analysis to help you set realistic expectations on what your apartment is worth.

Getting Ready to Sell

Before you call in the real estate agents for a price evaluation of your apartment, you must do some cleaning and polishing. People are inordinantly impressed by good decorating, cleanliness, and a spacious appearance; they often significantly overpay for a tastefully decorated, spotless apartment. And despite their experience walking through hundreds of apartments a year, real estate agents are just as impressed by a beautiful interior as ordinary people. You will get higher market evaluations and, more important, a more enthusiastic effort to sell your apartment if it is appealing and marketable.

But sometimes seeing what is marketable is difficult for the homeseller. We all become accustomed to our living quarters and tend to see rooms as warm and comfortable when others might see them as cluttered. Sometimes our pathways become so habitual that we don't notice a newcomer's annoyance at walking around the recliner and its footstool in order to enter the dining room. It is important, therefore, to begin a selling experience by taking a fresh look at your apartment.

Experiment by taking things out. Try rearranging some of the furniture. You should aim for a sense of spaciousness. When a real estate agent shows your apartment he or she will be standing in the center of the room with one or two other people. Rooms look different from this perspective, busier, more crowded than when you're sitting in your favorite chair. Ask some of your friends to walk through your apartment with you. Try to get a sense of looking at it as one of a group on tour. In other words, put yourself in the role of a buyer.

Keep the rooms well lighted; buyers are put off by dark and gloomy. Keep the kitchen counters clear of clutter. The person who will work in that kitchen wants to imagine himself or herself with plenty of room to spread out his own cooking essentials. And if possible give your kitchen ceiling a coat of white paint. No one will notice that you've done this, but kitchen ceilings have a way of getting discolored over the years and a bright, clean ceiling will make the room more appealing (perhaps subconsciously, but still more appealing).

Above all else, bathrooms should be clean. Potential real estate deals have died because someone pulled away the shower curtain and saw black grime creeping from between the tiles. And think about a new shower curtain. You can take it with you when you move, but it makes the bathroom *look* so much more appealing.

Remove the clutter from the bedroom closets. A cascade of boxes from the top shelf onto the real estate agent's head may be comic relief, but it won't help to sell your apartment. Under the bed is a good place to store loose items; no one ever picks up the bedspread to look there.

What about redecorating? Don't go overboard. If your walls are particularly marked or discolored, a new paint job might add several thousand dollars to your selling price, but paint in neutral colors. If you must repaper, keep the patterns quiet. Splashy decorating will turn more people away than it will attract. An extra plant or two, a new bedspread, a painting on the wall, or a silk flower arrangement on the hallway table will usually do more for your sale than $40-a-single-roll wallpaper.

Carpeting? This is a problem in real estate. For some reason buyers seem to regard wall-to-wall carpeting as about as permanent as the walls themselves. They will turn away from a potential purchase because the carpet is the wrong color. You can avoid this stumbling block by noting on your listing that the wall-to-wall carpeting is negotiable. If the buyers want it, they will say so when they make their offer (this gives you an extra negotiating point); if they don't want it, they won't feel guilty that they are going to have to throw out perfectly good carpet that they have had to pay for. The buyers will think they are getting your apartment for less money without the carpeting even if the price would have been exactly the same, and meanwhile, you can sell that carpeting or take it with you to use in your next home. Contrary to popular belief, wall-to-wall carpeting *can* be removed and reinstalled elsewhere.

And if your carpeting is very worn? This is always a problem for real estate agents who have to practice their footwork in order to stand on the worn spots. Seriously, threadbare carpeting is a major turnoff to buyers. Somehow they equate it to poor quality, shabbiness, and they proceed to look for evidence of shabbiness elsewhere in your home. They usually convince themselves that they have found it too.

If your carpeting is in bad shape, consider pulling it up and having your floors sanded and stained. Everyone is impressed by shiny, newly finished floors with an area rug here and there. If you can't afford to redo your floors, invest in some small areas rugs and place them strategically over the worn spots. Even if you state clearly to the buyers, "The carpet is worn through under the area rugs," it does not seem to register. What the eye sees (a lovely, well-kept room with area rugs) seems to negate what the ear hears (the carpet is threadbare and we're taking the area rugs with us).

Replace burned-out light bulbs. Clean and organize the inside of your kitchen cabinets and the linen closets. Why people open these we can't understand, but they always do and crowded and/or sloppy counts for many minus points in their minds. And be sure that all your doorknobs are secure. A doorknob that falls off in a buyer's hand when grabbed screams "Poor maintenance!" and frightens him or her off beyond rational recall.

Once you have your apartment clean and marketable, you must gather several pieces of information in anticipation of questions from serious potential buyers. Do not leave these documents on the dining-room table where they might be shuffled through by every casual walk-through apartment-hunter, however. Put them in a convenient cabinet or drawer and take them out only when needed. You may want to make copies of some of this information in the event that a buyer wants to take it home to read.

The financial statement of the condominium or cooperative. This is a most important document in effective selling. It graphically demonstrates the stability of the corporation or condominium association by listing the exact operating expenses, expenditures, and revenues of the past year. Prospective buyers want to be assured that their monthly maintenance fees will not jump drastically, and that what you tell them is indeed true. A readily available financial statement avoids the embarrassing position of questioning your veracity, puts the buyer at ease, and usually gets the sale rolling.

Names. Have ready the names and phone numbers of the president and other officers of the board of directors. Many buyers will want to talk to other people in the building and you will win confidence points by having these names available for the asking.

Heating costs. If your heating costs are billed separately (most commonly done in garden- or patio-plan communities), obtain the exact amount of last year's heating bill from your supplier and file it. "How much does it cost to heat?'' is a little like kicking tires in a used-car lot, but you should be able to answer the question when asked.

Mortgage information if applicable.   Can your mortgage or co-op loan be assumed? Have you made arrangements with your lender to write a new mortgage on your property at below market rates? Is your apartment eligible for FHA-backed financing? Are you willing to assist with financing in any way? Purchase money mortgage? Second mortgage loan? Now that financing has become a major problem for most homebuyers, you should provide as much advance information as you can possibly gather. Pointing a buyer in the right direction might well keep a faltering deal together.

Approvals.   When selling a co-op apartment, type a statement as to the policy of your building on approving new buyers. Will they have to appear before the board of directors? Do they need personal references? Should they bring credit references? Last year's tax returns? Employment references? If you are selling a condominium, check to see if the board of directors holds a right of first refusal. If it does, you should notify your buyer.

House rules.   Buyers will want to know about children, pets, guests, subletting, swimming pool and other recreational facility rules, parking-lot regulations, and any unusual restrictions. Machine-copy the house-rules list or type a list of the rules that you can copy and give to them.

Personal property.   Most important of all, prepare a list of those items of personal property (appliances, chandeliers, draperies, and so forth) that are specifically included in the sale, those that are not included, and those that are negotiable. Your list of items that are definitely included should be as short as possible. Your list of negotiable items as long as possible. If you prepare this list in advance of putting your apartment on the market, it will facilitate the process of listing with an agent, showing your property, negotiating the sale, and drawing the legal contracts to purchase.

Do You Need an Agent?

It depends. Will you be at home most of the time to show your apartment? What's the real estate market like in your area? Are apartments in demand and selling quickly? Or do they stay on the market for several months? Where is your apartment located? Is it on a main thoroughfare that most buyers would easily recognize? Or is it out-of-the-way, in a picturesque but difficult-to-find place? How comfortable are you with strangers? Can you show your apartment for sale without being self-conscious? Can you ask questions about a potential buyer's finances without feeling awkward and embarrassed? Are you experienced in negotiating? Do you have a lawyer who will represent you as a seller? Can you advise potential buyers on financing and help them to find it?

Most people need the services of a real estate agent when selling their homes. (According to the National Association of Realtors, over 90 percent of the residential property sold in this country is sold through a Realtor.) If you felt positive about your answers to the preceding questions, however, there is absolutely no harm in giving selling on your own a try. You may save several thousand dollars in commission costs.

But do not overprice your apartment. Even if you are determined to sell on your own, you should invite several real estate firms in to give you a competitive market analysis. And *use* the information they give you. Inaccurate pricing, greed (trying to save the commission *plus* a little extra), and a misunderstanding of market conditions (*"Houses* are slow! Apartments are in tremendous demand"*) are the primary factors in the failure of most sellers to market their apartments successfully.

For Sale by Owner

If you decide to try to sell without an agent, give yourself four weeks of marketing time, and then stop. In your four weeks, you will draw to your apartment most of the active buyers in your price range who have the time and motivation to run after apartments on their own. After four weeks you will essentially have exhausted this market, and you will then need the services of an agent to bring out-of-town buyers and buyers who will not venture out on their own to your apartment.

Most of the buyers who answer a *For Sale by Owner* ad are usually excellent prospects. You will be able to spot the few "lookers" quickly; don't spend too much time with them. The people in genuine need of housing have usually been out actively hunting; they know what is available in the price range and they are very cognizant of value. If your apartment is accurately priced and attractive, you may well find yourself with an offer within the first week or so on the market.

Do not let this offer mislead you into thinking that your asking price is too low or that you are going to make a "killing" if you hold out longer. There is a saying among real estate agents that the first offer usually results in the best deal and most agents have witnessed many instances where sellers have refused to negotiate on an early offer and then waited months only to accept a still lower offer.

You should be quite certain of the value of your apartment before you put it on the market. If you get an offer on your own, negotiate toward that figure. As a seller who is not using an agent, you have the advantage of the entire amount of the commission as added negotiating space. Let's say, for example, that the consensus of the competitive market analyses set your apartment value at approximately $100,000. The most commonly acceptable commission rate for real estate agents in your area is 6 percent; $6,000 for your apartment if it were to sell at $100,000. An offer comes in at $90,000 to your $105,000 asking price. You could hold out for the $100,000. In fact, you should try. But don't lose the deal over the fact that the *value* of your apartment is $100,000!

If you see that $97,000 is absolutely the highest your buyer is willing to go after several negotiating sessions, take it. You are still making $3,000 *more* than the amount you would have netted from the sale of your apartment through a real estate agency.

How do you get to the delightful point of splitting the savings on the real estate commission with a savvy buyer? Use the following techniques:

Advertising

Your first task as a seller is to get people to come out to look at your apartment. You can put up notices on the office bulletin board or the community boards of your local grocery stores, you can put a line in your church bulletin, you can even call the major corporations in your area and list your apartment with their personnel offices, but you will get the most response from classified newspaper advertising. Your ads should be simple and direct. Unlike the real estate firms who are advertising in order to attract any and all possible buyers to their offices, *you* are advertising to attract only those people who are potential buyers for *your* apartment.

If you are located in a particularly attractive neighborhood or town, mention it in your ad, but do not give the exact address. You do not want to encourage drive-bys. Tell the number of bedrooms and the number of baths and any especially appealing features that would increase the value of your apartment. Always include the price; most potential buyers will not call on an apartment whose price is not mentioned. A good sample ad might read:

Two bedroom, 2 bath condo apt. in Burnham Park area. 19th floor, balcony, new kitchen. $129,000. By Owner. 555-0003.

The words *by owner* are not absolutely essential, but they set the ad apart. People genuinely in need of housing usually search the classified sections of their newspapers for new by-owner ads, often hoping to find a bargain. You might also include in your advertising the square footage of your apartment, and you might mention any special recreational facilities such as swimming pools or tennis courts available to your complex. But don't try to write a short story to be published as a classified ad. When sellers get carried away, you read:

Executive family must move across the country. Their beautiful 1½ year old condominium with its own private patio surrounded by roses must be sold. You will look out upon the verdant greens and rolling hills of the Lakeside Golf Course (perfect for sledding in the winter) from your elegant picture window. Our dining room seats 12 easily. The children's stockings will hang by the fireplace in the family room at Christmas with lots of room for an eight foot tree! Call for more information. Owners: 555-9999.

This ad is an all-too-common example of overkill, and it would draw surprisingly few responses. In the first place, it limits its appeal to families, closing off marketing to singles, childless couples, and older people. It makes judgments based upon personal perspective that cut away potential buyers. Keep your advertising as broad in appeal as possible; let the buyers decide if the apartment is too big for them. Despite its length and cost, the ad above does not mention how many bedrooms or baths are in the apartment! And worst of all, the words *must move* or *must sell* are an invitation to low bids. Do not use them; they reveal too much of your negotiating hand before you even begin to play.

Answering the Phone

Real estate brokers spend many office hours teaching new agents how to answer the phone. Why? Because inefficient phone technique eliminates more potential buyers than any other mistake an agent is likely to make.

When a potential buyer calls on an ad, he may think he is looking for an apartment, but usually he is looking to eliminate that particular apartment from consideration without bothering to search it out and inspect it. The person who answers the phone, therefore, must make the apartment enticing enough to bring the buyer out to see it. He or she must also make it easy for that buyer to find the apartment.

Before you put the ad for your apartment into the newspaper, prepare several sets of directions, one from each of the main streets in the vicinity, or if you are in a suburban area, each of the main highways near your town. Go out and drive the routes by which a prospective buyer would approach your apartment. Count traffic lights, blocks, or cross streets; note landmarks; even get accurate odometer readings; and write it all out carefully and clearly. If a certain route takes the buyer past undesirable sites or areas, give directions by another route. The buyer will probably discover the undesirables you are avoiding on his own, but first impressions are lasting and you do not want your apartment eliminated *en route* to it!

Type out your various directions, machine-copy them, and then keep a complete set near each phone extension. You want to avoid your prospective buyer hearing, "Mabel, this guy's coming from Cooperstown. Get me the directions from Route Twenty-four, will ya?" Much of your success in selling your apartment without an agent will depend upon the sense of professionalism that you convey to the buyer. Don't let your selling take on the tone of a Ma and Pa candy store.

In your marketing, do not give directions on the phone without making an appointment for a showing and taking the name and phone number of the prospective buyer. Anyone unwilling to give his name is an unlikely buyer. If you have difficulty asking for a name, you might try the line, "May I have your name and phone number so that I can reach you in case our apartment is sold before the appointment or if I have to cancel for some other reason?" This works virtually every time and puts a little pressure on the prospect to boot.

When your FOR SALE BY OWNER ad first appears in the newspapers, you will receive many calls from real estate agents seeking listings. If you were satisfied with the work of one or more of the agents who came to your apartment to give you the competitive market analysis, you may be planning to give the listing to his/her firm in the event that you do not sell in the time you have allowed yourself. In this case, simply tell the agents who call that the listing is promised. They won't bother you further.

If you have not decided upon a real estate agency, you can invite the agents who call to your apartment, talk with them about marketing it, and evaluate their services. Do not, however, allow them to show the apartment on an open listing while *you* are marketing it. (We'll explain open listings in just a few pages.) The customer that an agent brings tomorrow might have called you himself next week. If he buys, your nod to the agent's "Just let me show it to this one buyer that I'm working with" has cost you the amount of the commission.

Showing

When prospective buyers finally arrive at your door, invite them in and proceed to show your apartment professionally. Treat them as prospective buyers, not as guests. You do not need to offer them coffee or even ask them to remove their coats.

Walk through the rooms at the buyers' pace. It will be slow when there is great interest; fast when there is little. As you enter each room, do *not* say, "This is the living room" or "This is the kitchen." *What* a room is usually needs no explanation. Try instead to make conversation, or appear to make conversation. You might say for example, "We enjoy the fireplace in here during the winter." This effectively says, "This room has a working fireplace." Or "My wife really enjoys spreading out all her utensils when she's preparing a gourmet dinner," which is a way of saying that the kitchen is large and works for a gourmet cook.

Offer to show the common areas of the building or complex. This is another effective way to gauge buyer interest. Casual buyers out on tour or those who have already decided that they do not want to buy your apartment will usually refuse to take the additional time. Those who are considering your apartment seriously, however, will be eager for the tour. Point out to them any recent improvements such as a new elevator or roof. Knowing what has already been done will ease some of their fears about future assessments.

While you are showing your apartment and/or the entire building or complex, ask some questions. You might gather information on occupancy dates, employment history, family needs, interests, goals in purchasing, all of which you may use later in your negotiating. But most important of all, try to find out if the prospective buyers can actually afford to buy your apartment. A good way to do this is to focus upon monthly costs. You might say, "Maintenance fees for our apartment are $_____ a month. We figured that with a $_____ down payment, which is the least most banks will accept, and a mortgage at sixteen percent, a buyer would need an annual salary of $_____ in order to carry all the monthly payments. Are you comfortable in that ball park?" They might tell you that they have three times that down payment, which throws your figures out, but at least you have opened the subject. You and the buyer have each acknowledged that affordability is a factor, and the subject will be easier to open again at a later time when you are negotiating in earnest.

This kind of questioning fills in for the "qualifying" procedure by which an agent would check to be sure that buyers could afford to buy what they were looking at. The information is crucial to the success of a sale, yet many people (including some real estate agents) find it extremely difficult to ask the necessary questions. Some who don't ask pay heavily for their reticence. Their apartments are tied up in contract and off the market for many weeks while waiting for buyers to get financing that will be refused.

If your prospective buyers are seriously interested, they may also ask you some very specific questions about the building's operating expenses, mortgaging, taxes, house rules, and management. This is a good time to suggest that you go back into your apartment where you have the various documents and papers that will answer their questions.

An excellent tool for use with interested buyers is a homeowner's listing sheet. You and your apartment are competing with professionally marketed apartments. Information on most of these other apartments is gathered on neatly printed listing sheets or in an appealing prospectus. You should compete therefore by providing your prospective buyer with the same information, clearly typed, and organized in a format as close as possible to that being used in real estate offices. (You will become quite familiar with the form of local listing sheets through your observation of the competitive market analyses of your apartment.)

Prepare your homeowner's sheets well in advance. Machine-copy at least twenty copies and keep them in the drawer with your other documents. Give a sheet to any buyer who seems moderately interested. Be sure that your name, address, and phone number are on the sheets.

Negotiating and Contracts of Sale

You will miss the services of a competent agent most during the negotiating process. Coming to a meeting of the minds on a face-to-face one-on-one basis is difficult without a mediator, as any labor-union officer or corporate executive will tell you. But there are some universals that are effective in every real estate negotiation and you should be especially aware of them when negotiating on your own.

- *Never get angry.* And never take low offers as a personal affront. The buyers are trying to purchase your property for the least amount of money with the best possible terms, which is exactly what they should be doing. You are trying to get as much money as you can and arrange the terms to your benefit, which is exactly what you should be doing. Think of the entire process as a business deal. You do not have to like the buyers and they do not have to like you, but you should always be both courteous and respectful. (This is not to say that you can't occasionally crack a joke during negotiations. Comic relief is often helpful.) If you feel yourself getting angry, however, back away. Tell the buyers you must do some thinking or that you wish to consult with someone (your lawyer, accountant, father-in-law) and that you would be happy to continue the discussion tomorrow. Let everyone cool.

- *Never say never.* An absolutely rigid buyer or seller is extremely difficult to bring to a point of agreement. A statement like "We would never consider helping with the financing" slams the door before you know what's in the other room. Leave as many options open to exploration as you can. Discount offers or suggestions only after careful consideration. And take whatever time you need for that consideration; don't be pressured into a spur-of-the-moment decision.

- *Leave room for response.* "This is our counteroffer. Take it or leave it!" backs your buyer into a corner. Many apartment-hunters do not have the courage to say, "I can't afford that, but I am willing to go to $ Perhaps we can make some arrangements that would make that figure appealing to you." Instead they take you at your word and leave the counteroffer and the apartment, even when they might have planned to go higher.

  It is better to respond simply, "We can't accept that offer." If you feel that the buyers are serious and that you are not too far apart to start closing the gap, you might add, "But we would consider $." This new number may still be more than what you had decided would be your rock-bottom figure and it keeps the talking going.

- *Use factual information.* When negotiations seem to be hung up, you can often give them a push by bringing out facts and figures that you have gathered. You might use the sales prices of nearby apartments that were recently sold. (It is an excellent tool to have copies of old listings if you can get them.) You might use information from the financial statement that demonstrates the solidity of the co-op or condo community. You might use information on financing that you have worked out to show monthly living costs. A real estate agent would use all these methods in an attempt to help buyers realize the fair market value of the property and their ability to carry it.

  Factual information is best brought forth when people are fresh. So if you have been negotiating for a period of time and people are feeling tired and frustrated, beg off until the following day. Your facts and figures will make more of an impression.

- *Use extras and occupancy.* Gaps of $2,000 and $3,000 between buyers and sellers have been bridged by draperies, chandeliers, carpeting, or even a washing machine. Negotiating is rarely an entirely rational process and a token gesture on the part of a seller, "I'll come down $500 and leave all the draperies in the apartment" might prompt buyers to sign for several thousand dollars more than they had planned, thinking that they are getting something extra.

Occupancy date is the other trump card in your hand. Try to find out early in the deal whether the buyers want or need to move in soon or would prefer to wait several months for the closing. Then use that information as though it were money. "We can only come down $1,000 in price, but we are willing to vacate in thirty days." Or "Our price is firm but we are willing to schedule the closing four months from now. That should give you plenty of time to raise the extra money you need."

- *Leave the contracts to the lawyers*. Once you have agreed upon purchase price, occupancy, date, and extras, shake hands. There is no need to exchange money at that moment or to sign anything. Give your buyers the name, address, and phone number of your attorney and take down the name, address, and phone number of theirs. The attorneys will contact each other and work out the details of the contract, who holds the monies, what contingencies apply, and so forth.

If you don't sell your apartment after four weeks on the market, you should seek out a real-estate agency to handle it. Or, if you do not need to sell immediately, you might withdraw it from the market for two or three months and then try advertising it again to a new crop of apartment-hunters.

Choosing a Real Estate Agent

It is extremely important that you trust the real estate agent that you choose to market your property. In fact, legally the relationship between broker and seller is defined as a fiduciary relationship—that is, one of trust. You will work with your agent supplying information, arranging showings, negotiating, and perhaps even drawing contracts of sale. You must be honest and cooperative with him or her, and for your peace of mind, you must have confidence in his or her honesty, ability, conscientiousness, and positive attitude toward your property.

So which agent should you choose? The agent who raves about your apartment, tells you his office has seven different potential buyers for it right now, and promises you that his firm can get you $10,000 more than any other area firm is rarely your best choice. You may not be speaking to him six weeks into the listing term.

Choose rather to work with an agent who inspects your apartment carefully, who takes the time to look at the common areas of your building, who asks many questions and records the answers, who is accurate and honest in evaluating the worth of your property, and who knows the local financial marketplace intimately. You should be certain also that the agent you choose is a full-time professional. Your neighbor, who is a chemistry teacher and works in real estate evenings, weekends, and vacation days, may be intelligent, witty, and a good friend, but he cannot compete in a fast-paced, complex marketplace with agents who are making their livings in real estate.

Your agent's office should be located as close to your apartment as possible. Real estate is still a local business and listings are best serviced by agents familiar with their neighborhood. And that office should be a *residential* real estate firm that does a large part of its business in the type of apartment that you are selling. A significant trade assures you of the agency's familiarity with their product (your apartment) and an ample supply of customers seeking that type of housing.

Listing Your Apartment

Financially, listing with an agency usually means that you agree to pay a commission when your property is sold. The details of that agreement, however, are spelled out in the listing contract you will be asked to sign. Read it carefully; it is a legally enforceable document.

As you read the listing contract, check to be sure that you are listing your property for a clearly stated length of time. The expiration *date* of the listing contract should be written out *(e.g.,* June 29, 1984). Do not accept vague statements such as "four months after signing of this contract" as an expiration date. If your second cousin appears on June 30, offers to buy your apartment without an agent at close to your full asking price, and signs a contract that day, you may wish "four months" were spelled out as *ending* on June 29.

Most agencies will try to convince you to sign a listing for a term of six months or more. Don't. There is no minimum length of time for a listing contract. Three months is probably best; it gives you the opportunity to evaluate the services of the agency and leaves you the option of changing agencies within a reasonable time if you are not satisfied. If you are satisfied with your agency's services but your apartment has not been sold at the end of your listing term, you can extend the listing contract on a month-to-month basis.

How much, why, and when you pay the agency commission should also appear in your listing contract. The commission that you agree to pay is not predetermined; it is always negotiable between each seller and each broker. It can be a set figure or a percentage of the sales price. Percentage has been the traditional arrangement for many decades, with the going rate for residential property almost invariably 6 percent. Today, however, some agencies are working for 4 or 5 percent; others are asking 7 or 8 percent. Be sure you discuss with your agent exactly what you are getting for your commission dollar. Does a higher commission rate buy you more services? Are some services eliminated at the lower rate?

Be sure also that your listing contract states the terms under which a commission is due and payable. Most contracts state that commission is considered earned if the real estate agency produces a ready, willing, and able buyer for the property at a price and terms acceptable to the seller. This means upon the signing of contracts commission is earned. If the buyer defaults at the closing, the seller gets to keep the down payment but must pay the full real estate commission. Therefore it should also be clearly stated in the listing contract that the commission is to be paid *upon closing*. This clause protects you from being asked to pay the commission upon signing of the contracts and then possibly facing a buyer who refuses to close on the property. You might sue the buyer in this case, but your commission money would be difficult to retrieve.

Before we go on to discuss the types of listing agreements generally available, we'd like to mention the fee broker. Abundant only in scattered areas throughout the United States, the fee broker advertises that his or her office will market your property for *x* number of dollars. That number can be anywhere from a few hundred dollars on up, but it is always considerably less than conventional brokers are charging. This fee, however, is payable *in advance*. The broker receives his money whether or not he sells your property. Needless to say, this arrangement stimulates little incentive to work long or hard for the seller. It also effectively cuts the seller out of any possibility that his property will be sold by a cooperating broker, for most conventional agencies will not share listings and sales with fee brokers.

Whether you use a fee broker or a conventional broker, however, you are hiring an agent to sell your property under certain conditions and limitations. The rights that you give to your broker are spelled out in the listing contract you sign. The most commonly used types follow.

Exclusive Right to Sell

This is the listing contract most often used and most favored by real estate brokers. It gives to the broker the *exclusive* right to sell your property during the term of the listing. Under the exclusive right to sell contract, you cannot sell your apartment without paying a commission (not even to your widowed aunt). The broker, however, may share the listing with other brokers. Through such an arrangement, another agency may bring you a buyer. You would then pay the full agreed-upon commission to the selling agency, which in turn would send a part of the commission (usually 30 to 50 percent) to the listing agency.

Exclusive Agency

Under an exclusive agency listing, you give a broker the exclusive right to act as your agent in the sale of your property but reserve to yourself the right to sell it to a party not procured by the agent without paying a commission. With an exclusive agency contract you could sell your apartment to your widowed aunt the day after you sign the listing contract and not owe any commission. The broker in an exclusive agency contract may also choose to share the listing with other cooperating brokers and he would receive a share of the commission upon sale by another agency just as in an exclusive-right-to-sell contract.

Open Listing

Under an open listing you give the broker the right to act as your agent in the sale of your property but reserve the right to employ other brokers in the same capacity or to sell the property yourself. Brokers do not share open listings; most also will not advertise them.

Most real estate firms have simple forms available for a written open listing, but a few will still work under an oral agreement. The agent says, "I have just the person for your apartment, Ms. Seller. May I show it?" You nod. "Will you agree to a 6 percent commission at $80,000?" You were only asking $75,000, so you think it sounds fair, and agree. You have an open listing with that agent for that showing. The commission would be spelled out in the contract of sale if the agent did indeed sell the apartment.

Net Listings

Net listings are illegal in most states, but you may still run across them in certain areas and you should be aware of how they work. Under a net listing, a seller employs a broker to obtain from the sale of his property a certain dollar amount. Any amount above the stated figure becomes the broker's commission. For example a seller might say, "I want $90,000 from this apartment. I don't care what you sell it for." If the broker negotiates a sale at $93,000, his commission is $3,000. If he negotiates a sale at $119,000, his commission is $29,000.

Once you have signed a listing contract, your selling experience will be officially under way. The information about your apartment that the agent gathered will be printed on listing sheets and distributed to every other agent working in the firm. If your agency is a member of a Multiple Listing Service (MLS), a listing sheet on your apartment will be distributed to every member of the Realtor Board. Ask your agent to give you a copy of this listing sheet as soon as it becomes available. Check all the information on it for accuracy (especially your name, address, and phone number). If there are any errors have them corrected immediately; the first few weeks on the market are often your strongest selling time.

Showing with an Agent

Once you have turned your property over to a real estate firm for marketing, let them market it. Leave your apartment or remain in one room while it is being shown. Do *not* follow the agent from room to room, pointing out, explaining, and demonstrating; you will only make everyone feel uncomfortable, appear overanxious, and hurt your sale. If you are asked a question, answer as directly as possible and try not to get involved in an interrogation session. The agent should be able to answer most of the buyer's questions.

Again do not leave the packet of documents and information that you have gathered on the dining-room table for everyone to rummage through. Have your listing agent put a note on your listing sheet or leave a typed statement on the table saying something to this effect: *House rules for the co-op (or condominium) community, financial statements, names of officers on the Board of Directors, and other information regarding this property are available to interested prospective buyers upon request.* If the buyers are interested, they will ask the agent for the information. When he or she asks you, you will know there is interest in your apartment.

The Offer

Many agents will call a seller when their customers are "thinking about" buying an apartment. "Do you think he'll take $70?" says the buyer. "Let's make an offer and find out," replies the agent, and the phone call is placed. The seller's responding, "No, but we'll consider $78," is akin to giving everyone at a bridge table the chance to look at his hand before beginning to play.

Do not respond to *any* offer made by phone. If you do, you will begin your negotiating from a weak position. It is important that people sit down together to negotiate so that there can be space and time for silences and consideration, a place to write, the ability to read, eye contact, laughter, and discussion.

When an agent has a serious buyer, he should come to your home with a signed offer form (or in some areas a contract of sale) and an earnest money check. No matter how low or preposterous the offer seems to be, consider it. By "consider" we mean, "find out if the prospective buyer *can afford* to buy your apartment." The ability to buy and carry the payments on an apartment is much more important than the amount of the first offer. If the buyer is shaky, it is unlikely that the offering price will come up significantly; if, however, the buyer is well qualified, the low offer is likely to be a starting point in negotiations.

You can usually obtain the financial information that you need to evaluate the buyer by questioning the real estate agent and by carefully studying the offer form. How much down payment does the buyer have? How much will he need to finance? What kind of financing does he intend to get? At what interest rate? How much will the monthly payments be on that loan? Can he carry that plus the maintenance fee for this apartment? Where does he work? What position? For how long? At what salary? Does he have any other income?

If your buyer seems qualified, continue to ask questions at that initial negotiating session. Ask about the proposed closing and occupancy dates, the extras the buyer wants included in the sale, what he likes and dislikes about the apartment. Store all the information away in your memory and use it effectively later in the negotiating process.

If you think the buyer is an unlikely candidate, you can effectively shorten negotiating time by refusing to make a counteroffer. Only the most persevering buyers will come back after a flat refusal. If you are uncertain about the buyer, make a token reduction, a thousand or so, as your counteroffer. If you think your buyer is both serious and able, consider what your expected selling price might be, weigh how much negotiating space each of you has on either side of that figure, and begin to work toward a meeting of the minds.

When negotiating with an agent as mediator, the same principles apply as when selling without an agent. Remember them and *use* them.

When you reach an agreement, we suggest that you have your attorney draw the contracts. Many real estate firms advocate presenting the seller with a written offer form or a contract of sale executed by the buyer. This is fine, but don't sign it. Tell the agent that you accept the offer, but that you would like your attorney to review this contract or draft his own.

When you do sign a contract, be sure that it specifies who holds the escrow monies (ideally it should be *your* attorney and they should be held in an interest-bearing account for you). It should also specify when those monies will be released to you. In some states, by agreement, the seller is entitled to the monies as soon as all the contingencies of the contract are met. (This allows you, the seller, to use someone else's money as an escrow deposit on your next purchase.) The contract should also include cut-off dates for each of the contingencies (mortgage commitment, termite inspection, home inspection service, and so forth).

One of the most important elements of your contract should be a list of every item of personal property that is included in the purchase price and every item that is *not* included. Personal property is everything that is not permanently attached to the premises. Appliances, draperies, carpeting, chandeliers, lawn furniture, the mailbox, are but a sampling of the possibilities. By attaching this list and having all the parties concerned in the sale initial it, you will avoid many arguments at the closing table.

Closing the Sale

The closing is a meeting of all parties involved in the sale of a piece of property. Papers are signed, checks written, and title passes from the seller to the buyer. For you as seller, it is the time and place at which you will receive your money. Be sure that you have arranged to have your utilities disconnected and your mail forwarded. Check with your attorney that taxes and any special assessments have been prorated to the date of closing. Collect your check and go out for a toast to your future investments.

Note that not all closings take place on the date specified in the contract. Often people need a little extra time because of unforeseen circumstances. Therefore, we strongly suggest that the clause, "time is of the essence," should not be included in a contract by either a buyer or a seller. Always leave yourself room to breathe.

CHAPTER 11

Vacation Places: Time Share and Other Apartment Hideaways

The Endless Vacation is the title of an annual directory published by Resort Condominiums International (RCI), a corporation that arranges time share apartment swaps. The words of that title and, in fact, the words of all the subheadings in the book (Indian Summer in New England; Luau!; Glittering Coasts; and so forth), along with the enticing photographs of beautiful people having fun in beautiful places, are carefully chosen to appeal to the wanderlust in everyone. After all, who wouldn't like to vacation like the rich?

Elegant vacations—or more precisely future elegant vacations at today's prices—are the primary commodity being sold in the time share industry today. According to RCI, 71 percent of the over 200,000 time share owners who subscribe to its service bought their apartments for the exchange opportunity.

And who were these buyers, the new "beautiful people" exploring beautiful places? Middle-class Americans. Again according to RCI, 83 percent of time share buyers have incomes under $50,000 a year.

"But how can they afford it?" you ask. "An annual income of $30,000 or even $50,000 just won't buy a week in Hawaii, Aspen, Japan, Hilton Head, or Puerto Rico year after year."

It doesn't always. But we're getting ahead of ourselves. Despite the recent proliferation of articles about the time share industry (also called interval ownership) in local newspapers and nationally circulated magazines, there may yet be some readers who have not met this vacation concept.

What Is a Time-share Condo?

It's usually an apartment, but sometimes it's a detached cabin or house in a resort community, a stateroom on a luxury liner, a campsite, a yacht, or a hotel room. It's like the conventional condominium in the shared-space concept, but different in that it is also subject to shared time.

When you buy a time share unit, you buy the right to use that apartment for a certain time period each year. For example, you might buy the right to occupy Unit 441 at Mount Snow Apartments for the second week in February every year, or Unit 2B in Sky Lodge at Lake Tahoe for the second week in August every year. That week in that apartment is yours. It cannot be rented or used without your consent and knowledge.

"O.K., but do you really *own* anything?" the cautious buyer asks.

Yes, usually. Most time share- or interval-ownership developers or converters are selling the unit time outright—that is, they give the buyer fee simple ownership. He takes title to his one or two weeks per year in the unit and receives a deed. He must pay his share of the unit's real estate taxes (usually included in the maintenance fee) and he can claim for tax purposes his share (a tiny portion) of the unit's real estate deductions. He can (and should) obtain title insurance on his unit. And he can sell the unit for a profit (if he can find a buyer).

But—and there's always a but—some time share vacationers do *not* really own anything. Even newer than the outright time share unit sales plans are the right-to-use plans. "Buyers" of these condominium apartments never take title to their unit for the week or two a year that they claim as their own. What they actually buy is the equivalent of a long lease—that is, the right to use (and the obligation to pay maintenance fees for) an apartment for one or two weeks a year for an extended term (usually fifteen to thirty years). "Buyers" are attracted because prices for these units are considerably lower than those for the interval ownership units. When the term of the right-to-use lease is over, however, vacationers find that they own nothing.

Time Share Unit Costs

The price of time share units depends on the size of the unit, its location, and the season during which the time is bought. A week in November on Cape Cod may cost as little as $3,000 plus a $150-a-year maintenance charge.

A week in July in exactly the same unit may cost $11,000 plus the same $150-a-year maintenance fee.

Is it worth it? Salespeople will tell you that you will have the opportunity to vacation in this beautiful unit complete with, let's say, two bedrooms, two baths, a fireplace, and a fully equipped kitchen for the $150-a-week maintenance fee. "You can't beat that rate anywhere!" they'll assure you. "And think of the money you can save in restaurant bills by having your own kitchen!"

Sounds good. In most resort areas you can't get a back corner room next door to the kitchen for $150 a week. But is $150 the *real* cost of your time share vacation? Hardly.

Let's take the $11,000 week in July on Cape Cod. If you invested that $11,000 instead of buying your one-week time share apartment, you might well net 9 percent on your money after taxes. That's $990 of spendable income from your $11,000 investment. Your time share unit therefore costs you the $150 maintenance fee plus the lost $990 investment income, a total of $1,140 each year. Most people could rent an apartment at a resort of their choice for $1,140 a week.

"But buying an apartment is an investment too," retorts the salesperson. Yes, a time share apartment might appreciate in value over the years, but to realize that appreciation, you must be able to *sell* it. Currently, even time share resort executives admit that there is virtually no resale market in time share units. And besides the lost interest on the potential investment of the money used in buying the apartment, time share purchases are also at risk for another kind of loss. What happens if you can't take a vacation in a particular year? If you own a time share unit, you must pay your money for the vacation you didn't take.

Time share *as an investment* is profitable only to the sponsor of the conversion or the builder if it is a new development, and the management company. Just to give you some idea of *how* profitable, let's work through some numbers.

Arthur and Pamela Wright bought a one-bedroom unit for one week a year in Miami Beach at a cash price of $6,000. Their maintenance fee is $160 a year. In their condominium resort only fifty weeks a year are sold, two weeks are left vacant for maintenance and refurbishing.

If all fifty weeks were to sell at $6,000, the sale of the Wrights' apartment would gross the seller $300,000 ($6,000 × 50 = $300,000). But the purchase prices for the Wrights' apartment were allocated to certain weeks according to seasonal demand. Therefore, sale of all available weeks would bring the following return:

Christmas season
    2 weeks at $10,000 a week ....$ 20,000
Jan., Feb., & early March
    10 weeks at $9,000 a week 90,000
March, April, last 2 weeks of June, July, August,
November, and three weeks of December
    25 weeks at $6,000 a week 150,000
May, first 2 weeks of June, September, and
two weeks of October
    13 weeks at $4,000 a week 52,000
Total $312,000

"Wow!" you say. "Pretty good for a one-bedroom apartment."

But read on. A year-round condominium apartment comparable to the Wrights' two blocks south on Collins Avenue is priced at $110,000. If the entire time share year in the Wrights' apartment is sold, therefore, it will gross $202,000 *more* than a comparable unit sold as a full-time ownership condominium.

And let's take the figures a step further. There are 100 units in the time share resort, all priced alike. If the resort sold out, the seller would gross $31,200,000. If there were 100 units, all priced at $110,000 in the conventional condominium complex, the total gross income from the sale of those units would be $11,000,000. Theoretically, therefore, sale of a resort as a time share condominium would bring in $20,200,000 more than the sale of a comparable property as a conventional condominium.

"Wow!" again. But the real scenario is not quite so simple, nor quite so profitable. In many time share developments, some weeks are virtually unsalable at any price. Few people want the South Florida coast in May; even fewer want Cape Cod in November. Being left holding virtually all the apartments in a complex for a number of weeks out of the year can cut significantly into the gross profits of a seller. Time share sales are profitable, very profitable, but exactly how much return they bring on an investment dollar is dependent upon the circumstances that are unique to each individual property.

But we also said that time share was profitable to the management company. Let's look at maintenance fees. The maintenance fee on the $110,000 condominium on Collins Avenue is $1,200 a year. Multiplied by 100 units the maintenance income for the complex is $120,000. In the time share unit, the maintenance fee is $160 for one week times 50 weeks or

$8,000. Multiplied by 100 units, the gross maintenance income is $800,000. That's $680,000 more per year than the conventional condominium.

Before you quit your job to start a time share management firm, remember that the time-share maintenance fees include real estate taxes, maid service, and periodic refurbishing and refurnishing of the apartments.

The cost of keeping the time share units bright enough so that the owner of each week's stay is proud to enter his unit each year is very high. Although time share owners "own" their units, they do not treat the property as though it were theirs to have and to hold. In terms of wear and tear on the units, all occupants are vacationers. Sand is tracked in and ground into the carpets; people newly oiled for sunbathing plop down on the living-room chairs; children sleeping in strange places wet the beds; shower curtains are left outside the tub to drip upon the floor . . .

The two weeks allowed for refurbishing usually means a complete paint job and much redecorating. Carpets are replaced at five-year intervals, furniture and furnishings even sooner.

This is not to say that management companies do not make handsome profits on time share units. They do. But it is not quite so handsome and headache free as gross-income figures would indicate.

Should You Buy?

Since we've told you that time share units are *not* a good investment purchase for the one- or two-week-a-year buyer, that they are priced at a premium, that the maintenance fees are high, and that in many instances you could vacation quite nicely on the investment income from the money required to buy them, you may well be wondering why we would title a section "Should You Buy?" Well, believe it or not, interval ownership is right for some people. If you truly love the unit and the location, plan to return frequently over the years, and are not counting upon resale for a profit, you should consider time share ownership. In other words, buy a time share apartment if it fills your emotional and/or recreational needs.

The concept of vacation is one of those needs. For many people the fact that they have bought an apartment and must pay the maintenance fee forces them to take their vacation. A week "away," which might otherwise be put off month after month, year after year, because "I'm too busy" or "We can't afford it," is taken. How much, then, is a guaranteed vacation worth in terms of mental and physical well-being?

Some people buy time-share units knowing full well that they are paying a high price and consider that price worth it. They are buying the privilege of returning to a favorite place each year without ever having to worry about maintaining their vacation home.

Let's take the $11,000 ownership of a week on Cape Cod as an example. You and your spouse were both born in Massachusetts. You met during summer vacations on the Cape, and for the first eight summers of your married life you vacationed there. Your children built sand castles and caught fiddler crabs and played tag among the dunes. Then you were chosen for a fabulous promotion. Your new office, however, was in Salt Lake City, Utah. Is a one-week-a-summer-vacation condominium on the Cape worth $11,000 to you?

You could not buy even the flimsiest cottage for that price. And even if you could, you would not be "there" to watch your property 53 weeks of every year. Who would clean up after the September northeaster? Who would drain the pipes to shut the water off for the winter? Who would handle rentals? Fix the leaky faucet? Contract to have the five shingles that blew off the roof replaced? Yes, there are real estate agents and property management firms available to do these tasks. But you must pay them *and* they are not you; they are not maintaining (caring for) their own property.

The relative high price of time share units is a price paid for the freedom from care; for maintenance work that is accountable to the many "owners" who are there each year; and for the security of knowing you will have familiar and adequate accommodations even at the height of the season every year.

Before you buy a time share apartment, however, you should evaluate it by all the criteria we have listed in the previous chapters. It is still a real estate purchase and should be judged as such. You should also take pains to check on the reputation of the management company.

The International Apartment Swap

Our Cape Cod story is an idealized example, but for many people spending a week a year for seven, eleven, or nineteen years at the same place in the same apartment can become pretty humdrum. Enter, therefore, the time share equivalent of an in-group travel club. Most time share resorts offer optional membership in one of the two giant computerized apartment exchange agencies, Resort Condominiums International and Interval International.

For a yearly membership fee ($40 at this writing) and an additional fee of $40 per swap, either of these two corporations will try to find the time share apartment owner an acceptable week in another location. The majority of resorts are located in the United States, but places are available virtually around the world with Mexico, South America, Canada, the Caribbean, Western Europe, the Middle East, the South Pacific, Africa, and the Far East (especially Japan) all represented.

Sounds great again, doesn't it? You're thinking that maybe that $3,000 week on Cape Cod in November isn't such a bad deal after all. You could swap it for a villa in Spain during Christmas vacation.

Not quite. Your ability to swap your vacation week is dependent upon the desirability rating of that week, which also determines to a great degree how much you must pay for your time share slot. Owners of the most expensive and desirable vacation time can exchange their week with any of the equally or less desirable vacation-time slots around the world. Owners of less desirable weeks can swap only at their own level or below. That means your week in November on Cape Cod will get you a week between January 1 and March 31 in Minnesota or Oregon, and precious little else to choose from. So if you do choose November on Cape Cod, or its equivalent, you should do so with the intention of vacationing in your own time share unit most of the time.

For those of you interested in examining the time share exchange concept more closely, both exchange companies will send free information upon request. Write to:

Interval International
7000 S.W. 62nd Ave. Suite 306
Miami, Florida 33143

or

Resort Condominiums International
9333 N. Meridian P.O. Box 80229
Indianapolis, Indiana 46280

Time Share Sales Programs

Despite the obvious drawbacks of the purchase, most of those people who buy a time share unit thoughtfully—that is, knowing what they are buying and why—are satisfied with their purchase. The great outcries of dissatisfaction come from those buyers who were enticed into high-pressure sales programs. Their stories usually begin with a letter. The following letter is similar to four received during one six-week period at the Jumpatit household.

P O BOX 987654321   # Mail-E-Gram
WASHINGTON D C 20041

THIS IS OFFICIAL NOTIFICATION OF BEING SELECTED AS A
RECIPIENT IN THE LATEST AWARDS PROGRAM CONDUCTED BY
THE AWARDS DEPARTMENT OF VERIFICATION, ON BEHALF OF
MOSSY MANSIONS. THIS IS NOT A LAND SALES PROMOTION.
THERE ARE NO HIDDEN CONDITIONS.

-111-BE   YOUR AWARD NUMBERS
JOSEPH J. JUMPATIT   ARE:
92 COUNTRY ROAD   *** 1030 & 1081 ****
MIDDLETOWN, KANSAS 00000

YOU WILL DEFINITELY RECEIVE TWO OF THE AWARDS FROM
BELOW:

CATEGORY 1

$1,000.00 CASH
DELUXE GAS GRILL
LAS VEGAS VACATION

CATEGORY 2

TV HOME ENTERTAINMENT SYSTEM
GULF OF MEXICO VACATION
MICROWAVE OVEN

CATEGORY 3

HAWAIIAN VACATION
$2,500.00 CASH
POOL TABLE

TO DETERMINE THE CATEGORIES YOUR AWARDS ARE IN *CALL
NOW, TOLL FREE 1-800-555-7777,* GIVE US YOUR *AWARD
NUMBERS,* AND MAKE ARRANGEMENTS TO RESERVE A TIME TO
RECEIVE YOUR *CASH AND AWARDS.*

ALL WE ASK IN RETURN IS THAT, IF MARRIED, BOTH HUSBAND
AND WIFE LISTEN TO AN INFORMAL INTRODUCTORY
PRESENTATION OF MOSSY MANSIONS AND ITS OUTSTANDING
RECREATIONAL FACILITIES, WHILE VISITING THEIR LUXURY
VACATION RESORT . . . . WITHIN THE NEXT 21 DAYS.

*BE SURE TO BRING THIS MAIL-E-GRAM AND ENVELOPE WITH
YOU,* SINCE PROPER IDENTIFICATION WILL BE REQUIRED. WE
KNOW YOU'LL WANT TO HEAR ABOUT THE EXCITING DETAILS

OF A *VERY SPECIAL OFFER* AVAILABLE ONLY TO INVITED
GUESTS LIKE YOURSELF ON THE *DAY OF YOUR ACTUAL VISIT.*

FAILURE TO RESPOND WITHIN THE TIME ALLOTTED WILL
RELEASE YOUR CASH AND AWARDS FOR REISSUANCE, SO
CALL WITHIN THE NEXT 72 HRS TO MAKE YOUR APPOINTMENT
AND ARRANGE TO RECEIVE YOUR AWARDS ... *CALL NOW,
TOLL FREE 1-800-555-7777.* CALLS ARE ACCEPTED *9:00 A.M. TO
9:00 P.M. MONDAY THROUGH FRIDAY, SATURDAYS AND
SUNDAYS FROM 9:00 A.M. TO 5:00 P.M. (EXCEPT HOLIDAYS).*

BILL CANDIDE
DEPARTMENT OF VERIFICATION

P.S. ..... ON MONDAY THROUGH FRIDAYS ONLY, THE LESS
BUSY DAYS, YOU WILL RECEIVE *$10.00 CASH* TOWARD YOUR
TRANSPORTATION, AND AN *ADDITIONAL AWARD* ...... A
FOUR-PIECE FRENCH CRYSTAL STEMWARE SET *OR*
HOUSEHOLD APPLIANCE (RETAIL VALUE $24.95) .... *CALL NOW.*

And on the reverse side of that letter:

I certify that I have received the Award(s) check-marked below

☐ $1,000.00 CASH
☐ DELUXE GAS GRILL
☐ LAS VEGAS VACATION

☐ TV HOME ENTERTAINMENT SYSTEM
☐ GULF OF MEXICO VACATION
☐ MICROWAVE OVEN

☐ HAWAIIAN VACATION
☐ $2,500 CASH
☐ POOL TABLE

BONUS AWARDS

☐ $10.00 TRANSPORTATION
ALLOWANCE

☐ HOUSEHOLD APPLIANCE
(RETAIL VALUE $24.95)

☐ 4-PIECE FRENCH CRYSTAL
STEMWARE SET

OFFICE NOTICE OF RECEIPT FORM

This is to certify that the undersigned has received his/her award.
Received this ___ day of _____ 19 ___ Signature _____

NOTE: This is part of a marketing and advertising program being conducted for several sponsors. Participants will include persons from mailings made on behalf of all sponsors. This program is designed for persons between the ages of 23 and 65 years of age. Holder of this letter is entitled to take advantage of only one Mossy Mansions promotional program, within any 365 day period. You must be gainfully employed and a U.S. citizen and creditworthy. Mossy Mansions members, employees and persons previously visiting on any of the promotional programs are ineligible. This letter is not transferable; and proof of identification is required. No purchase is necessary. If married, both husband and wife will be asked to listen to an informal introductory presentation of the resort facilities while there.

The cash and awards are good only on the day of your actual visit. Only one set of awards will be given per Mail-E-Gram, auto or transaction. This offer is void where prohibited by law.

Your individual numbers have been selected for you by an independent promotional agency. The total number of awards to be distributed depends on the total number of participants. The more participants, the more awards that will be distributed. For a participant, the odds of receiving an award are as follows: $2,500 Cash: 74,790 to 1; Las Vegas Vacation for two, Accommodations and Air Fare: 57,114 to 1, value $1,480.00; Pool Table: 37,395 to 1, value $673.00; Deluxe Gas Grill: .99987 to 1; $1,000 Cash: 42,735 to 1; Hawaiian Vacation: 59,832 to 1, value $1,796.00; Microwave Oven: 37,395 to 1, value $542.00; T.V. Home Entertainment System: 59,832 to 1, value $1,625.00; Gulf of Mexico Vacation, transportation and meals not included: .99987 to 1. In the event all of the major awards are not claimed, random drawings will be held from among the participants of this and similar programs conducted by Gogo Printing and Mailing Services, Inc., Gold St., Rainbow, Virginia. This program ends December 31, 1982. You may request a list of all major award recipients by mailing a self-addressed stamped envelope to Gogo at the end of the program. Taxes on all major awards are not included. Names of award recipients may be used for publicity purposes.

There are several common elements in the letters being used as come-ons to a time share sales pitch. First, they all offer fabulous-sounding prizes. But what are your odds of winning and what do you really get? A little detective work among the fine print on the flip side of the letter will give you some pretty substantial clues. The odds of receiving a given award and the value of that prize are listed.

The $2,500 cash sports odds of 74,790 to 1; the TV home-entertainment system with a value of $1,625 lists odds of 59,832 to 1; and the Hawaiian vacation valued at $1,796 also comes in at 59,832 to 1. Hmmmmmm!

But the letter said we *won* two prizes, one from each of two groups, many people think. We must be a big winner! And the adrenaline begins to flow. Most of them missed the significance of two tiny and unobtrusive decimal points. The odds of winning the deluxe gas grill and the Gulf of Mexico vacation are .99987 to 1 for each, almost 1 to 1. The decimal point means that your chances of *not* winning these two prizes are approximately 13 in 100,000. In other words, everyone, except a few truly lucky people, wins a deluxe gas grill *and* a Gulf of Mexico vacation.

"Well, that's not bad," you say. "We'll listen to a sales pitch for a gas grill and a vacation. Seems like there's nothing to lose."

Perhaps, except the value of your time. Did you notice that every prize had a cash value accorded to it *except* these two? What's the gas grill worth? And the vacation?

When most people read these prize offerings among the others listed, they picture a freestanding patio grill and a week at a posh Mexican resort. What they often receive is the equivalent of a tabletop Hibachi and a week at a time share resort at, let's say, the mouth of the Mississippi, where an army of sales agents awaits their arrival. And did you notice that transportation to this resort and meals while you are there are *not* included in your winnings? Few people claim this prize.

Also common to such "prize" letters is the stipulation that if the "winner" is married, both husband and wife must appear together and listen to a presentation about the resort and its opportunities. There is always a time limit after which your "prizes" will be released.

And what happens if you show up to claim your "prizes"? Leon and Genevieve Marzek of Pontiac, Michigan, did so on an offer only slightly different from our Mail-E-Gram. They were given a wristwatch, a camera, and a strand of simulated cultured pearls, and were invited to a lunch of hot dogs and soft drinks. They were also assigned a "personal sales assistant" who watched a movie about the time share resort and worldwide exchange opportunities with them. The assistant then spent two hours talking price and terms.

The Marzeks were interested in a prime-time unit. It was priced at $9,600 for one week. When they balked at the figure, they were offered a $1,600 price reduction and the opportunity for financing of 80 percent of the purchase price over five years at 11-percent interest.

They said they had planned to pay cash, but they thought the price was still too high for one week a year. At this the sales assistant left them for a few moments, only to return with her supervisor. He talked awhile, left, and returned within two minutes. He had made special arrangements for them, he said. They could have the unit for $6,400 all cash, but this was a one-day-only offer. It would be canceled if they did not buy now.

The Marzeks had had some doubts about buying a time share unit at the

194   THE COMPLETE GUIDE TO CO-OPS AND CONDOMINIUMS

outset; their doubts were intensified by the one-day-only sales pitch. They did not like being pressured and got up to leave as the sales agent asked, "How can you refuse such a bargain? You're throwing money away!"

Two days later the agent called them again saying that, by special arrangement, the $6,400 offer had been extended for them. Their reply was "No, thanks."

Price reductions, offers of low rate financing, and today-only specials are common tools being employed in time share sales pitches across the country. Many people sign contracts to buy without ever having seen, much less inspected, the time share unit, without knowing the terms and conditions of their ownership agreements, and without having consulted a lawyer or even each other. They wake up the next morning with a long-term obligation they never wanted.

Most of the time share resorts that are genuinely desirable rarely use programmed sales pitches. Word of mouth travels and potential buyers seek out the resort rather than the resort seeking out the buyers. These buyers are usually familiar with the time share concept and have chosen it as a vacation option that suits their particular needs. If you would like to approach a time share resort as an informed buyer, you can obtain more information by writing to:

National Timesharing Council
1000 16th Street NW
Washington, DC 20036

or you may write to the Federal Trade Commission attorney investigating time-sharing complaints:

Alan Schlaifer
Room 264
Federal Trade Commission
Washington, D.C. 20580

Investment Vacation Places

Is there a way to lock in future vacation costs, assure yourself a place to get away from it all, and invest profitably too? Nothing is a certainty, but there are alternatives. In coastal resort areas, at ski and golf areas, around the nation's large recreational lakes, and in certain vacation cities such as Las Vegas, Orlando, and Los Angeles, investors are buying rooms and apartments in converted or newly built motels and apartment buildings and then renting their units by the day, week, month, or season. The price range and facilities available to investors and vacationers alike through these units is wide and growing rapidly.

On Florida's west coast, for example, a much advertised vacation resort is actually a grouping of several condominium communities and a resort hotel. The resort owns the main house with hotel rooms, the reception areas, the convention rooms, the roads, the restaurants, the marina, and many of the recreational facilities. Most of the rooms and apartments rented to vacationers, however, are privately owned condominium units.

The owner of an apartment at this resort may choose never to rent his unit or he may choose to participate in one of the two rental plans offered by the resort. The regular rental plan allows the unit owner to reserve as much or as little time in his apartment for his own use as he chooses. He may rent his apartment by procuring his own tenants; that way he pays no commission fees. Or he may turn rental for certain periods of time, or the entire year, over to the resort on a 50/50 split of the rental income.

Such rental plans are more or less typical, but there are many variations in rules, income divisions, and costs even from one resort to its neighbor. Therefore, if you choose this type of condominium investment, you must not only evaluate the apartment as real estate but also review the bylaws of the condominium carefully, talk with officers of the board of directors, and use a local attorney to represent you in your purchase. And *think*. Investment vacation properties are a condominium option that must be explored in light of the goals, needs, and financial resources of the individual investor.

CHAPTER 12

Strictly for Profit: Inside Advice for Investors

What's *your* dream? A sailing yacht? A Mercedes? European vacations every year? Odds are you'll have a difficult time finding the cash for your special dream in your annual salary. But eventually, taking a portion of that salary and letting the *money* work for you, you could generate sufficient cash. Successful investment is the stepping-stone between your hard-earned pay and your dreams.

Investing in shared-space housing could be your best bet; we'll give you a step-by-step guide to *how* to do it. But you may be surprised to hear us say that investment in condominium and cooperative apartments may not be for everyone. If your dreams and goals can be satisfied by investment in the currently available safety instruments (the money market funds, All-Savers Certificates, municipal bonds, the Individual Retirement Accounts, etc.), put your money there. While every investment carries with it some risk, the safety instruments are the least risky. Your chances of losing money are negligible, and you know your rate of return before you commit your money.

If your dreams need a sprinkling of magic to become reality, however, you may want to look toward investments whose return is less certain but potentially greater. Think of the available investment vehicles: real estate, stocks, commodities, antiques, Oriental rugs, wine, art, coins and stamps, theater productions, small businesses. *Residential* real estate demands little specialized knowledge (as opposed to rug dealing or wine collecting), requires little professional advice (as opposed to the stock market, where investment decisions are often best left to the broker), is most secure over the long term (as opposed to backing a theatrical production that might well fold in an evening), and pays only a courtesy bow to Lady Luck.

In a very real way, everyone has insiders' knowledge of his or her local housing market, for everyone is a consumer of the housing product. Perhaps subconsciously or perhaps despite ourselves, we are aware of the needs, attractions, limitations, and liabilities of housing in the area in which we live. And each of us can use this knowledge to stack the odds for successful investment in residential real estate heavily in his or her favor. Which brings us to the first and probably the most important of the investment guidelines that we will offer you in this chapter: *Invest in real estate close to home*.

If you found and/or bought the apartment or house where you now live, you have already done some of the work necessary to ensure a successful investment in condominium or cooperative apartments. You have at least a nodding acquaintance with the real estate market and you know your community. Since you've read this book, you also know the techniques of evaluation and the procedures for shopping, negotiating, and buying. Now you need only consider the investment potential of your money. Let's look at it. The traditional concerns of every investor are safety, liquidity, and rate of return.

Safety

The safety of an investment is more important than most people are willing to admit. No one wants to lose money. Many investors buy real property, however, with about as much care as they use in betting the horses. Luck and intuition (and a little bit of exhilaration in risk-taking) get them by. Often they win. Their intuition becomes sharpened and heightened by absorbed information. But the law of averages dictates that eventually they will meet with some serious losses. Thus our second guideline: *Give proper weight to the safety of your investment*.

To ensure that safety:

(1) Know the area in which you are about to invest intimately. Be familiar with the master plan for zoning and future development. (You can examine the plan and current zoning maps at the town hall.) Be aware of changes in the character of the neighborhood; trends toward revitalization, deterioration, growth, stagnation, increased or decreased desirability.

(2) Evaluate the property by all the variables that you would use in buying an apartment for your own use and occupancy, except that you need not "love" it.

(3) Negotiate the best price, terms, and financing possible, being certain that you can afford to carry your investment.

If you buy in an area with which you are familiar, take the time to evaluate your purchase carefully, and secure your cash flow within affordable limits, your money in shared-space housing will be invested in one of the potentially most profitable and safest opportunities available today. If you have doubts, go back and read Chapter 2 again. Supply and demand are on your side, along with a government that is both stable and supportive of private property ownership. There may be economic swings that will affect the value of your investment dollar, but in the long term, that dollar will grow substantially.

Liquidity

People will tell you that liquidity is the big problem with investing in real estate. And it's true, if you consider that there is no way you can withdraw your investment money from a piece of property with one day's notice. But you can often achieve virtually the same effect by borrowing upon that equity. It may cost you a few dollars in interest, but you *will* have money to work with almost immediately. Sometimes you can even postpone paying interest upon that equity loan until you can sell the property.

But what if the owner can't sell? What if there are no buyers? Borrowing on equity is usually a second mortgage, isn't it? That's expensive. If times are bad, the apartment owner could get stuck with an expensive loan and a nonliquid investment.

Most people think along these lines and ask exactly these questions, but liquidity is really a judgmental factor. Anything is salable at a price. For example, you couldn't sell a stock that was trading at $50 a share for $75 a share. If you demanded $75 a share, you would have a nonliquid asset. But if you were willing to sell at $48 a share, your money would be in your hands within a day at most.

So too with real estate, although the numbers are larger and the time spans somewhat longer. An apartment whose true market value is $50,000 won't sell for $75,000 even in the best sellers' market. It will sell for $40,000 in the worst of times. Thus, any asset is nonliquid when the price you are trying to realize from its sale will not materialize under present market conditions.

Apartments are quite liquid at the right price, and if you bought well (that is, below the market value in a neighborhood that was appreciating), you can afford to sell below market value a year or so later and still realize a sizable profit. And if you bought very well (''stole the place,'' as the saying goes), you may find that your apartment investment is profitably liquid on the very day you close on it.

In shared-space real estate investment, however, price is not the only determinant of liquidity. Financing and rental each also play a supporting or detracting role. Tight and expensive money depresses sales, but an offer of financing at below market rates can markedly increase the salability of a piece of property. Rental, on the other hand, can decrease the liquidity of an investment while assuring its safety.

If you consider your down-payment money (your investment) safe as long as the property is appreciating in value and you can make the monthly payments required to carry it, renting at a rate that will cover or nearly cover your monthly cash outlay relieves the pressure upon your income while allowing your investment to grow in value. It is more difficult, however, to sell an occupied apartment, especially if the term of the lease is a long one or if the occupants are protected by government rent controls. So what do you do? Is it necessary to give up liquidity for safety? Or safety for liquidity?

A little of each. How long do you plan to hold the apartment before selling? How rapidly is it appreciating? Will the rapid appreciation allow you to attract a buyer to the occupied apartment at a price below the market value but still very profitable to you? Two years from the date of purchase, will you be able to afford to carry an unoccupied apartment for the three to six months required to sell it?

We are certainly not advising that you refrain from renting your investment apartment. On the contrary, renting makes the apartment purchase possible for most people. There are, however, some guidelines to wise rental:

(1) Keep your leases short. Never more than two years.

(2) Screen your prospective tenants by requesting references and financial data.

(3) Be aware of political movements in your area that might bring about rent controls. You do not want to wake up one morning and discover that your tenants have the right to remain in your apartment for the rest of their lives, subject only to regulated rent increaes!

(4) And *never* offer your tenants an option to buy, or its cousin, a right of first refusal.

An option is one of the simplest and most misunderstood instruments in the real estate marketplace. Many sellers use it as an inducement to rent their apartments, yet it is almost invariably detrimental to their investment.

The option-to-buy clause in a lease gives to the tenant the right to purchase the apartment at an agreed-upon figure on or before some specified date in the future. But there is no *obligation* to buy whatsoever.

Here's how the option works against the seller: If the apartment has appreciated considerably during the term of the lease so that it is worth many thousands of dollars more than the option price, the wise tenant can exercise the option even if he/she has no intention of owning the apartment permanently. That tenant can then resell the apartment at or near market value for a profit and move on. Meanwhile, the seller has written himself out of long-term appreciation that should have been his.

If, on the other hand, the apartment does not appreciate in value as well as expected or if the real estate market is very soft when the lease expires, the tenant is under no obligation to exercise his option. It is a no-risk, potentially high-gain situation for the tenant, with no benefit to the owner/seller.

More important, the option also cancels out all potential liquidity in the investment. The owner *cannot* sell the apartment while the option is in effect, except to the tenant.

The right of first refusal is less well known, less often used, and slightly less detrimental to the apartment owner. A lease that contains a clause granting the tenants the right of first refusal gives them the opportunity to match the sales price agreed upon between the seller and another party and thus buy the apartment. Some condominiums have a right of first refusal to the board of directors written into their bylaws as a means of controlling to some degree the membership in their community.

You're probably wondering what's so bad about the right of first refusal. After all, you as the seller will get your money. What care you whether an outside buyer, or your tenant, or the board of directors of your condominium comes up with the agreed-upon purchase price?

You don't. But your buyers do. A right of first refusal on a property must be made known in listing that property for sale. Buyers seeing that notation on the listing sheet become very wary. They do not want to get tangled up in the process of negotiating for an apartment only to have that apartment bought out from under them at the price that *they* negotiated. Many buyers simply refuse to consider apartments tied to a right-of-first-refusal clause.

Liquidity in an apartment investment becomes a real concern only when you *need* to get your money out at a certain time. *For maximum safety and profit potential, therefore, you should not buy an apartment unless you can afford to keep it for a period of five years*. You may indeed sell your apartment profitably after six months, or eighteen months, but knowing when you buy it that you can carry it for five years will keep you from having to sell under pressure or in a poor market.

Rate of Return

Some investors who bought apartments in 1970 for $50,000 sold them for $250,000 to $300,000 in 1980.

"Wow!" you say. "They made five or six times their investment in ten years! That's not bad!"

No, it's not, but it's also not accurate, unless those investors paid all cash for their apartments. Actually most of them probably made a much greater return on their investment dollars. More than likely, each put down $10,000 (20 percent of $50,000) and financed the balance. That $10,000 investment, therefore, grew to a $250,000 to $300,000 return in ten years. Twenty-five to thirty times the cash at risk! Now that's a fabulous rate of return.

Not everyone scores that big. But these figures illustrate a well-known principle that contributes significantly to making real estate one of the finest available investment vehicles: *leverage*. Leverage is the use of a small proportion of cash at risk (investment dollars) to buy property while relying upon appreciation in value to far outstrip the carrying costs for financing. Thus the fabulous rate of return for our $50,000 investors.

But you still don't have the whole story and the numbers are still inaccurate. The real rate of return for these apartment owners depended upon a complex relationship between cash investment, carrying charges, income from the property, maintenance charges, tax advantages, and finally sales price.

Once you get into investment properties, we believe you will benefit from (if not positively *need*) the help of an accountant, but we'll go through some of the most common factors in calculating rate of return in order to make you conversant with investment language and to give you a base from which to figure the profit potential of an investment you might be considering.

Capital-gains Tax: The profit that you realize from the sale of an investment apartment is considered a capital gain. If you have owned the apartment for a year or more, it is considered a long-term capital gain. As such, the new tax laws (The Economic Recovery Tax Act of 1981) allow you to keep a large portion of your profit. The formula for tax calculation allows you to ignore (not pay any tax upon) 60 percent of your profit. You are then taxed upon the remaining 40 percent according to your regular tax bracket. Even in the 50-percent bracket, therefore, the highest amount of tax that anyone will be required to pay on a long-term capital gain is 20 percent.

Cash Flow: The income from the rental of your apartment is taxable, but maintenance costs are deductible, as are interest charges on your loan, real estate taxes, and the allowable depreciation on your property. Your costs (deductions) may well exceed the income from rental, which will give you a negative cash flow on paper, but not necessarily a real loss for the year since your deductions will significantly lower the tax dollars that you must pay.

Depreciation: Depreciation of a property for tax purposes is a complex and not always rational process. The federal government has decided that in theory the life of most investment property is fifteen years. [The accelerated cost recovery system, called ACRS, is described in the new IRS code (section 168, c, 1).] Which means that you, the investment apartment owner, can depreciate (take as a loss) 1/15 of the value of your apartment each year for fifteen years.

What do you do with the tremendous profit you realize on the sale of the investment apartment ten years after you buy it if you have used one of the accelerated depreciation systems?

You fill a lot of scratch pads with numbers. Those numbers and the section references to the tax laws get very complicated, which is but one of the reasons we advised you to use an accountant. To answer the question with much oversimplification: You will have to add the excess depreciation that you took as a tax deduction during the past ten years to your declared profit and pay taxes upon it.

So what is your rate of return? It all depends. You may show a negative rate of return in a given year because of the tax benefits that you chose or because of expenses for maintenance or capital improvement. You may know full well, however, that your long-term rate of return on that apartment will be very high. Or you may choose to buy an apartment where the rental income affords you a small cash profit each month, and thus has a rate of return that is tangible annually as well as over the long term.

Rate of return must be a significant factor in the choice of your apartment, but it should be weighed to fit your needs and goals. Whether you are seeking a paper tax loss or extra income, there are investment apartments available that will suit your needs and goals; you need only take the time to find them.

If you think you barely have enough down payment for an apartment to live in, and don't know where to find the extra cash for an investment, it may surprise you to learn that you can get the cash for your first investment from the apartment that you purchased for your own use and occupancy.

How to Get Started

The secret to using your first apartment/home as a means of breaking into the ranks of successful entrepreneurs lies in careful selection of that apartment. Choose one in an area that is being revitalized, or in a building that is in the early stages of conversion, or one of the first "paper" apartments to be sold by a builder, or a resale from sellers under pressure. In other words, choose an apartment where the initial purchase price is below market value and rapid appreciation is a high probability.

Live there for two or three years. Meanwhile, continue to go out into the real estate marketplace and look at all or most of the apartments in your area that are offered for sale. When you think you have spotted a number of investment properties equally as good as the one you now own, offer yours for sale.

Take your profit from the sale of that apartment, but *do not* buy a bigger and better apartment for your own personal use. Buy another apartment that is about the same size, perhaps even one that needs some tender, loving care, certainly one priced below market value and again likely to appreciate. Use *half* of your profit from the sale of your old apartment as a down payment on your new home. Use the other half to buy your first investment apartment, as near to your new home apartment as possible. In the same building is an ideal arrangement.

There! Three years from the day you bought your first place to live, you have become an entrepreneur. As long as you continue to buy horizontally rather than up, you can keep increasing the number of apartments in your portfolio. You will become more and more expert at spotting the best buys; and not only will you be on your way to that dream we mentioned at the beginning of this chapter, but you'll be able to buy up to that elegant apartment for your own use sooner than you ever dreamed possible.

Short-term Speculation

Sometimes you can gather a windfall profit with relatively little cash investment at risk and without ever closing on your purchase. You must look for buildings where the conversion process is just beginning and likely to take some time (at least six months, preferably a year) or new construction that is still in the planning stage.

You sign a subscription agreement in the case of a co-op conversion or a contract to purchase in the case of a to-be-built condominium. This firmly establishes the price that you will pay for the apartment. Meanwhile, you leave the smallest deposit that you can negotiate to hold your purchase. (The seller will try to get 10 percent of the purchase price, but anything is legally acceptable. See how little he will sit still for.) Also try to negotiate the following terms in your purchase contract or subscription:

(1) Ask the seller to allow you to deposit the earnest money in stages. For example, $500 at the signing of the contract, half of the balance a month later, and the remaining balance two or three months later. This process permits you to retain control of as much of your cash as possible for as long as possible.

(2) The right to assign your contract without penalty or review must be included in the purchase agreement. This clause is most important because it is the means by which you will realize your speculative windfall.

(3) As a safety device, include the right to sublet or rent the apartment that you have contracted to buy. This clause will protect your investment in the event that you must go through with your purchase. (The bylaws of most cooperatives prohibit subletting without the approval of the board of directors. However, in most conversions, the sponsor retains control of the board for a specified period of time or until a designated number of units have been sold. If this is the case in your investment purchase, you can negotiate a written commitment from the sponsor that he will vote approval of the subletting of your apartment.)

Now on to the nuts and bolts: If you chose your apartment investment wisely, the price of the other apartments in the building or area will rise sharply as the condominium complex is built or the cooperative conversion nears completion. Shortly before your scheduled closing, you can sell your right to purchase your apartment.

If your contract was written at a purchase price of $50,000, for example, and the same apartment on the next floor is now selling for $62,000, you should have no difficulty getting from $5,000 to $10,000 for the assignment of that contract, plus the reimbursement of your earnest money. You have $5,000 to $10,000 in profit while never having bought a thing; meanwhile the new buyer is happy to be able to buy the apartment at below market price. Your earnest money is your at-risk money and even that risk is minimal if you have the financing available to close on the apartment and rent it until you can resell at a good profit.

Opportunity in a Rent-controlled Area

New York City has grappled with rent controls since the 1940s and the legislation there today is among the most stringent in the nation. Some experts feel the controls are unnecessary, that the market would control itself, but cities in California, New Jersey, New York, Massachusetts, and other states have instituted controls; many, many others have considered or are considering them. When controls are enacted and when they allow tenants the equivalent of a lifetime lease, new building starts drop off sharply and investment in apartments becomes a whole new ball game.

But it is not necessarily a bad game for everyone. Today one of the best long-term investment opportunities in the nation is hidden among the tenant-occupied apartment's of New York City's cooperatives.

During the past five years there, many buildings have been converted on noneviction plans, with a trend still continuing toward an increasing number of such conversions. In these buildings, sponsors have sold as many units as possible to the current tenants, but are anxious to sell off the remaining units and withdraw from involvement in the property. The units, however, do not sell on the homebuyer apartment marketplace because homebuyers want occupancy with their purchase. They cannot get it when they buy a rent-controlled occupied apartment, so for the most part, they do not buy. Sitting unwanted upon the market, these apartments have become a plum to in-the-know investors.

In New York City at this writing a savvy investor can purchase a block of four or more occupied units at 60 to 70 percent *below* market value and often with below market financing from the sponsor. The buyer, however, must be willing to hold the units until the tenants vacate or until the apartment appreciates in value enough so that he can sell it profitably to another investor at below market value.

There are several keys to successful investing in tenant-occupied apartments. Watch these points:

(1) Choose the units wisely. They should be among the most desirable in the building and should be occupied by very elderly or very young tenants (both more likely to vacate than established midlifers).

(2) Choose units where the rental income covers or closely approaches the cost of carrying the apartment.

(3) Negotiate to put down minimal cash at the closing, thus obtaining the greatest leverage.

(4) Negotiate as long a term (at least five years) for below market rate seller financing as possible. Try also to persuade the seller to allow the financing that he offers you to be assumable in the event that you sell one or more of the units before the five year term is out. Assumable financing at below market rates is a prime sales incentive in today's market, even if it is short term. The seller's refusal to allow assumable financing, however, should not stop your purchase. When he refuses, ask for one year longer on the term of the financing; you'll probably get it.

(5) Test the property against all the variables discussed in Chapter 3.

(6) Be sure that you can afford to hold the property at least five years. If economic need forces you to sell, you may find that your selling will result in a loss.

Shared-equity Investment

How many parents or other relatives have felt squeezed during the past decade when young people came to them and asked to borrow all or part of the down payment for a home purchase? How many friendships have been strained by the same request? The questions are rhetorical, but the problem is all too real.

With shared-equity investment, however, a request for aid in a home purchase (whether it be an apartment or a detached house) can be an investment opportunity of unparalleled safety for the lender. It can also leave the borrower guilt- and obligation-free and a good deal wealthier. Here's how it works:

Tom and Pat Young have $5,000 saved for a down payment on a place of their own. They find exactly what they want—for a starter, at least—at $50,000. But they discover that they need $10,000 as a down payment (20 percent) and that they can't really afford to carry the payments on a $40,000 loan, the taxes on the apartment, the insurance premiums, and the condominium maintenance fees. They approach Pat's parents, and after some discussion the four come to an agreement.

Pat's parents will put up $5,000 toward the down payment and will pay one-half of the carrying costs on the loan, taxes, and insurance. Tom and Pat will pay the other half. The names of all four people will appear on the deed to the unit and upon the bank loan. (People with well-established credit as co-signers on a loan will often induce a lending institution to lend more money with less down payment.)

Since Tom and Pat have the advantage of living in the unit, they agree to pay the condominium maintenance fee and all utility costs. And all four buyers agree that they will sell the apartment in five years or sooner, the date to be decided upon by Tom and Pat.

When the unit is sold, each couple will be reimbursed their $5,000. Then any extraordinary improvement costs will be deducted from the profit. The remaining equity (profit) is to be split between Tom and Pat and Pat's parents. Tom and Pat can then use their share of the profit as a down payment on another apartment.

There are no complex legal documents necessary to facilitate such a shared-equity joint-ownership investment. A simple letter between the two parties (signed by both) stating that they are tenants in common, each with a 50-percent interest in the property (or whatever precentage arrangement has been agreed upon) and specifying a tentative schedule for the sale of the apartment is sufficient. The condominium deed or co-op stock certificate registered in the names of both parties is an added protection to everyone's investment.

Such shared-equity arrangements require a smaller capital investment than most real estate purchases and involve little risk to the investor since the tenants in the apartment are co-owners and therefore eager to protect their own investment. This arrangement is so potentially attractive that at least one national real estate franchise, Electronic Realty Associates, Inc. (ERA), has developed a plan called the ERA partnership mortgage for co-ownership between resident/owner and investor. Through local office files the firm will match apartment buyers and homebuyers with investors willing to share part of the down payment and/or part of the monthly payments in return for a share of the tax deductions and appreciation upon the sale of the property.

With the growing interest in such plans, tax questions have naturally come up. Chief among these are: To what extent is the apartment a residence and to what extent is it an investment? How are deductions calculated? Should the occupants of the apartment be paying rent? Should their payment of the maintenance fee and utilities be considered the equivalent of paying the "rent" on the apartment or at least part of it?

The new IRS code spells out most of the answers to these and other questions, but its strands can get pretty tangled to someone not familiar with tax laws and practices. So again we recommend that you consult an accountant familiar with shared-equity transactions before you file your first after-purchase tax return.

Starting a Friendly Syndicate

Running a real estate syndicate is somewhere near the pinnacle of entrepreneurship, but you need not have a stake in the Rockefeller millions to take the first steps toward this lucrative avocation (or perhaps even vocation).

You begin by finding an apartment that has excellent appreciation potential. Let's say it's a two-bedroom apartment in a well-maintained neighborhood. It's selling price is $55,000. The building is just going co-op and the closing is five months away. The subscription agreement requires a $2,000 down payment upon signing; the sponsor will not budge on that figure. Financing is being offered at 12 percent for five years on 75 percent of the purchase price.

You want the apartment. You see it selling for $80,000 within a year or two. But you do not have the $13,750 needed for the down payment. How do you get in on this deal?

First, study the property and write out an evaluation, using all the customary criteria of a real-estate appraisal: location, comparable sales, maintenance costs, and so forth (Chapter 3 again), along with some projected figures spelling out cash flow, depreciation allowances, and projected appreciation. You will need a copy of the prospectus and information on rental income, maintenance costs, taxes, financing, and the real estate market in general.

After you do a paper profile of the apartment, judge it again. If you are still certain that you have an excellent investment, you should put the $2,000 down and sign the agreement to purchase. (Be sure, however, that it contains the right to assign your subscription.)

Now you have five months or more to start your first "friendly" syndicate.

You're probably wondering why it has to be a friendly syndicate. It's a matter of paperwork and legal fees. Many states have so-called "blue sky" laws that restrict the ability of an individual to start a syndicate in which securities are offered to the public. The opportunity to invest with a group in the purchase of an apartment would be considered a securities offering.

But we haven't yet explained how the "friendly" part avoids paperwork and legal fees. It's a matter of size and membership. No state law anywhere prohibits three or four individuals from getting together to buy a piece of property. If you carefully restrict your first syndicate to your close friends, co-workers, and family, you circumvent the question of a *public* offering. No state government will question you if you approach less than ten people in an effort to raise less than $50,000 and those ten people are all personally well known to you.

So by beginning small with friends and family you can try on the role of entrepreneur. Approach three of your most likely prospects and show them each the paper profile of your investment apartment. If they express interest, take them to see it. Offer them the opportunity to join with you in the investment. If the apartment is as good as you think, you won't have difficulty finding your partners.

Here's how to make the syndicate work. Offer each friend a 25-percent share in the apartment for $4,500. You take a 25-percent share for your $2,000 down payment and the time, effort, and skill involved in locating the apartment and securing the deal. This gives your group a total of $15,500 in disposable cash. $13,750 is required for the down payment; the remaining $1,750 is a good working fund.

Like the shared-equity investor, you do not need complex legal documents for your friendly syndicate. A simple letter will suffice. It should state your names and addresses, the fact that you are tenants in common each with a 25-percent interest in the apartment. The authority to rent and sell should be delegated to you (the finder), although some cutoff date (five years is good) should be indicated for the sale of the unit so that the investors have some idea of when they will be realizing their profit.

Real Syndicates

Once you have successfully organized a few such investment partnerships, you may want to begin syndication in earnest. In states with "blue sky" protection laws, you will need the help of an attorney. In all probability you will be required to register with the state attorney general's office and explain the type of investment offerings you plan to handle. If you intend to limit your offerings to twenty to thirty people raising under $50,000, you may be able to qualify for an exemption from the requirement of filing a formal prospectus for each investment. If eventually your investment hobby becomes a substantial source of your income, however, you will have to comply with the paperwork requirements of your state. But you probably won't mind. By that time you'll have a staff of hundreds and work with million-dollar figures, right?

Hold the dreams a minute. Let's go back to you as a beginner with two or three successful friendly group investments. Word gets out. People begin to admire your judgment and ability. They want to join you and they are willing to pay for your opinion. Now you can begin to buy into investments by putting down only your time and talent.

If we take another $55,000 apartment with the same terms as were offered on your first venture, you will put the $2,000 down on the unit and then gather three investors willing to invest $5,000 each in your unit. Thus you will be reimbursed the $2,000 that you put down on the unit and be given a 25-percent share in the ownership of the apartment for no capital investment. Nice work. Go to it and good luck!

Converting a Building

Investing in a rental apartment building with the intention of converting it to condominium or cooperative ownership can be very profitable. It requires more capital investment, more patience, more work, and more professional assistance (lawyer, accountant, appraiser, real estate broker, engineer, insurance agent, and so forth) than investing in a single unit or block of units. The basic principles of real estate investment, however, are exactly the same. You must judge:

(1) Location: Will the apartments be appealing in the marketplace because they are located in an area where people want to live?

(2) Costs and capital investment versus rate of return: Will the investment be profitable in the short term? The long term?

(3) Demand: Is there a shortage of the kind of housing unit that you will have for sale?

(4) Safety: Can you afford to carry the building until the conversion is complete?

A Word About Fear

Many a person says, "I don't have the money to buy an apartment," when he or she really means, "I'm afraid to make the commitment, afraid of being in debt, afraid to take the chance." And almost always their fear is the by-product of their lack of knowledge.

With ignorance and fear as their advisers, potential apartment buyers sit upon their hands. Thus they leave more space in the marketplace for those who dare to enter it.

A Word About Success

No wealthy investor has been successful 100 percent of the time. Even the most sophisticated and experienced among us make errors. But two factors tremendously increase the odds of success in the real estate marketplace: knowledge and time.

In this book, we have tried to share with you the knowledge we two have gathered through our rather different involvements in the real estate field. Much of what we have written here has never before been printed. It is the kind of insiders' information that should set you upon the road to acquiring the specific knowledge and skills that are necessary to find and buy the unique piece of property that you are seeking. But it is not enough.

No real estate book can assure you success unless you are willing to add your time to the information on the printed page. Only time spent in your local marketplace can focus general knowledge upon your particular purchase. You must be willing to leave the comfort of your living room and shop for the home or investment that you want. Shop. And shop. And shop. Spend the time necessary to become intimately familiar with your local market, so you'll be able to recognize a fabulous deal when you see one.

Your time will be rewarded with success.

A Real Estate Glossary

A prospective real estate agent usually finds learning the language of the real estate world every bit as demanding as learning its laws. Buyers and sellers are often confused and intimidated by that same language. But the language is not difficult; it is merely extensive, specialized in its definitions, and unfamiliar.

Everyone entering the real estate marketplace should take the time to check the definitions of words that he/she doesn't understand. Do not let them pass, or you might find yourself committing your money under terms you never bargained for.

To help you, we have included here a selected list of terms that you might encounter in your apartment-hunting, negotiating, buying, or selling. For the most part we have not repeated those words that we have defined in the text.

Absolute fee simple: The absolute ownership of real property. Title that contains no stipulations, restrictions, or qualifications. This is the best title available, but in reality it is rare in today's world of governmental restrictions and utility easements. The term *fee,* or *fee simple,* is often used more loosely to mean ownership of property that is yours to use and/or sell at your discretion.

Abstract of title: A synopsis of the history of a title, indicating all changes of ownership and including liens, mortgages, charges, encumbrances, encroachments, or any other matter that might affect the title.

Acceleration clause: A stipulation in a mortgage agreement that allows the lender to demand full payment of the loan immediately if any scheduled payment is not made by a given time.

Access: The means of approaching a property.

Access right: The right of an owner to enter and leave his property.

Addendum: Something added. In real estate contracts, a page added to the contract. It should be initialed by all parties concerned.

Affidavit of title: A sworn written statement signed by the seller stating that he owns the property, has clear title to it, and therefore has the right to sell it.

Agreement of sale: A written agreement by which a buyer agrees to buy and a seller agrees to sell a certain piece of property under the terms and conditions stated therein.

Apportionment: The costs and expenses that are prorated between the buyer and seller at the closing. These may include taxes, maintenance fees, special assessments, and even oil in a storage tank.

Appreciation: An increase in the value of a piece of property.

As is: A term used in a contract to mean that the buyer is buying what he sees as he sees it. There is no representation as to quality and no promise of repair or fix-up.

Assessed valuation: An evaluation of property by an agency of the government for taxation purposes.

Assessment: A tax or levied charge on a piece of property to pay for a portion of a specific improvement.

Bona fide: In good faith, without deceit or deception.

Building codes: Community laws that regulate the construction of buildings.

Cancellation clause: Any clause in a contract that allows the buyer or seller to cancel the contract if a certain specified condition or situation occurs.

Cash flow: The cash income generated by a rental property after all expenses are paid. Negative cash flow is a situation wherein expenses generated by the property exceed its income.

Certified check: A check that is guaranteed by the bank upon which it is drawn. A certified check for the balance of the down payment is usually required at the closing.

Chattel: Items of personal property, such as furniture, appliances, chandeliers, that are not permanently affixed to the property being sold.

Closing: The meeting of all concerned parties in order to transfer title to a property.

Closing costs: The expenses over and above the price of the property that must be paid before title is transferred.

Closing statement: A written account of all the expenses, adjustments, and disbursements involved in a real estate transaction.

Cloud on the title: A defect in the title that may affect the owner's ability to market his property. This might be a lien, a claim, or a judgment.

Collateral: Security pledged for the repayment of a loan.

Consideration: Anything of value but usually a sum of money. A contract must have a consideration in order to be binding.

Contingency: A provision in a contract that keeps it from becoming binding until certain activities are accomplished. A satisfactory professional inspection report might be a contingency.

Contract: An agreement between two parties. To be valid a real estate contract must be dated; must be in writing; and must include a consideration, a description of the property, the place and date of delivery of the deed, and all terms and conditions that were mutually agreed upon. It must also be executed (signed) by all concerned parties.

Convey: To transfer title from one person to another.

Conveyance: The document by which title is transferred. A deed is a conveyance.

Deed: A written instrument that conveys title to real property.

Default: A breach of contract or failure to meet an obligation. Nonpayment of a mortgage is considered a default.

Depreciation: The loss in value of real estate, especially because of age, obsolescence, wear and tear, or economic conditions.

Discount: The fee charged to grant a mortgage or loan. Also called "points."

Duress: The use of force or unlawful coercion.

Earnest money: A sum of money that accompanies a signed offer to purchase as evidence of good faith. It is almost always a personal check rather than cash.

Easement: A right-of-way or access. The right of one party to cross or use for some specified purpose the property of another.

Eminent domain: The right of a governmental body to take property from a private owner when that property is needed for the public good. A fair price, which is fixed by professional appraisal, must be paid for the property and the owner must accept this price as just compensation.

Encroachment: A building or part of a building that extends beyond its boundary and therefore intrudes upon the property of another party.

Encumbrance: A right or restriction on a property that reduces its value. This might be a claim, lien, liability, or zoning restriction. The report of the title search usually shows all encumbrances.

Equity: The interest or value that an owner has in a piece of property above the amount of the mortgage and/or other monies owed on it.

Escrow: Money or documents held by a third party until specific conditions of an agreement or contract are fulfilled.

Escrow account: A trust account in which escrow monies are deposited and from which they are disbursed. Both lawyers and real estate brokers maintain escrow accounts.

Et al.: Abbreviation of *et alia,* meaning "and others." This term is often used in a contract concerning a piece of property that is owned jointly by several people.

Et ux.: Abbreviation for *et uxor,* meaning "and wife." It is preferable that the woman be named.

Eviction: The legal expulsion of a person from a property. Any breach of a lease can be a reason for an eviction.

Execute: To perform what is required to give validity to a legal document, usually to sign it.

Fee simple: See *Absolute fee simple*.

Fiduciary: A person acting in a position of trust.

Fixtures: Items of personal property that have been permanently attached to the real property and are therefore included in the transfer of real estate. The kitchen sink is a fixture.

Grace period: An allowed reasonable length of time to meet a commitment after the specified date of that commitment. For example, most lending institutions allow a two-week grace period after the due date of the mortgage payment before a late fee is imposed.

Ground lease: A lease of land alone, usually for a long term (99 years), upon which the tenant constructs a building.

Hand money: See *Earnest money*.

Inspection: The act of physically observing and testing a piece of property.

Installment sales contract: A sales contract for property in which the buyer receives possession of the property but does not take title to it until he makes regular installment payments to the seller and fulfills other specified obligations.

Instrument: Any written legal document.

Interest: A fee paid for the use of money.

Judgment: A decree of a court that states that one person is indebted to another and specifies the amount of the debt.

Lease: A contract that allows one party the possession of a piece of property for a specified period of time in return for a consideration (usually rent) paid to the owner of the property.

Lessee: The tenant; someone who rents under a lease.

Lessor: The landlord; someone who rents to another party through a lease.

Leverage: The effective use of money to buy property by using the smallest amount of one's own capital that is permitted and by borrowing as much as possible in order to obtain the maximum percentage of return on the original investment.

Liquidity: The ability to convert an asset into cash.

Lis pendens: Notice of a suit pending.

Listing: A contract or agreement for employing a real estate broker to sell a piece of property. Also a piece of property that is for sale.

Loan-to-value ratio: The relationship of a mortgage loan to the appraised value of a piece of property. Often expressed to the buyer in terms of how much the lender will loan—for example, 75-percent financing.

Market value: Generally accepted as the best price that a ready, willing, and able buyer will pay and the lowest price a ready, willing, and able seller will accept.

Marketable title: A title that is free from clouds and encumbrances.

Meeting of the minds: The mutual agreement of two parties who are ready to enter into a contract.

Mill: Equal to one-tenth of one cent. A mill is the unit of measure for property taxation rates.

Model apartment: A completed (and often decorated) apartment that a builder promises to duplicate at a given price in another location.

Mortgage: A legal document that creates a lien upon a piece of property.

Mortgagee: The party or institution that lends the money.

Mortgagor: The person or party that borrows the money, giving a lien on the property as security for the loan.

Multiple listing: An agreement that allows real-estate brokers to distribute information on the properties that they have listed for sale to other members of a local real estate organization in order to provide the widest possible marketing of those properties. Commissions are split by mutual agreement between the listing broker and the selling broker.

Multiple Listing Service (MLS): The office that supervises the printing and distribution of listings shared by members of the local Board of Realtors.

Notary public: A person licensed to authenticate documents and certain transactions.

Offer: A proposal, oral or written, to buy a piece of property at a specified price.

Operating expenses: All the expenses incurred to keep a property in usable and rentable condition. Operating expenses do not include mortgage payments or interest.

Origination fee: A charge by the lender for originating the mortgage.

Personal property: Also termed *personality*. Anything that is not permanently attached to the real property. Chandeliers, mirrors, and drapery rods are common examples.

Points: Sometimes called *discount*. A fee that the lending institution charges for the mortgage. One point is 1 percent of the face amount of the loan.

Power of attorney: An instrument in writing that gives one person the right to act as an agent for another in signing papers, deeds, documents, and so forth.

Premises: The land and everything attached to it; the property in question.

Principal: The amount of money borrowed; the amount of money still owed.

Real property: Land and buildings and anything permanently attached to the land and/or buildings.

Realtor: A real estate broker who is a member of the National Association of Realtors.

Refinance: To pay off one loan by taking out another on the same property.

Report of title: A document required before title insurance can be issued. It states the name of the owner, a legal description of the property, and the status of taxes, liens, and anything else that might affect the marketability of the title.

Reserve fund (general operating): Funds that are accumulated on a monthly basis to provide a cushion of capital to be used when and if a contingency arises.

Reserve fund (replacement): Funds that are set in escrow to replace or repair common elements, such as roofs or elevators, at some future date.

Restriction: A limitation to control the use of a piece of property.

Second mortgage: A mortgage on a property that is subordinate to a first mortgage. In the event of default, the second mortgage is repaid after the first. Also called a *junior mortgage*.

Specific performance: A court order that compels a party to carry out the terms of an executed (signed) contract.

Syndicate: An entity, usually a limited partnership, that is established for the purpose of making an investment.

Time is of the essence: A phrase used in a contract to indicate that specific dates are essential to the contract and that the contract terms must be performed on those dates. It is most often used in regard to closing dates.

Title: Actual ownership; the right of possession; evidence of ownership.

Title insurance: An insurance policy that protects against loss incurred because of defective title.

Title search: A professional examination of public records to determine the chain of ownership of a particular piece of property and to note any liens, mortgages, encumbrances, easements, restrictions, or other factors that might affect the title.

Trust deed: An instrument used in place of a mortgage in certain states; a third-party trustee, not the lender, holds the title to the property until the loan is paid out or defaulted.

Valuation: Estimated or determined value.

Variance: An exception to a zoning ordinance granted to meet certain specific needs.

Void: Canceled; not legally enforceable.

Yield: The annual percentage rate of return on an investment in real estate.

Zoning ordinances: Municipal ordinances that limit and regulate the character and uses of private property in a given area.

Index

Titles of Related Interest from PLUME

☐ **BUYING RIGHT IN COUNTRY REAL ESTATE by Jean Young and Jim Young.** A practical, up to the minute guide that answers all your buying questions: how to pick the best buying season, choosing a broker, understanding true value, handling a lawyer and appraisers, finding the best financing, cutting red tape in the purchasing process in every state, and even how to buy a solar house—in the one guide you'll ever need for considering country real estate.

(252172—$3.95)

☐ **FIVE ACRES & INDEPENDENCE: A Practical Guide to the Selection and Management of the Small Farm by M. G. Kains, B.S., M.S.** A back-to-the land underground classic that explores the opportunities and pitfalls of the rural wilds; examines questions of finance, water supply, sewage, livestock, the planting of crops; and counsels on tools, insect enemies, and much more! (252377—$4.95)

☐ **LIVING ON A FEW ACRES by the Department of Agriculture.** Covering every region of the country, here is essential advice on how to pick the most appropriate location; how to build or improve a house; its landscaping, outbuildings, animal shelters or wells; plus how to use land to stretch the family budget, from growing nuts to raising minks. With photos and line drawings. (252156—$4.95)

☐ **THE LOG HOUSE BOOK by Jack Kramer.** The do-it-yourselfer's guide to planning, building, or buying a log house—from a one room, hand-hewn cabin to kits for full-size, year-round homes. Illustrated with photos and line drawings. (253799—$6.95)

In Canada, please add $1.00 to the price of each book.

To order, use the convenient coupon on the next page.

PLUME Quality Paperbacks for Your Bookshelf

(0452)

☐ **THE FURNISH YOUR HOME BY MAIL CATALOGUE by Sarah Gallick with Mary Gallick.** Carefully arranged for quick and easy reference, this definitive catalogue gives you the names, addresses, toll-free phone numbers, products, price ranges, and credit card policies of firms all over America, and tells you how to acquire their lavish catalogues. (252911—$9.95)

☐ **COUNTRY FURNITURE written and illustrated by Aldren A. Watson.** "A handsome, readable study of the early American woodcrafter and his work . . . valuable to a woodworker and entertaining for the most casual reader."—*The New York Times.* With over 300 beautiful pencil sketches. (251303—$4.95)

☐ **FURNITURE OF THE AMERICAN ARTS AND CRAFTS MOVEMENT by David M. Cathers.** The first book to fully trace the development of mission oak style furniture—which provides a means for identifying, dating, authenticating, and evaluating individual pieces. "The definitive guide . . . for collectors of one of the most sought after collectibles in the antique market."—*Boston Globe* (253748—$9.95)

☐ **A FIELD GUIDE TO AMERICAN ARCHITECTURE by Carole Rifkind.** The first book of its kind to classify and illustrate every major form of American building style—from 17th-century wood houses to today's glass and steel skyscrapers. This invaluable handbook describes the historical background, construction materials, and basic structures and styles that will enable the reader to identify virtually any building in the United States. With over 450 black and white illustrations. (252377—$4.95)

In Canada, please add $1.00 to the price of each book.

Buy them at your local bookstore or use this convenient coupon for ordering.

THE NEW AMERICAN LIBRARY, INC.
P.O. Box 999, Bergenfield, New Jersey 07621

Please send me the PLUME BOOKS I have checked above. I am enclosing $＿＿＿＿＿(please add $1.50 to this order to cover postage and handling). Send check or money order—no cash or C.O.D.'s. Prices and numbers are subject to change without notice.

Name＿＿＿＿＿＿＿＿＿＿＿＿＿＿＿＿＿＿＿＿＿＿＿＿＿＿＿＿＿

Address＿＿＿＿＿＿＿＿＿＿＿＿＿＿＿＿＿＿＿＿＿＿＿＿＿＿＿

City＿＿＿＿＿＿＿＿＿＿＿State＿＿＿＿＿＿Zip Code＿＿＿＿＿＿

Allow 4-6 weeks for delivery.
This offer is subject to withdrawal without notice.

Quality Reference Books from PLUME and MERIDIAN

Architectural Guides from MERIDIAN